LOCATING LYNETTE ROBERTS

WRITING WALES IN ENGLISH

CREW series of Critical and Scholarly Studies
General Editors: Kirsti Bohata and Daniel G. Williams (*CREW*, Swansea University)

This *CREW* series is dedicated to Emyr Humphreys, a major figure in the literary culture of modern Wales, a founding patron of the *Centre for Research into the English Literature and Language of Wales*. Grateful thanks are due to the late Richard Dynevor for making this series possible.

Other titles in the series
Stephen Knight, *A Hundred Years of Fiction* (978-0-7083-1846-1)
Barbara Prys-Williams, *Twentieth-Century Autobiography* (978-0-7083-1891-1)
Kirsti Bohata, *Postcolonialism Revisited* (978-0-7083-1892-8)
Chris Wigginton, *Modernism from the Margins* (978-0-7083-1927-7)
Linden Peach, *Contemporary Irish and Welsh Women's Fiction* (978-0-7083-1998-7)
Sarah Prescott, *Eighteenth-Century Writing from Wales: Bards and Britons* (978-0-7083-2053-2)
Hywel Dix, *After Raymond Williams: Cultural Materialism and the Break-Up of Britain* (978-0-7083-2153-9)
Matthew Jarvis, *Welsh Environments in Contemporary Welsh Poetry* (978-0-7083-2152-2)
Harri Garrod Roberts, *Embodying Identity: Representations of the Body in Welsh Literature* (978-0-7083-2169-0)
Diane Green, *Emyr Humphreys: A Postcolonial Novelist* (978-0-7083-2217-8)
M. Wynn Thomas, *In the Shadow of the Pulpit: Literature and Nonconformist Wales* (978-0-7083-2225-3)
Linden Peach, *The Fiction of Emyr Humphreys: Contemporary Critical Perspectives* (978-0-7083-2216-1)
Daniel Westover, *R. S. Thomas: A Stylistic Biography* (978-0-7083-2413-4)
Jasmine Donahaye, *Whose People? Wales, Israel, Palestine* (978-0-7083-2483-7)
Judy Kendall, *Edward Thomas: The Origins of His Poetry* (978-0-7083-2403-5)
Damian Walford Davies, *Cartographies of Culture: New Geographies of Welsh Writing in English* (978-0-7083-2476-9)
Daniel G. Williams, *Black Skin, Blue Books: African Americans and Wales 1845–1945* (978-0-7083-1987-1)
Andrew Webb, *Edward Thomas and World Literary Studies: Wales, Anglocentrism and English Literature* (978-0-7083-2622-0)
Alyce von Rothkirch, *J. O. Francis, realist drama and ethics: Culture, place and nation* (978-1-7831-6070-9)
Rhian Barfoot, *Liberating Dylan Thomas: Rescuing a Poet from Psycho-Sexual Servitude* (978-1-7831-6184-3)
Daniel G. Williams, *Wales Unchained: Literature, Politics and Identity in the American Century* (978-1-7831-6212-3)
M. Wynn Thomas, *The Nations of Wales 1890–1914* (978-1-78316-837-8)
Richard McLauchlan, *Saturday's Silence: R. S. Thomas and Paschal Reading* (978-1-7831-6920-7)
Bethan M. Jenkins, *Between Wales and England: Anglophone Welsh Writing of the Eighteenth Century* (978-1-7868-3029-6)
M. Wynn Thomas, *All that is Wales: The Collected Essays of M. Wynn Thomas* (978-1-7868-3088-3)
Laura Wainwright, *New Territories in Modernism: Anglophone Welsh Writing, 1930–1949* (978-1-7868-3217-7)

Locating Lynette Roberts

'Always Observant and Slightly Obscure'

WRITING WALES IN ENGLISH

Edited by Siriol McAvoy

UNIVERSITY OF WALES PRESS
2019

© The Contributors, 2019

All rights reserved. No part of this book may be reproduced in any material form (including photocopying or storing it in any medium by electronic means and whether or not transiently or incidentally to some other use of this publication) without the written permission of the copyright owner. Applications for the copyright owner's written permission to reproduce any part of this publication should be addressed to the University of Wales Press, University Registry, King Edward VII Avenue, Cardiff CF10 3NS.

www.uwp.co.uk

British Library CIP Data
A catalogue record for this book is available from the British Library.

ISBN: 978-1-78683-382-2
e-ISBN: 978-1-78683-383-9

The right of The Contributors to be identified as authors of this work has been asserted in accordance with sections 77 and 79 of the Copyright, Designs and Patents Act 1988.

THE ASSOCIATION FOR
WELSH WRITING IN ENGLISH
CYMDEITHAS LLÊN SAESNEG CYMRU

Typeset by Marie Doherty
Printed by CPI Antony Rowe, Melksham

Contents

Series Editors' Preface — vii
Notes on Contributors — ix
Acknowledgements — xi

Introduction: Locating Lynette Roberts: 'Always observant and slightly obscure' — 1
Siriol McAvoy

1. The Scarlet Woman — 23
   M. Wynn Thomas

2. '"You have a Welsh name, are you Welsh?" he asked. "I don't know," I replied': Lynette Roberts and Elective Welsh Identity — 47
   Katie Gramich

3. 'I remember these things': Memory, Misrepresentation and Cultural Tradition in Lynette Roberts's 'Seven Stories' — 67
   Michelle Deininger

4. 'What changes break before us': Semi-peripheral Modernity in Lynette Roberts's Poetry and Prose — 85
   Andrew Webb

5	Welsh Literary Modernism, Lynette Roberts and David Jones: Unearthing 'a huge and very important culture' *Daniel Hughes*	101
6	'Crusaders uncross limbs by the green light of flares': Lynette Roberts's Avant-garde Medievalism *Siriol McAvoy*	121
7	Burnt Pain and Blasted Seashells: Lynette Roberts's Estuarine War Writing *Leo Mellor*	155
8	Listening and Location in the Poetry of Lynette Roberts *Zoë Skoulding*	177
9	Lynette Roberts's *The Endeavour*: a Generic Adventure *Charles Mundye*	197

Select Bibliography 219
Index 233

Series Editors' Preface

The aim of this series, since its founding in 2004 by Professor M. Wynn Thomas, is to publish scholarly and critical work by established specialists and younger scholars that reflects the richness and variety of the English-language literature of modern Wales. The studies published so far have amply demonstrated that concepts, models and discourses current in the best contemporary studies can illuminate aspects of Welsh culture, and have also foregrounded the potential of the Welsh example to draw attention to themes that are often neglected or marginalised in anglophone cultural studies. The series defines and explores that which distinguishes Wales's anglophone literature, challenges critics to develop methods and approaches adequate to the task of interpreting Welsh culture, and invites its readers to locate the process of writing Wales in English within comparative and transnational contexts.

Professor Kirsti Bohata and Professor Daniel G. Williams

Founding Editor: Professor M. Wynn Thomas (2004–15)

CREW (*Centre for Research into the English Literature and Language of Wales*)
Swansea University

Contributors

Michelle Deininger is Lecturer and Co-ordinator of the Humanities provision at the Department of Continuing and Professional Education, Cardiff University. Her interests include Welsh women's short stories in English from the mid-nineteenth century to the present. She has recently published an essay on ecofeminism in contemporary Welsh women's writing, and is preparing (with Claire Flay-Petty) a major monograph on women, writing and higher education in twentieth-century culture.

Katie Gramich is Professor of English Literature at Cardiff University. Her research has focused on rediscovering Welsh women writers. She has edited texts by Allen Raine, Amy Dillwyn, and Eiluned Lewis and co-edited a wide-ranging anthology of Welsh women's poetry for the Honno Classics series. Her monographs include *Twentieth-Century Women's Writing in Wales: Land, Gender, Belonging* (UWP) and *Kate Roberts* (UWP). Broadview Press published her new edition and translation of the poetry of the late medieval Welsh woman poet Gwerful Mechain in 2018.

Daniel Hughes is lecturer in modern and contemporary literature at Bangor University. His work has been published in *Wales Arts Review* and *The International Journal of Welsh Writing in English*. Daniel is preparing a monograph on anglophone Welsh modernism, as well as a co-authored monograph (with Tomos Owen), on the poet, critic and translator Tony Conran.

Siriol McAvoy is a writer and literary researcher. She teaches in the Department of Continuing and Professional Education, Cardiff University. An Honorary Research Fellow in CREW, Swansea University, she is also co-chair of Modernist Network Cymru. She completed a PhD at Cardiff University in 2017, and her current research projects focus on Anglophone Welsh poetry of the 1940s and 1950s and twentieth-century women's writing.

Leo Mellor is the Roma Gill Fellow in English and Director of Studies at Murray Edwards College, the University of Cambridge. He has published widely on modernism and twentieth-century literature, and is the author of *Reading the Ruins: Bombsites, Modernism and British Culture* (Cambridge University Press, 2011).

Charles Mundye is President of the Robert Graves Society and Fellow of the English Association. He is the editor of Keidrych Rhys's *The Van Pool: Collected Poems* (Seren, 2012), and Robert Graves's *War Poems* (Seren, 2016). He is currently Deputy Head and Head of Academic Development in the Department of Humanities at Sheffield Hallam University.

Zoë Skoulding is a poet and Reader at Bangor University. She has published several volumes of poetry including *The Museum of Disappearing Sounds* (Seren, 2013), and a monograph, *Experimental Cities: Contemporary Women's Poetry and Urban Space* (Palgrave Macmillan, 2013).

Professor M. Wynn Thomas holds the Emyr Humphreys Chair of Welsh Writing in English at Swansea University, and is the former Director and founder of CREW, the Centre for Research into the English Literature and Language of Wales. A Fellow of the British Academy and the Learned Society of Wales, he has published over twenty books on American poetry and on the two literatures of Wales. In 2018 he won the Wales Book of the Year Award for creative non-fiction with his essay collection, *All That is Wales*.

Andrew Webb is Senior Lecturer in Welsh Writing in English at Bangor University, where he is also currently Head of the School of Languages, Literatures and Linguistics. He is the author of *Edward Thomas and World Literary Studies: Wales, Anglocentrism and English Literature* (University of Wales Press, 2013).

Acknowledgements

A special thanks goes to Kirsti Bohata for her initial suggestion of a collection of essays on Lynette Roberts, and for reading versions of this book. This project could not have happened without her vision and support. Many thanks are also owed to Gareth Evans for his instrumental role in the design and conception of this volume. My gratitude is due to Angharad Rhys for her attentive reading of the manuscript and incisive observations, and to both Angharad and Prydein Rhys for their generous permission for the use of the material included in this book. Thank you to Daniel Williams, Katie Gramich, Jane Moore and Rob Gossedge for feedback on the material I used in my own essay in this volume. The input and reflections of attendees of the annual conference of the International Association of Welsh Writing in English following presentations on Lynette Roberts's work were also very helpful. Llion Wigley at the University of Wales Press has offered patient and meticulous guidance at all stages of the process. The publication of this book was supported by HEFCW funds allocated by Cardiff and Swansea Universities, and thanks are due to the School of English, Communication and Philosophy at Cardiff University, and the School of English Literature and Creative Writing at Swansea University, for making this possible.

The unpublished letter to Lynette Roberts by T. S. Eliot, 28 December 1953, is reprinted by permission of the Estate of T. S. Eliot at Faber & Faber. A letter to Lynette Roberts by Edith Sitwell, 31 January 1954, is reprinted by permission of Peters Fraser & Dunlop (*www.petersfraserdunlop.com*) on behalf of the Estate of Edith Sitwell, and correspondence between Robert Graves and Lynette Roberts is reprinted by permission of the President and Fellows of St John's College, Oxford. Letters from Lynette Rhys to David Jones and other unpublished writings by Lynette Roberts are reprinted with kind permission of the Estates of Lynette Roberts and David Jones. Gratitude is also due to the staff at the Harry Ransom Center at the University of Texas at Austin, and at the National Library of Wales.

Finally, I wish to express my heartfelt thanks to my family and friends for their unending support and encouragement in the preparation of this book, and their general enthusiasm for all things Roberts-related. Diolch yn fawr i chi gyd.

Introduction: Locating Lynette Roberts: 'Always observant and slightly obscure'

Siriol McAvoy

There is something unplaceable about Lynette Roberts. Her poetry baffles and beguiles; promises artless grace and offers 'calculated awkwardness'; aspires to plain-spoken social commentary while showing a predilection for 'intricate Imagistic play': longs for authenticity, but revels in a 'restless artifice'.[1] Composed mostly during the 1940s, when she lived in the small Welsh village of Llanybri, and the early 1950s, Roberts's writings – an eclectic assortment of poetry, short stories, essays and novels – share a focused, ethnographic interest in the particularities of culture and place. Though they sometimes express a 'premature nostalgia' for what might soon be lost to the tentacular forces of capitalist modernity, they are simultaneously invigorated by modern production, drawing inspiration from the flash of the galvanized sheds that punctuate the rural Welsh landscape, or the flight paths of planes that blur the boundaries between 'here' and 'elsewhere', shaping new patternings of global space.[2] Furthermore, if Roberts's representations of her west Wales location shine with the lucidity of the outsider's eye, her poems and stories are also immersive, inclusive, presenting the writing self as *part* of the culture and community being perceived – a culture that, while seemingly small and bounded, is never fully knowable, always in process.

Attentive to the unrealities of modern life in wartime, Roberts's poetry is yet lent a certain candour and distinctiveness by the fact that it is almost always anchored in her own, lived, experience. But for all her writing's rootedness in a particular time and place, her territorial affiliations are notoriously difficult to pin down, and critics have yet to agree on them. Her itinerant, cosmopolitan biography could seem to affirm her status as one of modernism's paradigmatic 'exiles' and 'émigrés', yet her particular spatial and cultural co-ordinates are far more complex than the model of the modernist exile would allow. Born Evelyn Beatrice Roberts on 4 July 1909 in Buenos Aires, Roberts was brought up in affluent colonial circles in the towns of Mechita and Ramos Mejía, to the west of Argentina's capital. While Dylan Thomas's rather snide conjecture that she had 'rich Welsh parents in South America (oil-driving or train-wrecking)'[3] was erroneous, her father, Cecil Arthur Roberts, had risen to become head of the Western Railway company in Argentina; the family owned yachts and racehorses, and lived in a large house with a tennis court and curlicue gate 'made of strapped and scrolled ironwork.'[4] Roberts greatly admired her father, a man popular with his employees and celebrated in his professional life for his modernizing zeal,[5] and she recalls the exhilaration of accompanying him across the country on official visits by train. The language in which she describes his journeys emphasizes his role in the expansion and development of Argentina: 'My father went on an expedition. It was to be virgin country. He was to look at the land with a view to extending the railway line. During his trip he took a geologist and water diviner'.[6] Although her relatively privileged status kept her at a certain distance from the lives of ordinary Argentines, she always took an interest in what lay beyond the confines of her iron gate, even as a small child. Her 'Notes for an Autobiography' and 'Radio Talk on South American Poems' often remark on the conditions of Argentina's poor or disenfranchised rural peoples, and her childhood sense of injustice at their treatment was to colour her response to rural Wales. Indeed, Roberts's early memories of South America were bound up, not only in the thrill of exploration and liberating expanses, but also in experiences of loss and dispossession. Her mother, Ruby Garbutt, died from typhoid in 1923, the day before Roberts turned fourteen. Her mother's memory – linked, perhaps, to her sensuous early recollections of the wide open pampas, the sound of innumerable birds, the 'fazenda shop clinking like ice in an enamel jug'[7] after the heat of the sun – was to haunt her throughout her life; Roberts later suggested that it was she who had inadvertently helped fetch her mother the water from the well that poisoned her.[8]

Roberts's parents' families had both come from Wales, via Australia; her father was from Ruthin in north Wales, her mother's grandfather a farmer from Pembroke, and both sides retained a certain pride in their Welsh ancestry. Yet, educated in a French and Spanish convent in Buenos Aires and later at a boarding school in Bournemouth, she had relatively little contact with Welsh culture while she was growing up.[9] Charismatic and friendly, she gradually assimilated herself into London's literary and artistic circles during the 1930s: she knew Wyndham Lewis and the painter Victor Pasmore, and was friends with Sonia Brownell, the future wife of George Orwell. As Katie Gramich suggests in her essay in this volume, it was only on meeting Keidrych Rhys – poet and 'flamboyant impresario' of Welsh letters – that Roberts was brought fully to reflect upon her Welsh cultural heritage.[10] They married on 4 October 1939 and moved to Llanybri, a small village in south Carmarthenshire, near to Dylan Thomas's Laugharne. Many of Roberts's poems read as ambivalent love songs to the country and community that offered her a prickly welcome during the war. Often adopting the guise of the returning 'native', her poetry charts her self-conscious construction, through language, of a sense of 'home' in Wales.

Yet, for all her longing to belong and keenness to participate in rural Welsh life, there was always an aura of eccentricity that hung about Roberts, reinforced by the theatrical red capes in which she wrapped herself and her children as protection against the cold Atlantic winds that whipped across the Taf estuary. This, at least, was poet Alun Lewis's impression when he met her, writing to tell his parents that 'She's a queer girl, very gifted, wears a red cloak and is unaccountable'.[11] Differences in class and culture, as well as an inability to speak Welsh, made integration into village life difficult at times; she was treated circumspectly by the inhabitants of Llanybri, and was even suspected of being a German spy during the dog days of 1942. Patrick McGuinness, the editor of her *Collected Poems*, presents itinerancy and outsiderness as keynotes of Roberts's life and work:

> Her poetry and its place in the poetic tradition are eccentric, and Roberts herself was an outsider in all sorts of ways: in terms of nationality and belonging; in terms of intellectual background; and in terms of life and location. An outsider, she was also marginal, hovering on the outskirts of the London literary scene of the 1940s and the first flowering of Welsh writing in English.[12]

Roberts's 'hovering', 'unplaceable' presence can partly be explained by facts of biography and geography; that she, as McGuinness explains, 'was from an expatriate family from Argentina and settled on the west coast of Wales in rented accommodation'; after her marriage with Keidrych Rhys broke up in 1948, she was even domiciled for a time in a caravan, first in the graveyard in Laugharne and then in Hertfordshire near her children's boarding school – a seeming embodiment of her nomadic sensibility.[13]

But Roberts, it has to be said, was also something of an insider, too. Her marriage to Keidrych Rhys drew her into the heart of the Welsh modernist formation that Daniel Hughes examines in his essay in this volume, and she quite often uses the first-person plural – 'ours' – to lay claim to her part in Welsh culture. In literary terms she was remarkably well connected: her correspondents included David Jones, T. S. Eliot, Robert Graves, Wyndham Lewis, and Edith Sitwell, to whom she dedicated her long 'Heroic' poem, *Gods with Stainless Ears*. It seems, then, that Roberts actively nurtured a patina of 'obscurity' as part of own poetic self-mythology. For her, it was at once an artistic performance and a lived commitment to marginal peoples and their practices.

The phrase that gives the title to this book – 'Always observant and rather obscure' – is taken from the poem 'Lamentation', originally published in Roberts's first collection, *Poems* (1944). Composed during the period 1939–44, the poem rehearses Roberts's own arrival and settlement in west Wales, beginning, fairy tale-like, with a mysterious arrival: 'To the village of lace and stone / Came strangers. I was one of these / Always observant and slightly obscure' (*CP*, 8). The voice quickly swivels between the point of view of the embattled Welsh community ('strangers') and that of the incomers ('I was one of these'). As Laura Wainwright has suggested, the speaker can here be seen to identify herself with the 'dispersive tide' of the Second World War – a group including refugees and the women and evacuee children posted to west Wales from urban locations during the conflict.[14] Similar to her poem 'Displaced Persons', which likens refugees 'to birds without winter food and dying of starvation', 'Lamentation' expresses a sense of solidarity with all of those who remain out of kilter or 'out of place', on the edges and fringes of the nation.[15]

In 'Lamentation' and throughout her writing, Roberts is attuned to war as a moment of encounter, when fixed categories of place and identity are suddenly pitched into radical uncertainty. Although destructive, this uncertainty also brings with it a strange freedom and sense of possibility, conjured when the speaker 'roam[s] the hills of birds and bone / Rescuing bees from under the storm' (*CP*, 8). The bee signals fragility and dispersal, yet also, in its mythic guise, offers a figure for industriousness and communal survival. In fact, the bee gathering honey emblematizes Roberts's self-assigned poetic 'work': eclectically collecting and conserving all that is good (*melys* or sweet) in Welsh culture, as a defence against annihilation.

The speaker's self-characterization as 'always observant' in 'Lamentation' underlines the importance of vision to Roberts's identity as a writer. The strikingly visual quality of her work, detected in its vivid, sensual play with form and colour, is partly indebted to her training as an artist at the Central School of Arts and Crafts in London. But it also has to do with her drive to write herself onto a new national and/or cultural map. As Jane Garrity has observed, modernist women writers in Britain remained subject to forms of national ideology that systematically excluded women from public life, while at the same time gendering the land as passive and feminine.[16] Scholars such as Katie Gramich, Jane Aaron and Deirdre Beddoe have similarly emphasized the status of twentieth-century Wales as an 'ideologically charged and gendered space', in which women had to struggle with the legacy of the 'land of my fathers'.[17] For Garrity, it is primarily through the gaze that modernist women writers attempt to reposition themselves at the centre of national culture: 'link[ing] the visual with territory', they 'imbue the gaze with redemptive agency' – both for themselves, and for the nation.[18] This resonates with Michelle Deininger's postulation, in this volume, of ethnographic observation as one of the primary modes used by Roberts in order to comprehend and situate herself in Welsh culture. In 'Lamentation', the speaker's self is at times almost entirely subsumed by her seeing eye – expressive, perhaps, of the move away from private interiority towards a more material, social world that has been seen to characterize late modernism.[19] In a related sense, Maggie Humm has argued that visuality and visual culture appear as sites for modernist women writers to approach the struggle 'between the public and the private, between the formally expressive and the everyday moment.'[20] The struggle or slippage between the public and private is an issue pertinent to Roberts's writing, and one that I take up in my discussion of her engagement with medievalist craft traditions in my essay in this volume.

If observation has to do with clarity and social legibility, then obscurity, conversely, has to do with that which is difficult to understand, enigmatic or ambiguous. Like 'unaccountable', the word used by Alun Lewis to describe Roberts, 'obscure' is suggestive of someone who doesn't quite add up, who refuses to conform to prevailing epistemological or economic structures. This is certainly the case when it comes to Roberts's political convictions. Socialist in inclination (in her diary, she admires the Welsh miners for 'how they fight for their rights', and vigorously denounces what she sees as the neglect and exploitation of Welsh workers by a bureaucratic and 'corrupt' government in Westminster),[21] she yet leans towards a Yeatsian idealization of feudal structures, noting appreciatively that Llanybri villagers seem to have retained 'all the natural and true qualities of an aristocrat.'[22] She told Alun Lewis in a letter that she felt 'very strongly AGAINST democracy', which 'as I see it will mass produce all creation' – a statement that betrays typically modernist anxieties about the global commodification of culture and the populist power of the 'mass'.[23] Further, while she undoubtedly shared her husband's enthusiasm for the cause of Welsh national self-definition, Roberts's interest in Wales sometimes appears as a synecdoche for her wider, internationalist concern with the plight of rural and minority peoples in the shadow of global modernity. Her political outlook, then, might best be summarized by Kristin Bluemel's definition of 'intermodernist' (or late modernist) writers as 'politically radical, "radically eccentric"', rebelling against the Manichaean politics of the 1930s and 1940s through a refusal to toe a single party line.[24]

Roberts's writing demonstrates a robust confidence in her right to participate in, and speak publicly for, a culture and community that both was and was not her own. But as many critics have noticed, an uncanny sense of unbelonging haunts her texts – glimpsed in their dislocated domestic realms, proliferating pairs and doubles, and use of 'countercanonical' literary forms such as the folk tale and fable.[25] All this resonates with the 'exilic' sensibility detected by Angela Ingram in the work of 'colonial' writers such as Doris Lessing and Jean Rhys – figures 'for whom the starting-place is no more – nor less – home that is the Mother England [or Wales] to which they exile themselves.'[26] Indeed, many of the essays in this book explore how the modern dialectic of belonging and unbelonging is complicated by gender. In light of Ingram's suggestion that 'women have had to deal differently from men with the specific workings of political systems designed to oppress and incapacitate those who cannot, or will not, subscribe to the central "home" ideology', Roberts's wilful 'obscurity' (or ex-centricity) could be read as a gendered strategy for critiquing and evading the demands of capitalist and imperial subjecthood.[27]

Roberts seems to have embraced rural Carmarthenshire as a space of what Robert Crawford has called 'empowering marginality', seeing in it a hybridity that mirrored her own sense of betweenness.[28] 'Obscure', when used to describe a place, means 'remote from observation; hidden'.[29] Rather like the seventeenth-century poet Katherine Phillips, it might be said of Roberts that her relation to Wales, paradoxically perhaps, enabled her as a poet by providing 'That private shade' from which she could engage with the world beyond.[30] But for Roberts, south Carmarthenshire was not a romanticized retreat from the anomie of the metropolis or the horrors of civilian warfare; rather, it was a living ecosystem whose rhetorical invisibility – its symbolic erasure from imperial cartographies of British national space – designated it a site in which to work out alternative national identities, and strategies of resistance.

Applied to a person, 'obscure' signifies 'not illustrious or famous; humble', or 'inconspicuous, little-known'.[31] In the context of Roberts's writing strategies, this definition points to her dismantling of the heroic pretensions of the avant-garde, through a close attention to everyday life and the language(s) of the working-class community among whom she lived (many of her poems challenge the conventions of high literary discourse by ventriloquizing the idiomatic speech of villagers whom she knew in Llanybri). But 'inconspicuous, little-known' also describes Roberts's allotted place in the history of twentieth-century British and Welsh literary culture, at least until relatively recently. She enjoyed a certain amount of literary acclaim during the 1940s and early 1950s; championed by T. S. Eliot, her editor at Faber, her writing was published in many well-known journals, including *Wales*, the literary magazine edited by Keidrych Rhys, *Life and Letters Today*, George Orwell's *Tribune*, *Poetry London*, *Horizon*, and American publications such as *New Directions*. But critical enthusiasm for her work underwent a gradual decline during the 1950s. A manuscript for a new collection of poetry, 'The Fifth Pillar of Song', was turned down by Eliot in 1953, and compounding this setback, an art project she attempted in the Chislehurst caves in Kent over 1955–6 had to be aborted when part of the roof caved in.[32] Roberts experienced a severe downturn in her mental health after this, when she was in her mid forties, and took relatively little interest thereafter either in her writing or her poetic reputation.[33] Although a few of her poems were anthologized in collections of anglophone Welsh and British poetry during the twentieth and twenty-first centuries,[34] it was only with the landmark republication of her *Collected Poems* in 2005 under the skilful editorship of Patrick McGuinness that the importance of her writing began to garner wider recognition. It is to this new wave of interest that this volume responds.

The handful of scholars championing Roberts's cause during the 1980s and 1990s had always insisted on the significance of her writing to the wider story of the development of twentieth-century poetry in the British Isles. John Pikoulis, for instance, saw her as 'one of the period's most distinctive voices';[35] Tony Conran, a poet who acknowledged Roberts's influence on his own praxis, underlined her contribution as a poet of the Second World War,[36] while Nigel Wheale emphasized the continued relevance of her writing to an understanding of postmodernity.[37] With its heightened attention to the emerging information and capital flows that were to characterize the later twentieth century, its celebration of particularity and 'petit récits' over grand narratives and preoccupation with historical traces and environmental degradation, Roberts's writing undoubtedly looks both ways, to an old world and a new.

What, then, were the reasons for Roberts falling off the historical map of anglophone literary culture in Britain, at least for the best part of the twentieth century? One theory is that her 'risk-taking exuberance' fell out of favour in the 1950s, when the vogue for radical experiment and excess gave way to the empiricist, plain-speaking strategies of the Movement poets.[38] Additionally, while the avant-garde energies of British poetry of the 1930s were accompanied by a decentralizing, Celtic impetus (a phenomenon captured in John Goodby's term 'surregionalism'), the Movement was more conspicuously Anglocentric.[39] In Wales, too, the experimentalism of earlier anglophone Welsh writing was eclipsed by a new form of English-language poetry, which, spearheaded by R. S. Thomas, espoused Welsh nationalist principles but was 'indebted to the plain-style, anecdotal English mainstream tradition'.[40] Roberts's 'uncompromisingly eccentric' use of form and language has been cited as another possible reason for her neglect:[41] her poems overlay arcane diction derived from chemistry, geology and botany, while the cadences of local speech forms, inflected by the Welsh language, lend her English a heightened and estranged quality. Similarly, her localist aesthetic – her delight in naming places and practices unknown to the rest of the world – has been seen as a possible obstacle to wider recognition; Conran underlines the 'obscurity' of her 'private reference[s]', while Pikoulis sees her texts as deliberately 'riddling'.[42] However, other modernists have won widespread acclaim for work that is equally, if not more resistant to straightforward interpretation: Mina Loy, a writer assimilated to the inner circles of the modernist canon in recent years, 'disrupts ordinary readerly procedures' in analogous ways, while Robert Graves's free-associative mythography is perhaps even more idiosyncratic than Roberts's.[43] Furthermore, as several scholars concede, she 'goes out of her way to explain to the reader what she's doing': rather than deliberately excluding her reader, or belittling or obfuscating its Welsh subjects, her work presents itself as a bridge or entry-point to cultural difference, experienced on its own terms.[44]

More likely, then, the lack of visibility afforded to writers such as Roberts is resultant from covert biases inherent to the field of modernist studies itself. These biases, of course, have traditionally been brought to bear on the activities of women writers. While the scope of twentieth-century culture in Britain has now been expanded far beyond the small coterie of white, middle-class men favoured in earlier definitions of modernism, as Jane Garrity has argued, 'there has been a simultaneous and persistent marginalization of non-canonical writing by female modernists since the institutionalization of feminist criticism in the 1980s – even as some women writers now have a certain caché [sic].'[45] Attention to gender and feminist approaches has been somewhat eclipsed by the academy's 'material' and historicist turn over the past two decades, while non-canonical women writers in particular have arguably been subject to what Sharon Marcus identifies as 'patterns of citation that favor male authors and critics';[46] in Wales, Roberts was for many years regarded chiefly as a satellite of the much better-known Keidrych Rhys, though Tony Conran paved the way for her feminist reclamation by presenting her as a member of 'the heroic generation of Anglo-Welsh women poets', alongside modernists Margiad Evans and Brenda Chamberlain.[47]

Lynette Roberts's exclusion from mainstream accounts of twentieth-century literary culture could also be attributed to some of the spatial and temporal presumptions attached to prevailing conceptions of the terms 'modernism' and 'modernity'. Susan Stanford Friedman has argued that 'generalizations about historical periods typically contain covert assumptions about space that privilege one location over others':[48] in other words, the conventional dating of modernism (usually from the mid 1890s to the 1940s) automatically privileges certain forms of Anglo-American modernism, in mostly metropolitan locations, and neglects modernism's efflorescence in different locations across the world later on in the twentieth century. Modernist Welsh poetry, identified by John Goodby and Chris Wigginton as a belated phenomenon in comparison to its Irish, English and Scottish equivalents (it arose in English-language texts in the late 1930s, and not until ten years later in Welsh-language writing) seems to have been victim to the spatial preferences embedded in modernism's usual periodization.[49]

The intellectual and methodological shifts inaugurated by the new modernist studies promise to benefit the reputation of writers such as Roberts. Most evidently, as Douglas Mao and Rebecca L. Walkovitz have observed, the expansion of modernism's spatial parameters beyond the Western metropolis has spurred 'the study . . . of texts produced in other quarters of the world or by hitherto little-recognized enclaves in the privileged areas', meaning that 'members of marginalized social groups have been encountered with fresh eyes and ears'.[50] In addition, the new attention to global patterns of circulation, translation and exchange (and their role in the formation of modernist cultures) offers a useful frame for understanding Roberts's writing, steeped as it is in concepts of 'migration, entanglement, and mix-up'.[51] The 'transnational turn' marks a departure from earlier, Eurocentric models of modernist internationalism by placing emphasis on modernism's transformative interaction with colonial and postcolonial struggles.[52] The issue of whether twentieth-century Wales can be understood as a properly 'postcolonial' space is still a contested one.[53] But there is a strong case for suggesting that Welsh modernists, who, like Roberts, were struggling with Wales's particularly uneven modernity while participating in rhetorical acts of nation building, stand to gain from approaches to modernist culture that spotlight 'the agencies of writers, artists, philosophers, and other cultural producers in the emergent postcolonial world just as their new modernities are being formed'.[54]

Transnational approaches might be seen to risk glossing over modernism's engagement with the national, regional and/or the local, all of which are important to Roberts's poetry. But as Neil Alexander and James Moran have argued, the new attention to specific questions of geography and location 'within a wider context of displacement and global flows' can actually bring the significance of the local into clearer focus.[55] Consequently, this book draws on Jahan Ramazani's transnational approach to modernist poetics, remaining alert to how modernist art and literature 'interlace localities and nationalities with one another in a globally imagined space'.[56] It takes as a starting point the suggestion that Lynette Roberts's 'obscurity' (ascribed, but also self-consciously performed) gives us an optic through which to reconsider some of the centralizing, metropolitan, Euro- or anglocentric paradigms that have been naturalized by modernism's self-mythologies.[57] As many of the essays in this volume show, her work encourages a reflection on the multiplicity and particularity of modernism (and modernity's) spaces, which in term invites us to reconsider the 'time' and tenor of modernist activity, too.

Why 'locating Roberts'? The essays included in this volume analyze the environments to which her writing responds, and tease out the interwoven skeins of her national, cultural and political affiliations. However, as Zoë Skoulding demonstrates in her essay in this volume, Roberts's writing actively questions the notion of an ontological connection between the writer and her 'place'. In fact, the hybridity or heterogeneity of Roberts's vision reveals some of the political tensions and problems inherent to the task of 'locating' a writer in the first place. As Chana Kronfeld has suggestively argued:

> many of the exclusionary practices of literary theory and historiography can be traced back to an optical difficulty with stereoscopic and kaleidoscopic vision: the difficulty to see writers like Kafka, for example [and Lynette Roberts, a similarly 'minor' writer, in Deleuze and Guattari's terms], as simultaneously maintaining multiple literary affiliations, and to view these multiple affiliations as partial, potentially contradictory, and ambivalent.[58]

This volume, then, is informed by the 'locational' feminist approach called for by Stanford Friedman: 'a critical methodology that attends to a "multiplicity of heterogeneous" spatial and temporal locations simultaneously (e.g. nation, region, race, class, and sexuality as well as gender.'[59] As the diversity of approaches collected here suggests, there are many different ways of 'locating' Lynette Roberts; she can be regarded as an 'elective' Welsh writer, in Katie Gramich's terms, a driver in what Daniel Hughes defines as a Welsh modernist 'formation' that produced such famous texts as David Jones's *In Parenthesis* (1937) and Dylan Thomas's *Deaths and Entrances* (1946). More specifically, she can be seen in relation to what both Gramich and Michelle Deininger perceive as a distinctive tradition of Welsh (and

Welsh-identified) women's writing, or, in light of Zoë Skoulding's essay, as a writer of place and the environment whose work anticipates contemporary shifts in ecological and posthumanist thought. As I have argued, she can be read as a 'colonial' woman writer whose work, like Katherine Mansfield or Jean Rhys, remains 'precariously positioned between categories of nation, race or ethnicity';[60] or, as M. Wynn Thomas suggests in this volume, she can be situated in a global context, as a poet whose unorthodox techniques often have more in common with American and South American modernisms than their British inflections.

This collection as a whole brings together some of the most original and innovative research to have emerged on Roberts over the past decade, following the publication of her *Collected Poems*. It is designed to offer a way in to her complex but rewarding prose and poetics, mapping out the themes, historical contexts and influences that undergird her work, and tracing the inter-cultural encounters and webs of literary relationships out of which it emerged. The essays follow a broadly chronological structure, beginning with an account of Roberts's earliest memories and experiences of her native Argentina, and culminating in an analysis of her later reinvention as a mid-century author of historical fiction. In this way, they provide a clear pathway through Roberts's heterogeneous literary oeuvre, and offer an understanding of how her aesthetic practice and poetic sensibility responded to, and encoded, the rapidly changing social, political, economic and literary contexts that shaped Wales and Britain in the early to mid-twentieth century. It should also be stressed that while Roberts frequently made her life part of her art (a factor that renders biographical approaches to her work important), the essays collected here represent a series of different viewpoints on her writing, rather than any one definitive line on Lynette Roberts and her life experiences.

M. Wynn Thomas opens the volume with a response to the claim that Roberts 'is not so much Anglo-Welsh as American-Welsh'.[61] Drawing on an overlooked radio talk and verse drama, *El Dorado*, he argues that Roberts's early impressions of Argentina 'were not simply filed away in memory to be retrieved as nostalgia' but remained an active, shaping force throughout her time in Llanybri. Roberts's poetics, he suggests, can be seen as resolutely 'compound' – the product of complex transactions between memory and observation, 'old' and 'new' worlds. His original analysis demonstrates that, as Stanford Friedman puts it, '[t]raveling and intermixing cultures are not unidirectional, but multidirectional; not linear influences, but reciprocal ones; not passive assimilations, but actively transformative ones'.[62]

The following group of chapters takes up Wynn Thomas's exploration of hybridity and adaptation, from the perspective of gender. Katie Gramich considers the implications of Roberts's 'elective' Welsh identity, arguing that she utilizes her chosen identity as a Welshwoman to address a critique of imperialism and war. For Gramich, the theme of hospitality is central to Roberts's lyric poetry. Seen as 'an ethical encounter . . . transformative of both self and other', hospitality (given and received) is shown to offer a new model for inter-cultural relations. The relationship between 'modernism, robust cultural exploration and the outsider form of the female-authored short story in Wales' is given sensitive treatment in Michelle Deininger's essay. Situating Roberts's collection *An Introduction to Village Dialect With Seven Stories* in relation to a broader tradition of women's short fiction in Wales, Deininger suggests that Roberts's short stories harness ethnographic techniques to capture 'the moment at which cultural traditions seep back into modern life', and to reflect upon questions of cultural memory, loss and preservation, particularly as they pertain to women's lives.

The subsequent group of essays elaborates on Roberts's cultural politics and complex engagement with the past. Andrew Webb's essay takes as its focus the interplay of material forces that shape the sites of Roberts's writing, suggesting that the concept of the 'semi-periphery' – a space shaped by 'conflicts between a globalizing capitalist modernity and a surviving, or reinvented, indigenous culture' – offers a useful model for understanding the temporal instability and multi-scale geographies that characterize Roberts's writing. Focusing on *Gods with Stainless Ears*, his essay illuminates Roberts's search 'for a poetic form adequate to the task of capturing the two poles of . . . [her] historical context' – the local and the global.

Daniel Hughes takes on two of Welsh modernism's megaliths: David Jones's *In Parenthesis* and Lynette Roberts's *Gods with Stainless Ears*. Jones's formative influence on Roberts has been detected by several critics,[63] but Hughes's essay is the first to excavate their affinity in depth. Drawing on archival evidence, he argues that both writers saw themselves as central players in the construction of a 'modern Welsh culture' – a project reflected in a poetics that is at once centripetal and centrifugal, oriented simultaneously toward an archaic past and an emergent future. My essay takes a closer look at the role of the residual in Roberts's writing, arguing that a revisionary engagement with the culture of the Middle Ages is the cornerstone of her unique avant-garde. Citing modernism's engagement in discourses of national retrenchment and regeneration during the 1940s, I suggest that the medieval past appears as an imaginative frame through which to participate in, and reimagine, Welsh tradition, from a liminal, gendered point of view; emphasizing a sense of history as matter and masquerade, Roberts presents the performing female body as the basis for recasting national tradition as a whole.

The next two essays consider the geographical and ecological dimensions of Roberts's writing, examining how her awareness of Llanybri as a living bioregion catalyzes the transformation of poetic perception in her work. For Leo Mellor, Roberts's 'wartime work is fundamentally shaped by the particularities of the estuarine, a space that is both a boundary and always itself in cyclical flux.' The rhythms of the 'estuarine' or 'intertidal' link village life with wider, inhuman forces beyond it, and are used by Roberts (and other writers of the 1940s) as a mode of 'apprehending the terrifying uncontainability of modern warfare'. Zoë Skoulding posits listening as central to the process of adaptation enacted in her work. Observing how new sound technologies encouraged 'a reflexive awareness of the listener's role', she suggests that Roberts's attention to the many sounds and languages that impinged on her speaks of a 'perception of her environment [that] is neither passive nor static, but an active means of participation'. In Skoulding's account, '[to] be listening', following Jean-Luc Nancy, 'is always to be on the edge of meaning': listening to the Welsh landscape is an attempt to decipher the future, as much as the lived complexities of the present.

Charles Mundye directs attention to Roberts's incarnation as a prose writer, a late stage largely neglected in critical accounts of her oeuvre. Focusing on *The Endeavour* (1954), a dramatic reimagining of the first major journey of Captain Cook, he demonstrates that the text 'provides a unique opportunity to re-evaluate the contested and evolving understanding of mid-century literary thinking and practice, especially as it relates to modernism and its aftermaths.' Charting Roberts's interactions with Robert Graves and Edith Sitwell, he claims that *The Endeavour*'s 'generic restlessness' – its amalgam of autobiography, natural history and travelogue – is symptomatic of the challenges involved in carving out a role as professional woman writer at mid century.

The aim in assembling these essays in one volume is not to offer a unified or comprehensive theory of Lynette Roberts's writing, or of Welsh modernism more broadly. Instead, the book offers a series of new interventions that – for the first time – address the full gamut of her literary endeavours, not only as a poet, but as a short story writer, novelist and broadcaster, too. All of the contributions call attention to the range and ambition of Roberts's thinking, described by Mundye as 'interdisciplinary and international before such requirements would become the sine qua non' of modern scholarship. It is perhaps fitting, then, that this volume as a whole should also look to the future: posing as many questions as it does answers, it looks forward to the new readers and new readings generated by the wider dissemination and discussion of Roberts's work.

All this resolves itself into the simple question: why Lynette Roberts? The recent rediscovery of her poetry, as Mellor has observed, has begun to change a number of critical narratives – about Welsh and/or anglophone modernism, or the complexity of a (still overlooked) 1940s culture of poetic verve and experimentation. This book reflects on and extends these ongoing critical conversations. As the essays collected here show, Roberts's writing illuminates the impressive range and ambition of literary responses to the cataclysm of World War II in Britain, as well as the cultural impact of the geopolitical changes attendant upon the contraction of the British Empire. Furthermore, as many of the essays also reveal, Roberts can be seen as one of those 'less familiar players and locales that are nevertheless crucial to understanding women's participation in that burst of creativity that later became known as modernism',[64] and thus any volume on Roberts necessarily participates in a wider, ongoing drive to reconsider women's contribution to twentieth-century literary culture.[65]

Roberts's self-consciously situated poetics reminds us that '[s]o much depends ... on place, proximity, position.'[66] As I have suggested, reading her work invites us to re-read dominant narratives of British and Anglo-American modernism 'from the [position of the] deprived hinterlands' – a process that promises to reveal the localism and diversity of even canonical forms of high modernism.[67] Harnessing 'countercanonical' forms and the rhythms of everyday life, her writing shows how late modernists sought to uncouple modernism from urban elitism through a cultural 'return to the folk'.[68] Yet, it does not just stage a conflict between rural and metropolitan versions of modernity: with its emphasis on patterns of recurrence and cyclical return, her style also resonates with Edouard Glissant's conception of a 'circular nomadism' that 'makes every periphery into a center . . . it abolishes the very notion of center and periphery'.[69] Her writing, then, encourages us to decentre and devolve how we think about modernist cultures, to focus in on the particular. It also points to the 'heteroreferentiality' of national cultures in the British Isles and beyond – their formation through confrontations and minglings across *and within* national borders.[70] Its value lies in challenging nostalgic and monocultural myths of nationhood, and in asking us to imagine more flexible, materially embedded, creative models of belonging, suitable for our complex, post-digital world.

Notes

[1] John Goodby and Chris Wigginton, 'Welsh Modernist Poetry: Dylan Thomas, David Jones, and Lynette Roberts', in *Regional Modernisms*, ed. Neal Alexander and James Moran (Edinburgh: Edinburgh University Press, 2013), pp. 160–83 (p. 175); Miranda Hickman, 'Modernist Women Poets and the Problem of Form', in *The Cambridge Companion to Modernist Women Writers*, ed. Maren Tova Linett (Cambridge: Cambridge University Press, 2010), pp. 33–46 (pp. 42–3).

[2] The term 'premature nostalgia' is Alexandra Harris's; see Alexandra Harris, *Romantic Moderns: English Writers, Artists and the Imagination from Virginia Woolf to John Piper* (London: Thames and Hudson, 2010), p. 175.

[3] Dylan Thomas, *The Collected Letters of Dylan Thomas*, ed. Paul Ferris (London: Dent, 1985), p. 418.

[4] For accurate information on Roberts's life, see Patrick McGuinness's introductions to *Lynette Roberts: Collected Poems* (Manchester: Carcanet, 2005), especially pp. xi–xix, and *Lynette Roberts: Diaries, Letters and Recollections* (Manchester: Carcanet, 2008), especially pp. vii–xi. Allusions to some of these details are also found in her 'Radio Talk on South American Poems', in *Collected Poems* (p. 109), and 'Notes for an Autobiography', in *Diaries, Letters and Recollections* (p. 192). Extracts from this document were originally published as 'Parts of an Autobiography' in the *Poetry Wales* special issue on Lynette Roberts, 19/2 (1983), 30–50. While several of the contributors here draw on these notes to illustrate their discussions, McGuinness has nevertheless advocated caution in the light of the circumstances under which they were written, pointing out that Roberts had experienced significant difficulties in her mental health during this period. See his notes in *Diaries, Letters and Recollections*, p. 228.

[5] Reporting on a lunch held for Cecil Roberts on his retirement from the Midland Railway, the *Buenos Aires Herald* quoted a speech by C. Gerez in which he emphasized the staff's 'affection for the man'. Another speaker, Mr Diego Pettigrew, claimed that the company 'found in our guest of honour

a splendid guardian, one who has provided what we might call a double protection for the future.' 'Farewell to Mr Roberts', *Buenos Aires Herald*, 3 April 1936, 10.

6   Roberts, 'Notes for an Autobiography', p. 199.
7   Lynette Roberts, 'Royal Mail', in *Collected Poems*, ed. Patrick McGuinness (Manchester: Carcanet, 2005), p. 27. Hereafter the *Collected Poems* will be cited as CP. A mimeo typescript version of her 'radio ballad', *El Dorado* (1953), bears a handwritten note by Roberts describing how her mother would sing a Spanish lullaby to her as a child. The music, she writes, 'is most strange elusive & full of atmosphere a sea of green pampas filled with rising birds.' See Harry Ransom Center, University of Texas at Austin, Lynette Roberts Collection, 2.1, p. 18. As M. Wynn Thomas notes in his chapter in this volume, Roberts in 'Radio Talk on South American Poems' explains that she included with the radio broadcast a lullaby 'which my mother in Mechita sang to me' (*CP*, 113).
8   These events are narrated in her 'Notes for an Autobiography': ' "It's so hot, I'd love a cold drink from that well. Ask Alfredo to bring us some." She drank it and said it was most refreshing. "Would I have some?" "No thanks Mummy" I replied.' See *Diaries, Letters and Recollections*, p. 192.
9   See Patrick McGuinness, 'Introduction', in *Collected Poems*, p. xiii.
10 M. Wynn Thomas, *Corresponding Cultures: The Two Literatures of Wales* (Cardiff: University of Wales Press, 1999), p. 84.
11 Alun Lewis, letter to his parents (1941), quoted in John Pikoulis, 'Lynette Roberts and Alun Lewis', *Poetry Wales*, 19/2 (1983), 9–29 (14).
12 McGuinness, 'Introduction', in *Diaries, Letters and Recollections*, p. vii.
13 McGuinness, 'Introduction', in *Diaries, Letters and Recollections*, p. vii. Roberts inhabited the caravan in Laugharne for a period during the summer of 1949, following her separation from Keidrych Rhys. After her divorce from Rhys in 1949, she moved to London, later moving the caravan to the Hertfordshire countryside to be near her children's boarding school (it eventually ended up by the Chislehurst caves in Kent). At the same time they had a fixed London address, at 3 Kent Terrace NW1. For further biographical information on Roberts's caravan, see Charles Mundye's chapter in this volume, 'Lynette Roberts's *The Endeavour*: a Generic Adventure'.
14 Laura Wainwright, 'New Territories in Modernism: Anglophone Welsh Writing, 1930–49' (unpublished PhD thesis, Cardiff University, 2010), p. 69.
15 Lynette Roberts, 'A Carmarthenshire Diary' (26 June 1940), in *Diaries, Letters and Recollections*, ed. McGuinness, p. 25.
16 Jane Garrity, *Step-daughters of England: British Women Modernists and the National Imaginary* (Manchester and New York: Manchester University Press, 2003), pp. 1–2, 27.
17 Katie Gramich, *Twentieth-Century Women's Writing in Wales: Land, Gender, Belonging* (Cardiff: University of Wales Press, 2007), p. 5.
18 Garrity, *Step-daughters of England*, p. 27.
19 See, for example, Tyrus Miller's suggestion that late modernism 'reopens the modernist enclosure of form onto the work's social and political environs', in *Late Modernism: Politics, Fiction, and the Arts Between the World Wars* (Berkeley, Los Angeles and London: University of California Press,

1999), p. 20. For an analysis of the intersections between late modernist culture in Britain and contemporary developments in anthropological and cultural thought, see Jed Esty, *A Shrinking Island: Modernism and National Culture in England* (Princeton: Princeton University Press, 2003). Kristin Bluemel's *Intermodernism: Literary Culture in Mid-Twentieth-Century Britain* (Edinburgh: Edinburgh University Press, 2009) considers modernism's involvement with the documentary form and Mass Observation movement during the 1930s and 1940s, while Samuel Hynes's influential *The Auden Generation: Literature and Politics in England in the 1930s* (London: The Bodley Head, 1976) sees British literature of the 1930s as symptomatic of 'a private self becoming aware of the public situation' (p. 143).

[20] Maggie Humm, 'Women Modernists and Visual Culture', in *The Cambridge Companion to Modernist Women Writers*, pp. 146–59 (p. 154).

[21] Roberts, 'A Carmarthenshire Diary', pp. 4, 17.

[22] Roberts, 'A Carmarthenshire Diary', p. 17.

[23] Roberts, unpublished letter to Alun Lewis (undated, *c*.1940–1), Alun Lewis Collection, National Library of Wales, Aberystwyth (pp. 3–4).

[24] Bluemel, *Intermodernism*, p. 1.

[25] Jane Marcus, 'Alibis and Legends: The Ethics of Elsewhereness, Gender and Estrangement', in *Women's Writing in Exile*, ed. Mary Lynn Broe and Angela Ingram (Chapel Hill and London: University of North Carolina Press, 1989), pp. 269–94 (p. 285).

[26] Angela Ingram, 'Introduction', in *Women's Writing in Exile*, p. 5.

[27] Ingram, *Women's Writing in Exile*, p. 6.

[28] Robert Crawford, 'Macdiarmud in Montrose', in *Locations of Literary Modernism: Region and Nation in British and American Modernist Poetry*, ed. Alex Davis and Lee M. Jenkins (Cambridge: Cambridge University Press, 2000), pp. 35–56 (p. 55).

[29] *Oxford English Dictionary*, adj. and n. obscure (4): *www.oed.com* (last accessed 4 February 2018).

[30] Katherine Philips, 'To my Lord Archbishop of Canterbury his Grace 1664', in *The Collected Works of Katherine Philips, the Matchless Orinda*, 3 vols, ed. Patrick Thomas, Germaine Greer and R. Little (Stump Cross: Stump Cross Books, 1990–3), I. p. 239, ll. 1–10. I draw here on Sarah Prescott's discussion in ' "That private shade, wherein my Muse was bred": Katherine Philips (1632–1664) and the poetic spaces of Welsh retirement', *Philological Quarterly*, 88/4 (2009), 345–64.

[31] *Oxford English Dictionary*, adj. and n. obscure (6): *www.oed.com* (last accessed 4 February 2018).

[32] McGuinness, 'Introduction', in *Collected Poems*, p. xviii.

[33] McGuinness, 'Introduction', in *Collected Poems*, p. xviii. Diagnosed with schizophrenia, Roberts was to be committed four times under the Mental Health Act to St David's Hospital, Carmarthen.

[34] These include Kenneth Rexroth's *The New British Poets* (1949) and, much later, the *Anthology of Twentieth-Century British and Irish Poetry*, ed. Keith Tuma (2001), *Welsh Women's Poetry 1460–2001*, ed. Catherine Brennan and Katie Gramich (2003), *Twentieth Century Anglo-Welsh Poetry*, ed. Danny Abse (2004), and Deryn Rees-Jones's *Modern Women Poets* (2005).

INTRODUCTION

35 John Pikoulis, 'The Poetry of the Second World War', in *British Poetry, 1900–50*, ed. Gary Day and Brian Docherty (Basingstoke: Macmillan, 1995), pp. 193–207 (p. 205).
36 Suggesting that *Gods with Stainless Ears* is one of the first large-scale poems in English to articulate the experience of modern warfare from an explicitly gendered, female perspective, Conran argues that there is a 'case for claiming [the text] . . . as the greatest war-poem of the 1939–45 war, and, for that matter, as the war-poem to be expected from that war'. Anthony Conran, *The Cost of Strangeness: Essays on the English Poets of Wales* (Llandysul: Gomer, 1982), p. 201.
37 Nigel Wheale, 'Lynette Roberts: Legend and Form in the 1940s', *Critical Quarterly*, 36/3 (1994), 4–19 (4).
38 Conran, *Cost of Strangeness*, p. 197. Correspondence between Roberts and the BBC informs that her unpublished novel the 'Book of Nesta' was turned down for radio broadcast in the late 1940s because the commissioner felt its avant-garde tendencies were no longer to the taste of a mass audience. See Harry Ransom Center, University of Texas at Austin, Lynette Roberts Collection, 3.7, Letter from P. H. Burton, Features Producer (Wales) at the BBC, to Lynette Roberts, 17 November 1948.
39 For a discussion of this concept in relation to the poetry of Dylan Thomas, see John Goodby, *The Poetry of Dylan Thomas: Under the Spelling Wall* (Liverpool: Liverpool University Press, 2013).
40 Goodby and Wigginton, 'Welsh Modernist Poetry', pp. 160–83 (p. 161).
41 Conran, *Cost of Strangeness*, p. 197.
42 Anthony Conran, 'Lynette Roberts: The Lyric Pieces', *Poetry Wales* (special issue on Lynette Roberts) 19/2 (1983), 125–33 (125–6); Pikoulis, 'The Poetry of the Second World War', p. 205.
43 Hickman, 'Modernist Women Poets and the Problem of Form', pp. 33–44 (p. 36).
44 Conran, *Cost of Strangeness*, p. 196. McGuinness argues that, unlike high modernists such as T. S. Eliot, Roberts's style has an unironical directness that speaks of 'an enabling – and in the best sense unsophisticated – belief in language's sufficiency' ('Introduction', in *Collected Poems*, p. xxxvi).
45 Jane Garrity, 'Modernist Women's Writing: Beyond the Threshold of Obsolescence', *Literature Compass*, 10/1 (2013), 15–29 (16).
46 Sharon Marcus, 'Feminist Criticism: A Tale of Two Bodies', *PMLA*, 121/5 (2006), 1725.
47 Anthony Conran, *Frontiers in Anglo-Welsh Poetry* (Cardiff: University of Wales Press, 1997), p. 165.
48 Susan Stanford Friedman, 'Periodizing Modernism: Postcolonial Modernities and the Space/Time Borders of Modernist Studies', *Modernism/modernity*, 13/3 (2006), 425–43 (426).
49 Goodby and Wigginton, 'Welsh Modernist Poetry', p. 160.
50 Douglas Mao and Rebecca L. Walkowitz, 'The New Modernist Studies', *The Modern Language Association of America*, 123/3 (2008), 737–47 (737–8).
51 Mao and Walkovitz, 'The New Modernist Studies', 738–9; Rebecca L. Walkowitz, *Cosmopolitan Style: Modernism Beyond the Nation* (New York: Columbia University Press, 2006), p. 6.

[52] Mao and Walkovitz, 'The New Modernist Studies', 745; Stanford Friedman, 'Periodizing Modernism', 427.
[53] While historians have noted Wales's historical involvement in (and sometimes complicity with) British/English imperialism, the upwelling of nationalist consciousness that saw the foundation of Plaid Genedlaethol Cymru, the Welsh National Party, in 1925, coincided with (and was indirectly influenced by) 'home rule' movements in former British colonies including Ireland and India. Kirsti Bohata's *Postcolonialism Revisited* (Cardiff: University of Wales Press, 2004) offers an eloquent reflection on Raymond Williams's perception of Wales as a colonized nation. Demonstrating the relevance of postcolonial critical paradigms to an understanding of anglophone Welsh writing, Bohata indicates the problems posed by Wales to the 'progressive-linear' models according to which the postcolonial is usually understood.
[54] Stanford Friedman, 'Periodizing Modernism', 427.
[55] Alexander and Moran, *Regional Modernisms*, p. 4.
[56] Jahan Ramazani, *A Transnational Poetics* (Chicago: University of Chicago Press, 2009), p. 15.
[57] For instance, Chana Kronfeld has argued that many seminal studies, including Hugh Kenner's 'The Making of the Modernist Canon' (1984), portray modernist culture as an overwhelmingly deterritorialized yet centralized phenomenon. See Chana Kronfeld, *On the Margins of Modernism: Decentring Literary Dynamics* (Berkeley, Los Angeles and London: University of California Press, 1996), p. 9. Malcolm Bradbury presents modernism as an 'art of the cities', arguing that while figures such as Joyce and Hemingway retained certain local affiliations, these were always refracted 'from the distance of an expatriate perspective of aesthetic internationalism'. Malcolm Bradbury, 'The Cities of Modernism', in *Modernism 1890–1930*, ed. Malcolm Bradbury and James McFarlane (London: Penguin, 1991), pp. 94–104 (pp. 96, 101).
[58] Kronfeld, *On the Margins of Modernism*, p. 12.
[59] Susan Stanford Friedman, *Mappings: Feminism and the Cultural Geographies of Encounter* (Princeton: Princeton University Press, 1998), p. 5; Garrity, 'Beyond the Threshold of Obsolescence', 15.
[60] Maren Tova Linett, 'Modernist Women's Literature – an Introduction', in *The Cambridge Companion to Modernist Women Writers*, pp. 1–16 (p. 12).
[61] Conran, *Cost of Strangeness*, p. 188.
[62] Friedman, 'Periodizing Modernism', 430.
[63] See also Conran, *Cost of Strangeness*, p. 195. McGuinness has observed that 'perhaps the nearest to her in vision and conception is David Jones, another poet who created from, and was created by, war and Wales.' ('Introduction', in *Collected Poems*, p. xxxvi).
[64] Linett, 'Modernist Women's Literature', p. 11.
[65] As exemplified in recent years, for instance, by *The History of British Women's Writing* series at Palgrave Macmillan, under the editorship of Jennie Batchelor and Cora Kaplan; the expansive *Routledge Encyclopedia of Modernism* (2016): www.rem.routledge.com also includes a significant number of entries on lesser-known modernist women writers and artists, such as Valentine Penrose (1898–1978), Lesbia Harford (1891–1927), Dalia Rabikovitch (1936–2005) and Catherine Carswell (1879–1946).

66 Laura Doyle and Laura Winkiel (eds), *Geomodernisms: Race, Modernism, Modernity* (Bloomington and Indianapolis: Indiana University Press, 2005), p. 1.
67 Raymond Williams, *The Politics of Modernism: Against the New Conformists* (London and New York: Verso, 2007 [1989]), p. 47; Kronfeld, *On the Margins of Modernism*, p. 5.
68 Daniel Williams, 'Welsh Modernism', in *The Oxford Handbook of Modernisms*, ed. Peter Brooker, Andrzej Gasiorek, Deborah Longworth and Andrew Thacker (Oxford: Oxford University Press, 2010), pp. 797–816 (p. 810).
69 Edouard Glissant, *Poetics of Relation* (1990), trans. Betsy Wing (Ann Arbor: University of Michigan, 1997), p. 29, discussed in Charles W. Pollard, *New World Modernisms: T. S. Eliot, Derek Walcott, and Kamau Brathwaite* (Charlottesville: University of Virginia Press, 2004), p. 5.
70 Irene Ramalho Santos, *Atlantic Poets: Fernando Pessoa's Turn in Anglo-American Modernism* (Hanover: University Press of New England, 2003), p. 4.

1

THE SCARLET WOMAN

M. Wynn Thomas

Lynette Roberts and Keidrych Rhys were married in Llansteffan on 4 October 1939. The very same month her poem 'To Keidrych Rhys' was published in *Wales*, the brash harlequinade of a literary journal established and edited (up to this particular number) by her colourful, buccaneering, incorrigibly errant new husband. 'I have seen', she there declared with a bardic claim to omnipresence that later, no doubt, she would have recognized made her unconscious kin to the ancient Taliesin, legendary poet-prophet of her adopted country:[1]

> light birds sailing
> A ploughed field in wine
> Whose ribs expose grave treasures
> Inca's gilt-edged mine; . . .
> I have seen, the mountain of pumas
> Harbour a blue-white horse.
> The tinsel-rain on dog's coat
> Zebra shoes at night.[2]

It reads like an ecstatic epithalamium, while its title, 'To Keidrych Rhys', seems also to turn it into a gift-giving ritual; a bride's ceremonial public display of her lavish dowry. That dowry, as the poem makes clear, is all the exotica of her 'foreign' imagination. And it is this largesse, in all its richness, that is again flaunted in the 'Poem' she published in the next (winter) issue of *Wales*:

For my house is clothed in Scarlet.
Scarlet my household, Scarlet my mind, spiced herbed and cherished,
   all alcoves wine
Laughter in corners, winks on air chasing shadows on ceiling bruins
   in lair.
Plush lacquered incense, open flowers on wall, frothed milk bread
   and honey to overcome falls
So come myth children, no longer fear, the winter is impotent under
   my care
For my house is clothed in Scarlet.[3]

Roberts had already lived an extraordinary life, peripatetic, adventurous and not just international but intercontinental. From the beginning, the solid privileges and comforts that were hers thanks to her father's career as manager (and later director) of Argentina's Western Railway had been offset by his rather louche, freewheeling personal conduct.[4] A family life supportive enough but rather rickety and improvisatory had been permanently destabilized by the early death of her mother. Thus partly, perhaps, in self-defence, Roberts early developed a restless, daring, unconventional spirit of her own. Resilience and adaptability had been hard-wired into her. As a girl, she'd survived sleazy boarding houses; as a young woman in Buenos Aires, she'd acted as her father's companion on formal occasions while also holding her own 'soirées' for artists and intellectuals; in London, she'd dabbled in bohemia yet acquired diplomas for interior decoration, completed Constance Spry courses in flower arranging, and run her own florist business.

There is therefore, in retrospect, something rather poignant about this defiant poem by a gutsy autumn bride about to start her married life at the outbreak of war in a damp, cold, bleakly windy corner of rural Wales, in a tiny stone cottage with an earthen floor. At least she had her 'myth children' to comfort her and to nourish her imagination, and from these she was to draw some of her solace in the challenging years ahead. But at times it was hard. 'I feel chequered with energy', she noted in her journal in the spring of 1940: 'Full of positive red squares and black negative ones. What shall I do?' (*DLR*, 8) And later that March, she recorded: 'The wind was cold. I drew my scarlet cape around me and walked leisurely, as village people do' (*DLR*, 9). It was an early attempt to adapt herself to her locality; to adopt its normalities (that leisurely walk) for camouflage, but without entirely repressing her creative energies – that defiantly scarlet cape that she took to wearing on all her walks became a blazon of her quietly scandalous internal difference, as did the 'scarlet letter' of Hesther Prynne in Nathaniel Hawthorne's celebrated novel. In a letter to Alun Lewis written during the early years of the war, Lynette Roberts gently corrected his supposition that the line 'my house is clothed in Scarlet' was influenced by Yeats. With characteristic directness, she informed him that it was in fact derived from the Bible – specifically, a line from Proverbs 31:21: 'She is not afraid of the snow for her household: for all her household *are* clothed with scarlet.'[5] She had been inspired, she told him, by 'the idea that the people for keeping warm in the winter clothed their house with scarlet', and had 'used snow as the contrast and the raging storm beating outside at the time.'[6] The poetry of the next few years was to show her devising strikingly original strategies of adaptation that would guarantee the creative survival of her singular identity. But, vivid with its own irrepressible idiosyncrasies, that poetry, too, became a kind of scarlet cape that kept her shivering 'foreign' imagination warm.

In the same October issue of *Wales* that saw the publication of his new wife's 'study in scarlet', Keidrych Rhys published a poem of his own, 'The Van Pool, Tichrig'. Which 'Van' he had in mind isn't entirely clear – 'fan' ('ban' in its original, non-mutated, form) being simply the Welsh for peak. 'A peak' is 'Y fan' ('f' in Welsh being the 'v' sound in English), and the Brecon Beacon peaks that loom over Keidrych Rhys's native district of the Ceidrych valley are known in Welsh as 'Bannau [plural of 'ban'] Brycheiniog' – the Breconshire peaks. But there is one 'b/fan' adjacent to the localities identified in Rhys's poem that stands out in popular imagination as in cultural memory, along with the pool at its base. The latter is known as 'Llyn y Fan Fach' ('the lake of the small peak') – a neighbouring peak being named 'y Fan Fawr' ('the Great Fan'). Attached to the spot is a well-known and greatly loved legend; that of the Lady of the Lake. She it is who lived under the pool's waters until she was wooed ashore by the entrancing rhymes of a young shepherd, whom she duly agreed to marry. Together they had several sons, but she had warned her human husband at the outset of the strange unbreakable conditions on which their unlikely alliance was based, and when, somewhat unthinkingly, he broke each of these in turn over a period of years, she sadly gathered about her all the cattle she had brought out of her native depths as dowry and departed back to the waters from which she had briefly emerged.

Whether Rhys, who wrote several poems about the 'Van Pool', actually had that specific lake and its legend in mind is immaterial. What is significant is that Lynette Roberts was to become enchanted by it. Noting this, critics and commentators have, unfortunately, been led to suppose that the phrase 'Hal-e-bant Fan Fach', in the poem 'Plasnewydd', is an allusion to the tale. It is not. 'Fan' (abridgement of 'Fanny') was a very common name for a Welsh sheepdog, and in her 'Carmarthenshire Diary' Roberts specifically mentions that her great friend and neighbour, Rosie Davies, had two sheepdogs, 'Fan and Tips' (*DLR*, 64). The phrase in the poem is therefore a record of the everyday instruction to a sheepdog – Fan ('fach' being simply here a form of endearment akin to 'dear') – to 'Hal-e-bant': that is 'Send [or shoo] him [cow or sheep, or naughty cat – 'pussy drwg'] away.' After all, for the incomer Roberts the mundane minutiae of Llanybri constituted a new exotic.

No, the significance of the Llyn y Fan legend probably went much deeper with Roberts than that. Could she have failed to recognize key aspects of herself in the tragic, seductive figure of that fey, faery lady? In that denizen of a strange, alien, beguiling world? Didn't that instinctive early gesture of presenting herself to her husband and his world at the very moment of her marriage as a 'scarlet woman', a visitor from a distant, foreign, scandalously opulent world, come to rhyme eerily in her ears with the story of the ill-fated Lady? Might it therefore not prove prophetic of a similar fate for herself? And might not her poetry bear witness to her predicament? What follows is a reflection on precisely such possibilities.

* * *

The poem with which Lynette Roberts announced her mature arrival as 'Welsh' poet to the world could scarcely have been more different from 'To Keidrych Rhys'. Her first collection, *Poems* (1944), opens with 'Poem from Llanybri', a title that designedly and deservedly represents Roberts as grounded in her adopted village. In it, she – who had lived in the village for fewer than two years – confidently presents herself as an insider, a native well versed in local customs and thoroughly (even nonchalantly) au fait with the patois; indeed as someone already 'authorized' to act as the confident voice of her community and to speak on its behalf. Hers is an impressive impersonation – for such it surely is – of cultural authority. But fully to appreciate its performative aspects and to value its complex, hard-earned, achievement one needs to acquaint oneself with writings by Roberts of an entirely different kind and place: those related to her earliest years in Argentina. It is, after all, no coincidence that the collection that opens with 'Poem from Llanybri' draws to a conclusion with a suite of poems about South America, before ending with a return to Cwmcelyn, the bay overlooking Laugharne across the Taf river. As she noted in July 1941, 'I have a backward glance at the Argentine[,] my father and Mechita [where she grew up]. I start a series of poems which were written here in Tygwyn but they are a South American group' (*DLR*, 218).

'Here are cucumbers in flower, tomatoes and sweet corn [*sic*],' she noted in her journal on 13 July 1941, 'but in my home – my South American home – we have bee-like humming-birds, flamingos wandering in the paddock, white peacocks, and the sun's resilient rays' (*DLR*, 37). No doubt sensitized anew by such nostalgic recollection, her eye was caught just two days later by the scarlet that seemed always to take her back in imagination to Argentina, prompting her to plan a 'Poem on moorhen and its scarlet garters' (*DLR*, 38).[7] She had nevertheless settled into her Welsh village with impressive resolution, had already grown to love aspects of life there, had started to master, through hard physical labour, some of the important skills and crafts of subsistence country living, and had begun to investigate her physical surroundings with a formidably 'scientific' analytic and forensic thoroughness even while appreciating its aesthetic and compositional aspects, brilliantly registering its characteristic forms, colours and textures with an artist's subtlety and sensitivity.

With the passing of time, she obviously came to feel real solidarity with the locals, and in particular to value the 'sisterhood' of women, strengthened by wartime conditions when, as she discovered through her own experience, they were left to survive traumas from childbirth to bombing, while struggling to keep body and soul together not only for themselves but their whole families. It was this practical experience of tough woman-power that led her, on VJ day, to declare angrily that 'War will exist until women become freed from slavery . . . it will exist until they become no longer the slaves of men but their leaders towards a preservation of life' (*DLR*, 69). And her campaigning identification with her subjugated gender, implicit in many of the poems in her 1944 collection, strengthened her inclination to identify with the Welsh as a subjugated people (*DLR*, 68). Her poetry was designed to promote liberation on both fronts.

Yet the value of Llanybri lay for her in its abiding, irreducible 'foreignness'. To the last, she remained what sociologists would label 'a participating observer'. To the very end she had to work hard to 'read' the locality – indeed omnivorous reading became an indispensable means, alongside constantly heightened observation, of gaining a clarity of understanding. And clarity was, for her, not just a passion but a consuming craving. She demanded of herself exactness of verbal and perceptual definition – her writing was underpinned by an obsession with classification and categorization that led to her autodidact's love affair with all the 'ologies' – anthropology, mythology, etymology, entomology, geology, mineralogy, ornithology, lepidopterology, and several more. Her appetite for clarity understandably made her impatient of the vague Celtic Twilight maunderings of Ernest Rhys, that irrepressible veteran of the 1890s (as well as unlikely friend of Whitman, Yeats and Pound) who turned up on her doorstep like a cheerful, irresponsible tramp.[8]

Her taste for dispassionate precision was no doubt in part inherited from her engineer father – she inclined to treat poems not as organic secretions but as complex functional assemblages, rather no doubt as he viewed railways. But it may also have owed something to her early exposure to the clarity of Argentine light, particularly in the region of the Andes. She commented with characteristic exactitude on the contrasting light of Wales, when mist and soft rain suddenly lifted and creatures, things and objects, caught in a 'magnesium light', stood out as if elementalized, washed clean of all superfluities:

> The rain, the continual downpour of rain, may also compensate us indirectly, by giving us that pure day which precedes it . . . During those intervals the rain water is reflected back to us through a magnetic prism of light . . . Here, then, in Wales, we frequently get three concentrations of light, where normally most countries only have two. This third eye, or shaft of light, gives us the same privilege as many of our scattered islands hold, which are devoted to the Saints. The light magnifies, radiates truth, and cleanses our dusty spirits. (*DLR*, 130)

She also valued the way the slow tempo and leisurely rhythm of life in a rural community enhanced awareness of every detail of ordinary living (*DLR*, 64). And then there was the contrast with the 'rich, mellow tones of English farmhouses' that meant she, like other English visitors, felt 'estranged and left singularly apart' (*DLR*, 127). She even felt that, in its clear-cut geometrical forms and simple colours, the village of Llanybri resembled a Cubist painting: 'the sharp outline of the whitewashed farms and houses as they stand against the skyline; the way in which the walls project geometrical planes of light that resemble still-life models of squares and cubes' (*DLR*, 127).

Like Hopkins, Roberts revered the sacred quiddity and inscape of bird, stone, leaf and flower and, again like him, she came to believe that the strict-metre poetry of traditional Welsh *barddas* was perfectly consonant in its 'hardness' and disciplined exactitudes of sound and metre with the society and landscape to which it was truly 'native'. She came to view traditional Welsh rural crafts and architecture in the same 'light'. There was percipience in her early comment that the poetic form of the Welsh *englyn* – which she proceeded to approximate in English – was 'itself like the village, like a piece of quartz' (*DLR*, 5).

The foreignness of Llanybri was, then, indispensable to her creativity. While empathizing strongly with a village community in which 'every home [is] a separate unit . . . of the nation's culture' (*DLR*, 130), she was aware of the secretiveness and peasant tricksiness of her neighbours. 'The continual subjugation of the Welsh by conquerors has made them distrustful of strangers', she noted sympathetically: 'They have grown accustomed to using their wits' (*DLR*, 68). Even as the village genuinely became a deeply loved home, it was not entirely 'my home', which was still 'my South American home'. In the summer of 1941 she could still feel 'lonely and homesick for the Argentine' (*DLR*, 37), recalling the pampas, the Incas' mountain grave, her railway-engineer father, the great River Plate (*Río de la Plata*) region, the convent where she was educated, and Mechita where she was raised. 'I had the strong desire', she frankly admitted, 'to leave the village and go to South America.' A year earlier, she had confessed to feeling 'cramped and barred from life', 'tired of reading the *Western Mail* every day. The only news from the outside world. I'm tired of reading the poems of puny poets and want to do something. Something. I don't know what' (*DLR*, 9). The fall of France in the summer of 1940 had prompted a revealingly impassioned response:

> I felt like running off to France and selling my British status. And I could do this, since I held an Argentine Passport and could demand protection from the Argentine Embassy. If it were not for the understanding and knowledge of most of the people here in Llanybri, there, and everywhere, I would REBEL and mightily. The villagers are superb in thought and

action, and strangely enough there is considerable unity in their thoughts and approach to the war. They are far more intelligent and efficient than most of the ways and means of Parliament. (*DLR*, 17)

A prison Llanybri could seem at times for her spirit – some of the locals even briefly suspected her of spying – even as it was becoming a refuge and a place of sanity in a mad world, and a catalyst of creativity. Even in Llanybri, the New World was ever present at the deepest levels of her being, although it was not until war's end that she explicitly began to address the formative significance of her native South America in her writings.

* * *

Her sensuous memories of Argentina retained an almost hallucinatory intensity for Roberts ('Memory widens our senses', she was later suggestively to write of her New World recollections) (*CP*, 28), partly perhaps because her periods of living there were ephemerally brief and partly because they marked emotionally charged experiences in her family life. Her heightened powers of sensuous attention and recall were in any case always the most stunningly impressive aspect of both her personal life and her creative imagination. 'One of my earliest memories', she wrote in her bewitching radio talk on the origins of her South American poems, 'was to wander out of the gate and stare at the South American pampas.' 'The New World', she hauntingly admitted, 'with its strange subtlety absorbed me with its vivid impressions, the spinning windmills irrigating the *quintas*, and as the corrugated containers filled with water, I bathed in them within shadow of the peach trees' (*CP*, 107).

But these impressions were not simply filed away in memory to be retrieved as nostalgia; they actively informed her responses even to Llanybri, eventually finding issue in her creative work. The suite of powerful poems included in her 1944 collection offer overt evidence of this. But more intriguing, if less arresting, are the examples available in the same collection, as in her journal, of more covert forms of indebtedness to her South American past. Later, in her radio talk, she was to place on public record her indignation at what was happening to the traditional lifestyle of the 'peasants/peons' of her native land:

> The small pueta where people lived with their horses tethered to the wooden posts outside their shacks, their songs, knife-fights, guitars, the

dark shadows the peons cast as they gamble behind clouds of dust as the horse race took place. They were and still are at the root culture of the Argentine soil. So when the thatched roofs were torn down and corrugated roofs placed in their stead and values were placed on the wrong issues, I rebelled and wrote to establish belief in these people in my poem called 'The New World'. (*CP*, 107–8)

That poem, published in her 1944 collection, opens by evoking the original life of the peons, before they were forced first to flee 'unwanted further on into the land' (*CP*, 28). There, where 'Spiders lifted the lids of their homes and slammed them back' – the detail is taken directly from her own earliest memories of the dusty end-of-the-line township of Mechita where she spent her childhood – 'they / strove, the harder not to be seen.' (*CP*, 28–9) But to no avail. Modernity, in the form of a rapacious capitalism, caught ruthlessly up with them:

> Lost now. No sound or care can revive their ways:
> La Plata gambles on their courage, spends too flippantly,
> Mocks beauty from the shading tree, mounts a corrugated roof
>   over their cultured hut. (*CP*, 29)

The anger in these lines was magnified when her uncomprehending London editor asked her to alter the phrase about the corrugated roof, because 'it was so ugly. He did not see that that was the purpose of the whole poem. The *estancias* were being sold or mortgaged and the money drifted into the Casinos at La Plata. The peon or gaucho and the land were left in despair' (*CP*, 109).

In 1872 the gaucho's colourful, violent style of living had been famously glorified by José Hernández in *Martín Fierro* (1872/9), the 'national epic' that came to be regarded as epitomizing 'the root culture of the Argentine soil.' (*CP*, 108) And Roberts's memories of both gauchos and peons were themselves clearly rooted, as her radio talk shows, in a very small child's frustration at having been debarred from knowing more about their tantalizingly close but mysteriously 'other', seemingly 'authentic' and 'indigenous' world.

In fact, as we can now see, her 'instinctive' sense of that world's 'otherness' had a cultural provenance. She grew up within the extensive immigrant, settler, community of an 'Anglo'[9] professional class and was thus very largely isolated not only from the indigenous cultures but from the dominant Hispanic culture of the country. Her response to the countryside, even, was mediated by the works of enormously influential 'Anglo-Argentine' writers like W. H. Hudson, to whose books Hispanic as well as British children were routinely introduced at school. In this respect, her positioning within Argentina was, like her situation in Llanybri, largely that of a participating outsider.[10] And the Eurocentricity of her outlook is everywhere marked.

It had, of course, been a common practice of European artists and intellectuals for two centuries to attribute sterling, precious, even redemptive qualities to a 'peasant' existence, valued for its supposed 'authenticities'.[11] But in Roberts's case such an ideology had a distinctive individual relevance and a corresponding intensity that made it a valuable creative asset. As we shall see, her sympathy with the dispossessed peons and gauchos fed into her gradual awareness that the Welsh – particularly the 'peasant' Welsh speakers of Llanybri and the rest of rural Wales – were a long subjugated people, their traditions variously threatened by mummification, barbaric modernization and obliteration.[12] Her empathy with their plight also fed into her poetics, central to which was the attempt at a sympathetic melding of old and new.

But it was not only the peons and gauchos of Argentina with which she imaginatively identified. An interest in the indigenous peoples is manifest in an interesting poem she wrote for radio about a notable incident in the early history of the Welsh colony in Patagonia. In 1883, eighteen years after the first landing in Puerto Madryn, four young men from what was still at that point an exclusively coastal settlement ventured prospecting along the Chubut river. Two of them penetrated inland some 400 miles, as far as the Andean foothills, where a couple of Araucans (members of the indigenous ethnocultural group nowadays known as the Mapuche) alarmed them with an invitation to visit their encampment. Rapidly retracing their steps, they had almost reached the safety of the settled region when they were ambushed. One of them was killed, but the other, John Evans, managed a Douglas Fairbanks escape by frantically spurring his horse into a prodigious leap across a canyon and then making his solitary way back through desert storms to the colony. Glyn Williams, a modern authority on the Welsh in Patagonia, has set the incident in context:

> This was the first sign of hostility by the native people against any member of the Welsh Colony in eighteen years of contact. There had been

several occasions when they had expressed dissatisfaction with the Welsh occupancy of their territory, but the evidence suggests that any threat of hostility by one of the groups against the Colony resulted in discussion by one of the other groups. The probable reason for this lies in the cruel genocidal campaign carried on against the native people independently by both the Argentine and Chilean armies between 1879 and 1885. It has been suggested that the Indians were a group of Northern Araucans who were driven south by the military and took the opportunity of strengthening the Argentinean harassment.[13]

It was to this episode, relayed to her by Cadvan Hughes, the son-in-law of John Evans, that Roberts turned when, at the end of the war, she began to consider ways in which she might put her childhood experiences in Argentina to creative advantage. Rejecting as too hackneyed the idea of a book of memoirs, she resolved instead to write a ballad about the Patagonian story, but '[i]n it of course [to use] many of my own memories, as a background, or reconstruction of the event' (*CP*, 112). She itemized some of the sensuous recollections of the pampas she particularly wanted to record:

> The quality of the thistles which they used for fuel and making rennet, their hollowness and crack, seeing iguanas as they flashed past from before the horses' hoofs, the legends, the racoon that I found on my dressing table, and who later was found curled up in sleep on my bed, the nutrias in hundreds, and flight, colour and song of the myriad birds, these I wanted to recreate. (*CP*, 112–13)[14]

As for the ballad form for which she opted, she undoubtedly appreciated its origins as a 'peasant', 'folk' form and its long history of local storytelling. But, given her enthusiasm at this time for the old Welsh *penillion* (simple stanzas of folk experience and wisdom to be sung to harp accompaniment) she may also have felt the ballad provided a rough but acceptable English cultural equivalent. 'I still have an ardent PASSION for *penillion*', she wrote to Robert Graves in 1947, 'I want to write *penillion* . . . I believe it is the most authentic and most wholesome material from which to build up any rural poetry. It is never sentimental in its original state' (*DLR*, 185).[15] And, since the poem makes explicit mention of Hernández's *Martín Fierro* ('*O ghost of Martín Fierro aid us*' (*CP*, 122)), it is further possible she may have felt the ballad form had a 'folk' pedigree and popular authority corresponding to the *payadas* of the *gauchesco*.[16] Indeed, the most adept because best adapted of the four Welsh adventurers whose story she tells is specifically commended for having learnt gaucho skills: 'He looked the gaucho in "wide awake" hat, / And lived that life as "guide" ' (*CP*, 119). In her autobiography, she specifically associated her ballad with the gaucho figure. Noting that a friend had sent her a record of native music for use in the radio broadcast of 'El Dorado', she added: 'He also sent a large book of national Gaucho implements which has been very useful' (*DLR*, 202). Given this mixture of sources, then, she may have viewed her ballad as a fruitful cultural hybrid; a mix of Welsh, English and Argentine cultural forms; a creative blend of old world and new.

That the poem connected Lynette Roberts to her earliest childhood in a particularly intimate way is underlined by its concluding with an old Spanish lullaby 'which my mother in Mechita sang to me' (*CP*, 113). She likewise identified strongly with the first Welsh settlers of Patagonia – although her personal wish to 'identify' as Welsh (if only partially) was a recent phenomenon, the product of her stay in Llanybri. It was evidently important for her to establish that the friendly relations the Welsh enjoyed with the native tribes marked them apart from the Spanish, and for that matter the English. The band that attacked the four Welsh prospectors are clearly identified as a maverick group of avengers, outraged by the wholesale slaughter of indigenous peoples by General Julio Argentino Roca and his forces during the infamous genocidal 'Conquest of the Desert'. In pointed contrast, Roberts gives pride of place to one of the colonists' key 'myths of origin', as related by Davies:

> '*Not long ago when we lived in caves,*
> *And Indians stood bare . . .*
> *From nowhere . . . My father spoke:*
> *The Chief stood back with care.*
>
> *Suddenly the Indian's wife bent down,*
> *And with thorn and thread as sinew,*
> *Without a word Father's trousers tacked*
> *And repaired the tear as new.*' (*CP*, 121)

The Patagonian equivalent of the Pocahontas story, this episode serves much the same purpose: it suggests that in welcoming the Welsh, the indigenous tribes implicitly bestowed a blessing on their invasion of the land. And in highlighting this 'myth',[17] it is as if Roberts is claiming that same blessing for herself, in the name of the 'Welshness' she supposedly shared with those first settlers. Hers, thus, becomes an authentic, primal relation to the land, 'innocent' of the stigma of violent misappropriation that marks the relationship to it of colonists like the Anglos and the Hispanics. In this way, the Welsh connection helped assuage the guilt she felt at the possibility of having been, if only by virtue of the white skin that bespoke her Europeanness, complicit in the seizure of the land from its original populations. Had she not read as a girl 'that the Incas if they shot a white man buried him upside down' (*DLR*, 195)?

Not that Roberts's interest in Patagonia was entirely nostalgic. On the contrary. She concluded her radio broadcast on the Welsh connection with an impassioned plea for contemporary Wales to pay attention to what had been achieved in the face of substantial odds in 'Y Wladfa', because there was so much to learn from the courage, adventure, resources and enterprise of the early settlers. Broadcast in 1945, her comments therefore applied in part to the immediate postwar period. But by then her six-year stay in Llanybri had made her aware of a far older, indeed seemingly chronic, malaise of the Welsh psyche, a lack of self-confidence that was the consequence of 'continual subjugation . . . by conquerors', as she perceptively put it in a diary entry that same year (*DLR*, 68). As a result, she remarked in her broadcast, 'Wales seems oppressed partly through her own misdirection and partly through outside jurisdiction' (*CP*, 133). A concentration on Welsh Patagonia 'would help to extend [the country's] vision, which at the moment, through suffering has become too parochial. An exchange, I believe, on all matters, such as agriculture, political and cultural, would stimulate and help both Countries to develop' (*CP*, 133).

This (liberating) concern to bring out the international dimensions and connections of Welsh life both past and present finds interesting creative issue in Roberts's poetry. The grandiose pseudo-scholarship paraded by Robert Graves as he constructed his own ingenious personal poetic mythography in a series of articles that culminated in *The White Goddess* appealed greatly to her, as the sustained correspondence between Graves and herself confirms. His fanciful narrative seemed to 'prove' that ancient Wales had been firmly linked in to a mythic pathway that had extended along the seaways and trade routes all the way through the Mediterranean to the Aegean and onwards to India, the source of all Indo-European cultures. Ancient Welsh legend and poetry everywhere bore covert testimony, he claimed, to this esoteric international 'song line', in which was encoded the primal secret religion of the 'White Goddess', whose priests were the druids and whose initiates were the bards.

Roberts's poem 'The Circle of C' is one in which she connects herself as Llanybri poet to this supposed tradition, since her consciously 'bardic' imagination, having been initiated into Graves's secret lore, perceives the 'C' of 'Cwmcelyn' (and of 'cinder" and 'curlew', both words that play a key role in the poem) to be a letter from the sacred 'tree alphabet' of the Celts.[18] Cwmcelyn bay thus reveals its hidden druidic aspects to her. Accordingly, she assumes the role of a devotee and petitions the powers instinct in the sacred landscape to grant her prophetic insight so that she might foresee the fate of her lover (an allusion to Keidrych Rhys, then away on war duty guarding the east coast of England). The Delphic answer she receives is, of course, full of dark foreboding and delivered against the background of the baying of 'the Dogs of Annwn' (the Celtic underworld). The 'C' of the title seems also to refer to the belief she shared with Graves that the travels of the magical 'White Cow' (emblem and emissary, so to speak, of the White Goddess) traced a 'circular route' (*DLR*, 168). And her belief in the sacred significance of the letter surfaces again when, in her essay on village dialect, she mentions a 'reference by Giraldus to the circular dance of the Welsh and this is from his *Itinerium Kambriae*, 1188 AD' (*DLR*, 120).

The estuarine situation of Llanybri, which features so prominently not only in 'Cwmcelyn' but in her major poem *Gods with Stainless Ears*, fitted in perfectly with Graves's theories, since the myths that were the carriers of the White Goddess religion travelled along the ancient sea routes. Roberts homed in on *Finnegans Wake* because it made mention of the 'Celtic' link between the Liffey and the Towy: 'Joyce . . . linked up the close mythology and dialect between the peoples of Eire and Wales – the Liffey – "Towy I too" ' (*DLR*, 119). All this accorded well with Lynette Roberts's own deep respect for the sea, dating from her early experiences of ten transatlantic journeys between Britain and South America. 'For the British born in the Argentine', she wrote, 'there are many voyages', and in 'Seagulls' she captured the nexus of experiences that were, for her, the essence of these trips. Describing a typical stopover en route at a port in the Canaries, the poem artfully encapsulates the ambivalences of feeling about land and sea. While the former offers the stability of ties, those ties take the form of the greedy locals who come alongside in their rowing boats only to fleece the voyagers by selling them shoddy 'bargains'. As for the sea, that is wistfully associated with the 'seagulls' easy glide' but also viewed queasily as 'An ocean of uncertainty' (*CP*, 16).

Elsewhere, as if seeking for a magical sea route that would connect Argentina to Llanybri through a transatlantic extension of the White Goddess trail, she makes an interesting suggestion in a letter to Graves about the possible meaning of a phrase from a famous boast by the legendary poet, magician, priest and shape changer Taliesin:

> What puzzles me is what does he mean by I was born 'Under the region of the summer stars'. As the legend carries the tale in various versions that he was shipwrecked & found in a coracle, or like Moses cradled in reeds, I have often wondered if it may have meant under the Southern Hemisphere or tropical stars. (*DLR*, 173)

Partly motivated by stories like this, Roberts thoroughly researched the history of the Welsh coracle. Fascinated by its continuing use in the Llanybri vicinity during her period there, she campaigned strongly for the modest 'industry' it served to be publicly supported. She also wanted it to take advantage of modern synthetic textiles and for coracles to be 'machine-sprayed with ICI plastics' (*DLR*, 136). But at the same time her passion for the coracle was steeped in her poet's sensitivity to the numinous aura by which the little 'primitive' craft had, over many centuries if not millennia, come to be invisibly haloed: 'the coracle men working on the rivers, the play of magic, ritual, superstition, prophets of the sky and foretellers of the ocean bed, these attributes remained a force in their trade, both for their gain and their protection' (*DLR*, 68).

Her deep wish to connect Argentina to the Celtic world of ancient Wales is again manifest in her Patagonian ballad *El Dorado*, when Parry, one of the four young Welsh adventurers, imagines he sees a 'Welsh' horse in the wild herd that descends on them, almost trampling them underfoot as it sweeps madly past:

> . . . *And that white*
> *Horse with the black mane*
> *Ears, fetlock, muzzle, and tail,*
> *Is surely a Dynevor strain.* (*CP*,120)

The white cattle (with red ears) of Dynevor Park, Llandeilo are reputed to date back to the ninth century and the period of Rhodri Fawr (Rhodri the Great). Associated with them are various legends, such as their use in druidic sacrificial rituals, and the special protection accorded the breed in the tenth-century laws of Hywel Dda – supposedly confirming the sacred status the cattle had enjoyed in Celtic culture, as evidenced by mentions in old Irish saga. Lynette Roberts's letters to Graves include meditations on the significance of white creatures in Celtic legend and literature, particularly when combined with red (or russet) ears, as in the story of Pwyll Pendefig Dyfed in the *Mabinogion* (*DLR*, 168).

* * *

Lynette Roberts, then, partly 'read' Llanybri through Argentina, just as she came retrospectively to 'read' Argentina (for example, the settlement of Patagonia) partly through Llanybri. Hers was a hybrid imagination – no wonder she was so taken with the universal village practice of making 'pele' (Welsh for 'balls') for burning on the fire. A mixture of coal dust, clay and water (Roberts provides the 'recipe' in great detail (*DLR*, 7)) the 'pele' seemed to her perfect for burning in a homely hearth. And she was similarly attracted to the mixed, or hybrid, in her own poetics. A simple, striking example of her ambition to fuse the New World with the Old is provided by one of her early poems, 'Rhode Island Red'. Not only does the very breed of the chicken advertise its (North) American origins, in using the phrase 'Song of joy I sing' to render the crowing of the cockerel, Roberts deliberately invokes the Poet Laureate of both North and South America, Walt Whitman. But rather than use a 'New World' poetic form, Roberts turned in this text to what she (wrongly) thought of as an English equivalent to the Welsh *englyn*, a form she admired for its brevity, pithiness and intricate system of internal alliteration and assonance.

One of the deepest of the interests that were consonant with her hybrid imagination – the question of how paradoxically to respect traditional cultures by modernizing them, thus changing in order to 'conserve' – seems to have been born of her childhood anger at the way the traditional life of the peons was being crassly disfigured and thus effectively erased through the *wrong* kind of modernization inflicted on them as the River Plate conurbation rapidly expanded. But her anger was brought into sharp focus by her Llanybri experience, because within months of settling in the village it became clear to her she was confronting an unacknowledged crisis: 'the imposition of a bourgeois and shallow town culture forced on their wholesome ways. That is why I have such an interest in the village of Llanybri. I see that in the future it will be forced to change for the worse' (*DLR*, 17). This remained her unwavering opinion throughout the years she lived and worked there, and still vibrating through her (increasingly nuanced and sophisticated) concerns may be felt the anger of the child recoiling from the horror of what River Plate was doing to the peons.

Also from the very beginning, she was very clear that protecting Llanybri did *not* mean fighting to preserve the status quo of the 'traditional'. Adaptation to the modern was not only inevitable, it was highly desirable. But first it was necessary to identify and evaluate that which was distinctive and invaluable about not only the village but the whole locality and culture of which it was a part. The thoroughness and industry with which Roberts applied herself to the task of educating himself in this matter, even while raising two children virtually alone in a tiny cottage with minimum facilities, is as humbling as it is impressive. She had no water on tap and lived off the produce of back-breaking labour in her small, simple kitchen garden. That hers were the researches of an undirected autodidact and led her to rely on nineteenth-, and even eighteenth-, century sources that were unreliable when not wildly wayward was not her fault. And in any case such sources may have in some ways served her very well, since what a poet needs in order to assemble enabling fictions and effective operating systems is very different from the aims and purposes of a scholar.

Not only did she familiarize herself with the traditional architecture, crafts, dialect and literary culture of Llanybri and its environs, she also studied its natural habitat, becoming versed in local flora, fauna, bird, butterfly and animal life. And she went much further, exploring anthropology in order to understand the prehistory of human settlement in Wales, and further seeking to map the village and its environs in deep time by understanding its geology and mineralogy. In an aside to Robert Graves that throws interesting light on *Gods with Stainless Ears* and highlights the committed hybridity of her imagination she comments 'Today [1944] we need myth more than ever: *but not blindly*, only in relation to its scientific handling: in relation to today. You will help us here – just as David Jones is helping us with his paintings' (*DLR*, 169).[19] And in a crucial passage from her 'Carmarthenshire Diary' she makes clear her wish to produce, through a creative fusion of different forms of knowledge, a psychically healing, holistic, reintegrative vision of the world:

> The entomologists may learn the names of hundreds of insects entirely through their study of larva breeding and imago feeding. The ornithologist may notice the shape and leaf of trees; and when studying water birds in particular, the names of shells cast on the shores, the small fish rippling on the water-scales of the tide. And so, whether we are conscious of it or not, the intense and penetrating study of one or any of these branches in the field of a naturalist will in the end grow, until it covers an area of the whole field. Sky, plant, tree, animal and soil strata included. And in this way a natural conclusion and unity is reached, which politics, industrial problems and scientific research cannot achieve. (*DLR*, 62–3)

Gods with Stainless Ears can perhaps be read as a war requiem for the death, by grotesque distortion, of some such aspirational vision as this; as a terrible miscarriage of her lovingly conceived hybrid imagination. In a letter to Graves she explained she'd 'purposely set out . . . to use words in relation to today – both with regard to sound (i.e. discords ugly grating words) & meaning.' (*DLR*, 181)[20]

The following single brilliant detail, not from the poem but from a prose fragment vividly describing the terrible 1941 raids on Swansea as seen from Llanybri, must suffice to illustrate the process at work:

> A collyrium sky, chemically washed $Cu.DH_2$. A blasting flash impels Swansea to riot! Higher, absurdly higher, the sulphuric clouds roll with their stench of ore, we breathe naphthalene air, the pillars of smoke writhe, and the astringent sky lies pale at her sides . . . We, alarmed, stand puce beneath another flare, our blood distilled, cylindricals of glass. The raiders scatter, then return and form a piratic ring within our shores. High explosives splash up, blue, white, and green. We know all copper compounds are poisonous, we know also where they are. (*DLR*, 103)

The active interest Roberts had developed in mineralogy as part of her holistic surveying of Llanybri and its peninsula heightened her awareness that, for more than a century, Swansea had been one of the world's greatest metallurgical centres, and consequently dubbed 'Copperopolis'. The poisonous fumes emanating from the maze of great works had already blighted the landscape of the lower Tawe valley by the time a new petrochemical plant at Llandarcy was added to the deadly mix, and it's this new component that Roberts probably had in mind when referring to naphthalene (organic compound with formula $C_{10}H_8$) produced by the petroleum refining process. Specific reference is twice made ($Cu.DH_2$, copper compounds) to the copper industry for which the town was most famous. Particularly powerful is the envisaging of a malign 'collyrium' (normally a harmless eye-wash) that consists of a 'chemically washed' copper. The metallurgical theme is continued through reference to the blue crystal cyanite – an aluminium silicate. And, of course, following the three-night Blitz of 1941, the area is smothered in the poisonous clouds of sulphur dioxide released. A response to the violent disintegration of a whole landscape, the whole passage is therefore a darkly parodic version of the holistic, integrative vision Roberts was so hopeful her hybrid imagination might achieve in Llanybri.

One interesting question that will have to be postponed to some other occasion is how far hers was, in spite of all its good intentions, essentially a 'colonial' incomer's relationship with the village. As has already been noted, hers had after all been a 'settler' consciousness, virtually from her birth. One prominent aspect of Roberts's otherwise conscientiously thorough self-education in the cultural mores of Llanybri was her seeming lack of interest even in attempting to learn Welsh at a time when most of the villagers struggled with English as a decidedly 'second' language. But that Roberts came to value what she somewhat perversely, and perhaps tellingly, persisted in calling the 'Kymric' language is unquestionable. She not only scolded the English for routinely excluding Welsh-language literature when purportedly surveying the history of literature in the British Isles[21] but implicitly rebuked the Welsh themselves for needing to travel to distant Patagonia before they could muster up the courage to treat their language as vigorously living rather than moribund and dying. And she certainly made attempts to familiarize herself with Welsh-language poetry from the very beginning of the great strict-metre tradition of *barddas* (in the process actively experimenting with the *englyn* form, for example (*CP*, 83)) to significant contemporary poets such as R. Williams Parry. And, acknowledging the work of W. J. Gruffydd, Dyfnallt and others in her notes to *Gods with Stainless Ears*, she adds that 'I have intentionally used Welsh quotations as this helps to give the conscious compact and culture of another nation' (*CP*, 76). Yet she seems not to have been particularly concerned to learn the Welsh language by which she was daily surrounded.

Instead, her passionate concern (fuelled by her memories of the River Plate peons) for the kind of innovation and adaptation that alone could ensure that what was valuable in 'tradition' was made meaningfully available to the present and, in suitably modified form, transmitted to the future, concentrated on a host of other signature cultural practices, customs, products and artefacts of her immediate locality. The dynamic figure leading the rural conservationist movement in the Wales of the period was the prominent ethnographer Dr Iorwerth Peate, at that time working towards establishing an open-air folk museum at St Fagans on the progressive Scandinavian model (*DLR*, 128).[22] While significantly influenced by his classic study of *The Welsh House* (1940), Roberts was concerned his conservationism might be misunderstood either to license the wrong kind of modernization, or to promote resistance to every form of adaptation for contemporary use. She herself clearly and repeatedly argued for the courage to 'experiment and build with the most up-to-date materials' 'provided it harmonises with the surrounding rural architecture' (*DLR*, 129). Hence her attack on the reactionary ruralism of the likes of 'Professors, who seem to live backwards anyway' (*DLR*, 51). 'Tradition can be evil', she insisted, 'when the root of its repetition is associated, as it is so much today, with FEAR' (*DLR*, 52). She wanted smallholdings to have fresh water on tap, electricity, spacious kitchens, dry walls and solid floors. The fruits of 'modern research and scientific knowledge' should be used for 'the good purpose of humanity' (*DLR*, 52), and not used – as in the bombing of Swansea – for evil, destructive ends.

Her 'Argentine' instinct to associate creativity with hybridity and to understand tradition as harmonious change is thus apparent in her attitude towards both the practical affairs of rural life and her poetics. Indeed, by 1952 she was urging Welsh writers in both languages to find new forms of creative synthesis 'before the particularities of the Celtic imagination are once again submerged in an Anglicised culture.' (*DLR*, 142) In retrospect, it can be seen that her own poetry had constituted exactly such an enterprise – the prefacing of the different sections of *Gods with Stainless Ears* with epigraphs from Welsh-language poetry both old and new was calculated both to instance and to emblematize the kind of creative synthesis she already had in mind in the early 1940s.

'I grow [vegetables in wartime] for Llanybri, for Llanybri that I love and that has given me so much' (*DLR*, 21). Touchingly, Lynette

Roberts was 'putting down roots' in the village as early as June 1940, just eight months after her arrival there. Yet she was fated ever to be as much 'scarlet woman' as 'native'. Significant aspects of her consciousness had, after all, been formed by Argentina. Her passion for 'deep time' and its human equivalent – tradition – obviously owed much to an unconscious awareness that, although she herself was indeed 'native' to Argentina, her parents had only very recently migrated there, a late example of the great waves of European migration of peoples to the country during the nineteenth century. She had no claim on the 'aboriginal past', such as she came to feel in Llanybri. Likewise, her understanding of 'tradition' as itself always, at any given point, 'hybrid' in character – the moment when the past meets the future and is modified by it – obviously owed much to her own peripatetic life, and the experience of searching for some meaningful form of continuity in the face of constant, restless change.

Her situation as 'Llanybri' poet is thus symbolically captured in an observation she recorded in her diary on 18 May 1942:

> I noticed a large splash of brilliant scarlet, a secretive flight from tree to tree until whatever it was hid deeper and thicker among the leaves. This sudden sensation of flight in colour disturbed me considerably . . . I had no idea what this could have been. It was so large. The Scarlet Cardinals in Buenos Aires, yes I had seen many of those, and flights of wild emerald green paraquets, but this vivid flash . . . (*DLR*, 44)

It turned out to be a great spotted woodpecker. Lynette Roberts's attachment to scarlet, always bringing with it memories of her South American 'home' – she entitled one of her most evocative poems about the vast plains of the pampas 'Blood and Scarlet Thorns' – had once more creatively sharpened her eye for her immediate surroundings in her new Welsh 'home' of Llanybri. 'While she was dying, in rural Wales', her daughter Angharad Rhys has movingly written, 'she kept reverting to Spanish – though not her first language it was the language of her childhood' (*CP*, x).

Notes

[1] In her essay 'An Introduction to Village Dialect', she quotes one of Taliesin's famed boasts: 'I have been in the ark, / With Noah and Alpha; / I have seen the destruction of / Sodom and Gomorra; / I was in Africa' etcetera. See

Lynette Roberts, *Diaries, Letters and Recollections*, ed. Patrick McGuinness (Manchester: Carcanet, 2008), p. 108. Hereafter *DLR*.
2   First published in *Wales*, 10 (1939), 278–9. It is reprinted, but under the title 'Song of Praise', in Lynette Roberts, *Collected Poems*, ed. Patrick McGuinness (Manchester: Carcanet, 2005), pp. 81–2, where it is mistakenly identified as first appearing in *The Welsh Review* in October 1939. Hereafter the *Collected Poems* will be cited as *CP*.
3   *Wales*, 11 (1939–40), 302. Reprinted in *CP*, p. 82.
4   From the very beginning of the construction of the extensive Argentinian rail network British engineers and shareholders had played a dominant role in its development. Rails, locomotives and rolling stock were likewise usually of British manufacture. And when the Western Railway company was formed in 1855, its vice-president, David Gowland, was a Briton. Roberts therefore grew up largely within an expatriate, 'Anglo' community.
5   The Bible, King James Version, Proverbs 31. 21.
6   Lynette Roberts, unpublished letter to Alun Lewis (undated, *c*.1940–1), Alun Lewis Collection, National Library of Wales, Aberystwyth, p. 2.
7   Duly written, the poem was included in her first published collection, *Poems* (1944) (*CP*, 16). In it, she rejoiced that 'shocking the air / With scarlet bill and garter' – the word 'shocking' is there surely charged with the village experience of the scarlet-caped Roberts herself – the water-bird could 'draw a wreath of joy / From our pale reeded hearts'.
8   At first she found the vivacity of the 'old old man' [*sic*] who had turned up unannounced 'bubbling over with joy', invigorating and entertaining (*DLR*, 11–13). But she quickly grew annoyed at the 'mock Celtic Twilight' era at the turn of the century of which he was by then the lone survivor, because 'He was still caught up in its aura when he met us, and, frankly, this nauseated me.' (*DLR*, 13)
9   'Anglo', but by no means exclusively English. As well as representatives of all the nations of the British Isles, it also included 'colonials' such as Roberts's Cambro-Australian parents.
10 Although she, along with a friend, briefly held salons for writers, artists and intellectuals in Buenos Aires around 1930 – 'No English just Argentines were invited – philosophers, psychologists, journalists' (*DLR*, 202) – there is no evidence she was aware of the exciting new developments in contemporary Argentinian literature. At that time, *Modernismo* was being replaced by a new wave of writing perhaps most strikingly instanced in the work of the writers (who included the young Borges) associated with the *Ultraísmo* movement. She makes clear her indebtedness to European (and specifically English) writers when writing of Patagonia in her essay on that region, where she singles out not only W. H. Hudson for praise but also A. F. Tschiffely's *This Way Southward* (*CP*, 130).
11 'If we do not listen to the rural wisdom of the common man we shall be a lost Nation', she wrote in June 1940. What was dangerous alike in capitalism, socialism and communism was the 'imposition of a bourgeois and shallow town culture [which is] forced on their wholesome ways' (*DLR*, 17). In her further belief that 'The dignity and pride of the craftsmen and farm labourers should be permitted to prevail . . . I do not mean the retention of any arty crafty work of the past', she was echoing, as she shortly discovered, the

sentiments of respected Welsh ethnographers of the time such as Dr Iorwerth Peate (see below). She was also – as again slowly became clear to her – championing the cause of 'y werin', the reputedly devout and naturally cultured 'folk' of the rural, Welsh-speaking heartlands, whose way of life had come to be heavily idealized by such influential scholars as Sir O. M. Edwards. His classic *Cartrefi Cymru* (1896) (The homes / hearths of Wales) became a huge popular success and contributed to the cult of the Welsh rural village, the ramifications of which are brilliantly analyzed by Hywel Teifi Edwards in '"Y Pentre Gwyn" and "Manteg": from Blessed Plot to Hotspot', *Beyond the Difference: Welsh Literature in Comparative Perspectives*, ed. Alyce von Rothkirch and Daniel Williams (Cardiff: University of Wales Press, 2004), pp. 8–20. Roberts's essays 'An Introduction to Village Dialect' and 'Simplicity of the Welsh Village' fit squarely into this cultural milieu.

12 She believed the 'peasant' class to be an international phenomenon, and so easily set Llanybri in the context of her experiences elsewhere, including Argentina and Spain. Similarly, she believed this class of 'people of the soil' shared a vocabulary: 'in certain idioms there can be found relationships between peoples of the soil elsewhere; in Spain, Ireland, Italy, France, Iceland, Brittany' (*DLR*, 123).

13 Glyn Williams, *The Desert and the Dream: A Study of Welsh Colonization in Chubut, 1865–1915* (Cardiff: University of Wales Press, 1975), p. 104; see also Glyn Williams, *The Welsh in Patagonia: The State and the Ethnic Community* (Cardiff: University of Wales Press, 1991). There are several interesting differences of detail between the version of the episode recorded by Roberts and her informant and that offered by modern historians such as Williams.

14 It would be interesting to compare Roberts's version of Patagonia with that of Eluned Morgan, a Welsh Patagonian born and raised in Gaiman, whose *Dringo'r Andes* (1904) is a classic account of her subsequent journey across the desert to the high mountains.

15 In the notes to the *Collected Poems*, *penillion* are mistakenly described as a form of *barddas* (classic traditional strict-metre poetry). Around this time, the *penillion* were attracting much interest from such eminent Welsh-language writers and scholars as T. H. Parry-Williams, who produced an authoritative scholarly collection of them and wrote a poetry influenced by their colloquial rhythms and vocabulary. In addition, they fascinated 'Anglo-Welsh' poets such as Glyn Jones, who highly valued them as a 'people's poetry' and eventually translated a body of *penillion* into sprightly, rhyming English verse.

16 *Gauchesco* (or 'gauchesque') writing, claiming to use the 'real' language of the gauchos themselves, flourished roughly between 1870 and 1920. It would therefore probably be very much 'in the air' when Roberts was a child.

17 Recent scholarship has expressed considerable scepticism about such Welsh Patagonian claims to 'exceptionalism'. An underplayed history has been uncovered of tensions between the indigenous peoples and the Welsh settlers, and emphasis has been placed on the much wider history of colonization of which the Patagonian venture was demonstrably a part. For instance, the extension of the Welsh settlement as far as the foothills of the Andes, which constituted the epic second phase of the venture, was a multinational enterprise financed by business interests in Buenos Aires. And this aspect of

inland development is unconsciously prefigured in Roberts's ballad as, far from being innocent idealists, the four Welsh adventurers are hard-headed gold prospectors, whose values contrast strikingly with those of the Mapuche people on whose territories they trespass. Interestingly, Roberts's 'Notes for an Autobiography' records an early personal experience of the difference between immigrant white and native Inca attitudes towards gold (*DLR*, 195).

18 Graves was drawing upon the theories for the origins of Ogham outlined by R. A. S. Macalister in *The Secret Languages of Ireland* (Cambridge: Cambridge University Press, 1937). Macalister was later to revise his own theories, which, while still predictably popular in neopagan and New Age circles, have not found support among later serious Celtic scholars. Both Graves and Roberts were also in thrall to the writings of that enthusiastic druidophile, Edward 'Celtic' Davies (1756–1831).

19 The affinities between Roberts's poetry and that of Jones's remain to be explored thoroughly, as does her obvious respect for his work, although Daniel Hughes's essay in this volume goes some way to address this with a comparative interpretation of *Gods with Stainless Ears* and *In Parenthesis*. Roberts spent much of her time visiting T. S. Eliot in his Faber office in London recommending Jones's work to his attention and urging him to pay a visit to the recluse. (A deeply appreciative review of *In Parenthesis* by Vernon Watkins – 'unique writing' – had appeared in *Wales*, 5 (1938), 184.) Both Roberts and Jones shared a passion for reviewing and restructuring present experience in the light of 'deep time', and in naming their son 'Prydein' (the old Welsh name for Britain – 'Prydain' in modern Welsh – favoured in medieval chronicles lamenting the loss of much of the island to foreign invaders), Roberts and Rhys seem to have been signifying their own sympathy for Jones's vision of a modern post-imperial Britain that, no longer arrogantly Anglocentric, would be a genuine confederacy of all the peoples of the island.

20 Given Roberts's own admission that, in structure and texture, her long poem owed something to contemporary film, it might be interesting to compare *Gods with Stainless Ears* to a classic groundbreaking documentary of the period, *Listen to Britain*. Directed for the Crown Film Unit by Humphrey Jennings and Stewart McAllister, and released in 1942, this is a highly atmospheric montage of the sounds and sights of Britain at war, without any linking voice-over commentary.

21 '[T]here has been practically no acknowledgement of Welsh Literature in the past. This lack of recognition in the History of English [*sic*] Literature has yet to be adjusted' (*DLR*, 107). Such omission resulted, she added, in a 'tragic deformity'.

22 For a highly informative account of Peate, his vision and his accomplishments, see Catrin Stevens, *Iorwerth C. Peate* (Cardiff: University of Wales Press, 1986).

2

'"You have a Welsh name, are you Welsh?" he asked. "I don't know," I replied':[1] Lynette Roberts and Elective Welsh Identity

Katie Gramich

The title exchange comes from Lynette Roberts's recollection of her first meeting with her future husband, Keidrych Rhys, in a poetry reading in Soho in 1939. Roberts's uncertainty over her Welsh identity at the time is, perhaps, not surprising. Both her parents were of Welsh extraction, her father's family being originally from Ruthin and her mother's from Pembrokeshire, but Roberts herself had been born and raised in Argentina, and had lived in the south-east of England from her mid-teens, returning to live briefly in Buenos Aires before relocating to London in the 1930s, with considerable amounts of time travelling in Western Europe. It might be surmised that her Welsh ancestry had not, to date, figured largely in her sense of her own identity. However, under the probing gaze of the charismatic Rhys ('27 years old and good looking')[2] who was eager to publish her poems in his new magazine, *Wales*, she may well have been tempted to reply in the affirmative. That affirmative would, indeed, soon come to replace her noncommittal 'I don't know' as, very quickly, she decided to marry Rhys and move with him to a cottage in rural west Wales.

Just how utterly different from her experience of life so far the Carmarthenshire village of Llanybri was can be surmised from further details recounted in her 'Notes for an Autobiography'.[3] Roberts's father was head of the Western Railway in Argentina. He had a green 'touring Bentley', their house near Buenos Aires had a high gate and walls with scrolled ironwork, a tennis court, a bungalow for the gardener and a hut for the servants.[4] After her mother's early death, Lynette, the eldest daughter, 'would go out with my father to the British Embassy, out to dinners and out to open, as I did once the Western Railways Sports Club, and cut the ribbons.'[5] Her grandmother's house had 'silver tureens for breakfast on the sideboard.'[6] Lynette and her siblings were sent to private schools, her brother to Winchester College. However unreliable some of the information in these notes may be, the overwhelming impression of these recollections is of a young woman brought up in considerable wealth, and with a strong sense of the family's status in the community. With this background, Roberts came in 1939 to a tiny rented cottage in Llanybri, a village in Carmarthenshire, where she would live throughout the war in a state of constant anxiety about money. And yet, paradoxically, it was here that Lynette Roberts found her voice as a writer and embraced a new identity as a Welshwoman, endowing her work with a strong sense of Welsh cultural difference.

Lynette Roberts, then, elected a Welsh identity. Of course, in marrying Keidrych Rhys, she had acquired a Welsh identity by proxy, but that was by no means enough for the independent-minded Roberts. She set about learning about Welsh history, literature, mythology, architecture, customs, and natural history, acquiring books by persistent letter-writing to librarians and authors. She was tenacious and probably rather alarming for the established Welsh intelligentsia; in her memoirs, she repeatedly complains about the reluctance of the keepers of knowledge in Wales to reveal it to the world. In her correspondence with Robert Graves at the time when he was writing *The White Goddess* and finding Welsh scholars less than receptive to his theories, Roberts wrote:

> I understand your fury at the barrier all those people of authority put up. They *refuse* to help, & are even reticent in allowing you to see the *original documents*. Idris Bell was like this when I inquired to see early books of 1606 at the MB. I disturbed him in his iron cage, no doubt he locked the gate *twice* after I had left him.[7]

The comic tone of the letter notwithstanding, Roberts did feel that she was being deliberately excluded from the secret knowledge of

Welsh culture and society, and she seems to have set herself the task of overcoming those barriers through study and observation and writing. Her work so often foregrounds Welshness and champions Welsh difference, referring to '*my* people' and frequently adopting the first person plural voice, that the reader is forced to assume that this author not only 'has a Welsh name' but is, emphatically and unmistakably, Welsh.[8]

However, an ambivalence remains in Lynette Roberts's Welsh identity. At times, her writing refers to the Welsh as 'they', and she judges them to be a 'jealous' and 'distrustful' people, though she attributes this to their 'continual subjugation . . . by conquerors'. She sees an ambivalence about them, which she finds similar to the 'dual quality' of the Irish; they have 'two visions instead of one'.[9] Such an ambivalence is echoed in Roberts's own vision and attitudes. Clearly, some of her negative views of Llanybri have biographical origins: at one stage in the war, she was suspected by some of being a spy;[10] she felt like a stranger and excluded at times partly because of her inability to speak or understand Welsh; she suffered from poverty, isolation, and, in the spring of 1940, had a traumatic miscarriage, which she describes as being caused by 'worry and lack of money.'[11] This is movingly described in Part IV of *Gods with Stainless Ears*.[12] Sometimes, she expresses homesickness for her native Argentina.[13] Nevertheless, most of the descriptions of the people and places of Carmarthenshire in her prose and poetry are suffused with admiration and excitement. Domestic and farm activities, such as making 'pele' to burn in the fire, gardening, cooking, haymaking, tending the farm animals, are all described with a clear sense of the importance and even beauty of these everyday tasks. For the modern reader, it is sometimes jarring the way in which in her writing she often refers to the residents of Llanybri, including some of her closest friends, as 'peasants'. Clearly, at times, Roberts's usage of the word is meant to be positive, when she praises the dignity and wisdom of the peasantry.[14] Nevertheless, at times, her use of the word is unmistakably disparaging; in a 1944 letter to Robert Graves written in London, for example, referring to his 'MSS on bardic mythology', which she has left behind in Llanybri, she says: 'shall I try & make one of the peasants understand where it is & get them to send it up.'[15] Possibly which side of Roberts's 'dual' vision is expressed depends upon whom she is addressing; the letters to Graves are, after all, to a public-school-educated man of a not dissimilar social background from herself, thus the disparagement of 'peasants'. One suspects strongly that were she to write to Ernest Rhys, another of her correspondents, who addressed her as 'Lynette/ Eiluned?', she would be unlikely to fall back on that sense of social superiority, which, in itself, would have been a barrier to her attempt to integrate into Welsh life.[16]

The concept of national identity as an active personal *choice* is not in fact a new phenomenon, though it is often associated with revisionary theories of nationalism, which emphasize the constructed or even 'imagined' nature of community, belonging and nationhood.[17] The phenomenon of 'elective identity' is not unique to Roberts; interestingly, though, it seems to have been particularly prevalent in the early twentieth century and among modernist writers. Modernism is often associated with exilic identities, such as those of James Joyce or Jean Rhys; for these writers, and others, such as Ezra Pound and D. H. Lawrence, exilic or nomadic existence provided a facilitating sense of outsiderhood to their writing. In some cases new national identities, allegiances and languages are of course foisted upon individuals by historical circumstance or political pressures; writers like Conrad, or Nabokov, could be seen as representative here. Other 'elective identities' are more clearly a matter of personal choice: T. S. Eliot's election of a British identity or David Jones's election of Welshness would certainly fall into the latter category.

In their 2005 study of suburban communities in Northern England, *Globalization and Belonging*, Mike Savage et al. coin the term 'elective belonging' to describe an identification not with

> a fixed community, with the implication of closed boundaries, but [as something] more fluid, seeing places as sites for performing identities. Individuals attach their own biography to their "chosen" residential location, so that they tell stories that indicate how their arrival and subsequent settlement is appropriate to their sense of themselves.[18]

This theoretical construct is useful in understanding the way in which Roberts conceived of her relationship with Wales.

Although many Welsh writers have adopted convenient 'British' identities in order to enter the mainstream of anglophone literature, and, not to make too fine a point of it, to cash in on the lucrative possibilities of a large anglophone audience for their work, writers who adopt Welsh identities have been fewer, perhaps because the rewards for such an election are less obvious. Nevertheless, there have been writers who have forged an 'elective belonging' to Wales both before and after the time of Lynette Roberts. One interesting female forerunner was the nineteenth-century writer Anne Beale, who also settled in rural Carmarthenshire. *The Dictionary of Welsh Biography* states of Anne Beale (1816–1900) that 'Few English writers have written more appreciatively of Wales.'[19] Beale was the daughter of a Somerset gentleman farmer and his wife and first came to Wales as a governess for the three children of the Reverend David Williams, curate of Llandyfeisant, near Llandeilo in Carmarthenshire, in 1840 at the age of twenty-five. In her 1844 travel book, *The Vale of the Towey* (1844), she describes her first arrival in Wales like this:

> When I came hither, a stranger, I was struck by the loveliness of the country, as well as by the character, manners, and language of its primitive inhabitants . . . I was going into Wales for the first time, and . . . the novelty and beauty of the scenery, together with the pure mountain air, dispelled whatever feelings of sadness had seized upon me . . . I had not expected to be at once so much 'at home' as I felt myself when I arrived at my journey's end, nor had I anticipated the warmth and friendliness of manner that characterize the Welsh, who are neither distant nor cold, but easily approachable.[20]

Although Beale's prose is more conventional and, naturally, more old-fashioned than that of Roberts, it is striking how similar some of their responses to rural west Wales are: both are 'strangers',[21] both are struck by the beauty of the place and the distinctiveness of Welsh culture; both appear to feel 'at home' and both also express a perhaps unconscious sense of superiority – Beale's 'primitive' inhabitants could be compared with Roberts's 'peasants'.

It is clear from her writing that Beale was immediately attracted to her new environment and, in effect, fell in love with the place and its people, using them as subjects for much of her prolific later fiction, which appeared from the 1840s to the 1890s. And yet, Beale's attitude towards Welsh betrays some ambivalence; like Matthew Arnold some thirty years later, Beale seems to approve of anglicization, while at the same time waxing lyrical about 'the grand old Welsh language.'[22] She also refers to those 'among the native peasantry, particularly those who dwell in the mountains . . . who speak their fine ancient language in its original purity.'[23]

One of the aspects of Welsh life that prevents Anne Beale from identifying wholeheartedly with her adoptive home is the fact that she is separated from the 'Welsh peasantry' by a class divide, as was Roberts, to a lesser extent. Maintenance of her class position is clearly more important for Beale than for the more bohemian Roberts – Beale cannot afford to 'go native' completely because she cannot afford to compromise her status as a gentlewoman. Perhaps this is particularly acute as a result of her original, rather ambivalent status as a governess – neither quite of the gentlefolk, nor yet a servant (interestingly, the 1844 census lists Anne Beale separately from the three servants of the household). Beale observes that many of the people she calls 'the Welsh peasantry' are 'miserably poor', but she blithely goes on to say that 'my business is not with them', effectively distancing herself as a gentlewoman from the poverty of the working classes.[24]

Similarly, the adjectives 'primitive' and even 'primeval' are frequently used by Beale in describing both the landscape of the Towy valley and its inhabitants. Though we might regard this use of language as indicating a supercilious attitude towards Wales, it is evident that the adjectives are actually used positively in order to valorize place and people but at the same time they serve to underline their alterity, in a similar way to Roberts's use of 'peasantry'. At the same time, Beale is perfectly prepared to claim possession of a Welsh identity in telling usage of the first person plural – as does Roberts – for instance, in describing Llandeilo as 'our town' and to the habits of 'we country-folk', just as Roberts refers to 'our village'.[25]

Supporting Savage et al.'s contention that 'elective belonging' is 'critically dependent on people's relational sense of place, their ability to relate their area of residence against other[s]',[26] Anne Beale laments: 'Alas! That our sister England should send her most depraved children into Wales to teach them the art of populous cities, as yet but little cultivated in this Principality, where robberies are few and far between.'[27] Again, this positions Beale herself both in and of Wales, with a relation of kinship to England, 'our sister'. Wales is here seen as morally superior, while elsewhere it is seen as *culturally* superior to England in its retention of old folk customs, festivals, and legends that 'are fast going into forgetfulness in England.'[28] Again, there is an element of this ethnographic interest in Wales as a repository of old-fashioned crafts, customs, beliefs and stories in Lynette Roberts's work, too, as evidenced in her essays originally written for *The Field* magazine on 'Coracles of the Towy' or 'Simplicity of the Welsh Village'.[29]

In the second edition of *The Vale of The Towey*, reissued significantly as *Traits and Stories of the Welsh Peasantry* in 1849, Beale writes a preface to explain why there is no reference to what she calls the recent 'agrarian excitement' in south Wales, by which she means the Rebecca Riots. She states that these sketches were written before the outbreak of violence and, moreover, that such behaviour is completely untypical of the Welsh. Tellingly, she speaks of the riots as an outbreak of a 'disease' that has now been 'cured', asserting that 'our tranquil vales and mountains' have now returned to their former pacific state. It is interesting that she again uses the possessive 'our', indicating in this case not only her own sense of belonging to Wales but also, perhaps, a sense that Wales is now once more enfolded into the cohesive national identity of Great Britain. For this is surely the nature of Beale's particular construction of Welshness: while she is an enthusiastic admirer of Welsh difference and, to a degree, a participant in that different culture, she is also a proud Briton and an upholder of empire. Lynette Roberts also arrived in Wales in a time of strife – the Second World War casts its shadow on her experience of rural Carmarthenshire in the same way that the civil unrest of the Rebecca Riots disrupted Anne Beale's life there. And yet Roberts signally refuses to embrace a shared 'British' identity in time of war, and there is no sense of imperial pride or indeed British patriotism in her work, including her 'heroic' war poem, *Gods with Stainless Ears*. Indeed, Roberts's construction of herself as a Welshwoman can be seen as an overt and defiant *escape* from a Britishness identified with vestiges of empire, and from an inherited class position that brought with it expectations, privileges and restrictions. Instead, she constructs a specifically Welsh female identity and landscape in the voices of her poems and prose, voices that oppose war outright and point out its futility. Roberts often explicitly ventriloquizes one of her Welsh neighbours and friends in Llanybri, Rosie Davies, whose lively, dialectal speech is rendered by Roberts as the female voice of opposition to war in the poem 'Plasnewydd':

> WAR. 'There's no sense in it
> For us simple people
> We all get on so well.
> Hal-e-bant.
> The cows are on the move.
> I must be off on the run:

> Hal-e-bant. *pussy drwg*.
> Hal-e-bant Fan Fach
> Hal-e-bant for the day is long
> We must strengthen it:
> *Ourselves*:
> To the cows
> Fetch them in.'[30]

Here, Rosie's words, first recorded in Roberts's diary and then fashioned into a poem, have the immediacy of direct speech and the ring of authenticity because of the hybridity of the language. In west Wales English is often punctuated with Welsh words and phrases, and vice versa, and this is vividly captured in Roberts's poem. At the same time, the use of both languages may be seen as another facet of that 'dual aspect' or double vision of the Welsh character that Roberts comments upon elsewhere.[31] The repeated dialectal phrase '*hal-e-bant*', meaning 'send him away', is the kind of dismissal one would use of a naughty cat ('*pussy drwg*') but here transposed, somewhat surreally, to refer to the war. It is as if Rosie is being figured as a benign witch, banishing 'WAR' with her poignantly domestic conjurations.

Rosie plays a key role in offering Roberts a model of Welsh female identity. She is represented repeatedly in Roberts's work as an independent and capable woman who runs her own farm and who is not afraid to challenge conventional gender roles. (She will only agree to act in the village drama if she is given a man's role, for example.)[32] Above all, Rosie shows her generous hospitality, offering Roberts her daughter, Iris, to sleep with in order to keep warm when her husband is away at war, helping her to make coal 'pele' for the fire, and bringing her food when she is ill.[33] In fact, Rosie is seen flitting in and out of the kitchen of 'Tygwyn', Roberts's home, throughout her works, and she also accompanies her in her excursions on foot through the fields, as we see in the short stories of *An Introduction to Village Dialect With Seven Stories* (1944).

Like Anne Beale, whose construction of a Welsh elective identity comes into being from an act of *hospitality* on the part of the Welsh, who welcomed this English governess into their midst, Lynette Roberts's distinctive Welshness owes a great deal to the hospitality of Rosie Davies, 'my v. dear friend in Llanybri', as Roberts wrote on the back of a photograph of Rosie and her family.[34] Thus, the experience of 'coming hither, a stranger', and of being welcomed is essentially an ethical encounter that is transformative of both self and other in the work of Anne Beale and Lynette Roberts alike. The notion of hospitality is central to Roberts's best-known work, 'Poem from Llanybri', and the voice of the hostess there might be construed as the voice of one who is, as it were, inviting her readers back into Wales, a Wales that is domestic, female-centred, and full of rich poetic traditions.

Roberts was not the first woman poet to identify the domestic and the national; the Anglo-Welsh Romantic poet Felicia Hemans specialized in writing the nation, indeed the empire, from an implicitly female, domestic perspective. As Tricia Lootens points out:

> By 1812, in 'The Domestic Affections' [Hemans] personified 'domestic affections' as a female figure who 'dwells, unruffled, in her bow'r of rest, / *Her* empire, home!' while 'war's red lightnings desolate the ball, / And thrones and empires in destruction fall' . . . Domestic memories alone 'cheer the soldier's breast / In hostile climes, with spells benign and blest'.[35]

While the patriotic tenor of Hemans's work is unmistakable, there is still a similarity to Roberts's 'Poem from Llanybri', written to the soldier-poet Alun Lewis from her domestic hearth in west Wales. Roberts appears to inherit Hemans's female-centred, domestic redrawing of national maps but to reject the imperialist ideology that underpins them in Hemans's case; the same is true of Roberts's relation to Anne Beale: both writers adopt an elective Welsh identity, but Roberts is less inhibited by her class formation and shrugs off Beale's conciliatory Britishness.

Roberts constructs a distinctive sense of Welsh place in her work partly through stories of the past, Wales's history, culture, literature, music, and customs, and partly by contrasting Wales with elsewhere. She presents communal as opposed to hierarchical structures as characteristic of Welsh life: Llanybri people constantly cross back and forth into one another's territories (as previously mentioned, Rosie is constantly to be seen in the kitchen of Tygwyn, for example). Though Roberts's is undoubtedly an 'elected' sense of belonging, therefore, it is not based purely on an individual autobiographical narrative, as Savage et al. found when they undertook their sociological study of belonging in contemporary Manchester. On the contrary, Roberts's construction of her Welsh identity depends very strongly both on community and on a shared history, though her sense of the past is by no means disconnected from the technological present.³⁶ This conjunction of the ancient with the contemporary supports Savage's theory that elective belonging is not necessarily a defiantly local gesture against globalizing pressures. Roberts's cottage in Wales is simultaneously an embodiment of Wales's history and of her own autobiography as a cosmopolitan, much-travelled, avant-garde writer.

It is not only in the domestic interior that Roberts stages the drama of a Welsh homecoming, however. In the diaries, letters, prose writings and poetry, Roberts expresses a strong identification with the land and landscapes of west Wales, an identification that ranges from the humble wartime occupation of gardening ('digging for victory' as the slogans had it) to a more wide-ranging mapping of the 'milltir sgwâr' around her village home.³⁷ As Siriol McAvoy perceptively observes:

> Though she attained some familiarity with the language through the influence of her Welsh-speaking husband, Keidrych Rhys, Roberts was unable to speak Welsh . . . Reading the landscape . . . offered her an alternative 'way in' to Welsh literary tradition, providing a more direct, phenomenological, and imaginative relationship with Welsh history and culture.³⁸

While Roberts writes a handful of vivid poems about places in her native Argentina, the majority of the places evoked in *Poems*, *Gods with Stainless Ears* and *An Introduction to Village Dialect With Seven Stories* are in rural Carmarthenshire, in the immediate vicinity of Llanybri. As McAvoy suggests, Roberts's preoccupation with this distinctive landscape is not only an aesthetic appreciation of its strange beauty but also an attempt to stake a claim to belonging in that place. The intricate knowledge of the flora and fauna, as well as local customs and characters, suggest the vision of an 'insider', though Roberts was herself well aware of being viewed as an outsider by some of her neighbours. In this sense, the writing may be seen as a wish-fulfilment, an expression of desire, a narrative of belonging.

The best examples of Lynette Roberts's visions of belonging in rural west Wales are to be found in the short stories in the curious 1944 volume entitled *An Introduction to Village Dialect With Seven Stories*, published by Keidrych Rhys's Druid Press in Carmarthen. *Village Dialect* is an attempt to prove 'that there is both a tradition and root to the Welsh dialect',³⁹ doing so by reference to Welsh medieval sources and providing a number of examples of language use and folk customs that survive from medieval times to the present day among her neighbours in Llanybri. As a study of language, the work would hardly satisfy the scholarly expectations of a modern linguistician; however, as a quirky celebration of Welsh culture and a spirited attack on the Anglocentric scholarly neglect of Wales, it is interesting and often thought-provoking. In its sheer eccentricity it is the quintessence of Lynette Roberts-ness. Much more interesting, though, from a literary point of view, are the 'Seven Stories', which can initially appear as an afterthought tacked on to the *Village Dialect* to make it book-length. Yet when we examine these 'stories' we find that they are less stories than visually intense prose poems with a strong emphasis on the specificity of place and people. In style and tone these works are reminiscent of the short stories of Katherine Mansfield, where she attempts to conjure into life her native New Zealand from a position of exile and in a war-riven world of personal loss and suffering. Like Roberts's, Mansfield's literary work was also intensely visual and directly influenced by painting; in her letters, for instance, Mansfield talks of the shock and thrill of seeing Van Gogh's painting 'Sunflowers' in the famous 1910 post-Impressionist exhibition, and of how that painting 'taught me something about writing . . . a kind of freedom – or, rather, a shaking free.'[40] In another letter, to her friend the painter Dorothy Brett, she wrote of one of her stories: 'What form is it? You ask. Ah, Brett, it's so difficult to say. As far as I know it's more or less my own invention . . . You know, if the truth were known I have a perfect passion for the island where I was born . . . in the early morning there I always remember feeling that this little island has dipped back into the dark blue sea during the night only to rise again at beam of day, all hung with bright spangles and glittering drops . . . I tried to catch that moment'.[41] These remarks on form, place and technique are uncannily appropriate to Lynette Roberts's 'Seven Stories', which, though written some two decades later, and located in a different corner of the erstwhile British Empire, also display a distinctively female, affective modernism that is an assertion of personal identity and belonging in a fragmenting world.

In Lynette Roberts's 'Fox', we have a striking, atmospheric opening, conjuring up sunrise in Llanybri much as Mansfield conjures the island of New Zealand into being at dawn in the opening of 'At the Bay'. Roberts's prose is in the present tense, creating an extraordinarily vivid sense of being in a particular place and time; the description appeals to several senses, and the use of precise placenames draws the affective and actual co-ordinates of where the speaker is standing:

> The sky is green and transparent. It holds that sudden flash which announces the sun but has no tie with the living green of the soil. It is a green impaled by age, that knew the pagans stretched before their gods. Now the trees twice as tall, appear blacker than usual under this astringent light. Out towards the Mill Bridge, the valleys are ringing with water. Streams have filled overnight, and steep lanes that have turned into waterfalls flow close to the hedge. The sun rising, threads through every crevice of the Prescelly Mountains, flares up and over towards St Clears, Pembroke Bay, cutting out the outline of each wave and leaf as they sparkle with a million separate lights. The ploughed fields are sweating, drawing out a blue blaze the colour of a new ploughshare.[42]

The evocation of place is not merely sensual and aesthetically pleasing, however. The voice asserts a local knowledge that is not only in the present but which links her to the old inhabitants of this earth; presumably those pagans who once prostrated themselves upon this 'living green' were the druids who gave their name to the Carmarthen press that first published this work in 1944.

The similarities between this opening and that of Katherine Mansfield's 1921 story 'At the Bay' are striking:

> Very early morning. The sun was not yet risen, and the whole of Crescent Bay was hidden under a white sea-mist. The big bush-covered hills at the back were smothered. You could not see where they ended and the paddocks and bungalows began. The sandy road was gone and the paddocks and bungalows the other side of it; there were no white dunes covered with reddish grass beyond them; there was nothing to mark which was beach and where was the sea. A heavy dew had fallen. The grass was blue. Big drops hung on the bushes and just did not fall; the silvery, fluffy toi-toi was limp on its long stalks, and all the marigolds and the pinks in the bungalow gardens were bowed to the earth with wetness. Drenched were the cold fuchsias, round pearls of dew lay on the flat nasturtium leaves. It looked as though the sea had beaten up softly in the darkness, as though one immense wave had come rippling, rippling – how far?[43]

Just as Roberts refers to Mill Bridge and the pagans, so Mansfield names Crescent Bay and uses the Maori name of the plant, toi-toi, to indicate that this is a real place with an ancient history. Where Mansfield uses 'you' to draw the reader into the scene, Roberts uses the first person and the present tense. Then, just as Mansfield goes on to focus on the human figures who gradually emerge out of the mist, so Roberts focuses our attention, as the 'valley . . . is engulfed by the rising vapour of streams', on her neighbour, Rosie Davies, the vivacious heroine of Roberts's Llanybri writing. In the second half of 'Fox', Rosie takes over the narrative, telling her story of the fox in lively direct speech. The story clearly partakes of the folk tale, in that the fox is seen as a cunning and resourceful creature, a 'smart fellow' who often outwits the farmer (Rosie herself and her family) and steals her poultry. But the narrative is also personal and intimate, evoking a real memory and expressing an admiration for this creaturely neighbour that overcomes her annoyance at losing her livestock to him. The fox's 'lovely . . . rich, dark red' colour is emphasized and Rosie's mother eventually accepts the sacrifice of a duck and lets the fox family stay – 'Whist, I expect the young ones could do with it!'[44]

In the context of Lynette Roberts's own precarious, 'outsider' position in Llanybri – as a bohemian artist she frequently wore a dramatic red cloak when she strode about the countryside, probably increasing the farm folk's suspicions of her as a potential spy – it is tempting to read 'Fox' as an allegorical narrative of hospitality and acceptance.[45] Like the clever fox, Roberts is tolerated and even admired by her neighbours, allowed to stay where she is, to stake her claim to belonging. If we do read the story in this way, it is proper to note also that 'Fox' ends on a note of uncertainty, for two of the fox cubs are eventually taken away to become prey for the hunters on the Kylsant estate. This sense of precarious existence is fittingly expressed in this image, at a time when so many of the village's menfolk, including Roberts's own husband, had been taken away to take part against their will in the appalling blood sport of war.

The other stories in Roberts's collection can also be read as an assertion of belonging and a desire to be allowed to stay. *Village Dialect* itself, with its self-conscious documentation of quite obscure medieval Welsh works, alongside examples of the contemporary vernacular, stakes a similar claim: Roberts 'belongs' by virtue of her knowledge of Welsh history and the literary tradition, as well as by virtue of her participation today in Welsh life and custom. The stories, however, make a more subtle, and in some senses more poignant 'case to remain'.

Roberts is writing, after all, at a time when thousands of people are being forcibly displaced by war, both at home and overseas;

Alun Lewis, one of Roberts's correspondents, refers to these people in his 1940 poem 'All Day it has Rained . . .': 'we . . . thought of the quiet dead and the loud celebrities / Exhorting us to slaughter, and the herded refugees: / Yet thought softly, morosely of them, and as indifferently / As of ourselves'.[46] This identification between the herded refugees and the herded soldiers, morose, displaced, deprived of agency, points to the reason for Lynette Roberts's verse letter to Lewis, offering him home, sustenance, shelter and belonging in 'Poem from Llanybri'. This poem is another example of her assertion of belonging, in which she underlines her 'insider' knowledge of Welsh poetic, social and culinary traditions. One might almost argue that she is standing in for Rosie Davies in this poem, when she offers the displaced outsider some proper Welsh hospitality:

> At noon-day
> I will offer you a choice bowl of cawl
> Served with a 'lover's' spoon and a chopped spray
> Of leeks or savori fach, not used now,
>
> In the old way you'll understand.[47]

Here, again, Roberts incorporates some Welsh words. However, aspects of the poem do betray an uncertainty about the speaker's own position within Welsh culture. In the above quotation, for example, Roberts might be accused of choosing stereotypical images of Welsh culture, such as the *cawl*, the lovespoon and the leeks, images that are perhaps the easiest ones to reach for if the author is not as confident of her embeddedness in Welsh culture as she would like to be. Despite the poem's relative renown, then, it is perhaps best to remind ourselves that Tony Conran, who met Roberts in 1953, notes that 'She once told me she only wrote it as a poetic exercise.'[48]

Conversely, the stories included in *Village Dialect*, though published in the same year as *Poems*, certainly do not have recourse to the stereotypical. As suggested, they are strange and somewhat disorientating precisely because of their combination of modernist experimentation and folkloric orality. All, in different ways, are about an assertion of belonging in the midst of the uncertainties of war. In 'Steer', the third story, Rosie again takes the narrative reins and recounts the story of a white steer sold by her mother to a farmer in St Clears. Miraculously, the steer escapes and heads for home by swimming across the estuary of the river Taf; despite the currents and the distance he safely arrives home. Again, the strange marvellous animal here, like the fox in the earlier story, can be seen as analogous to Roberts herself, determined to belong, determined not to be sent away. The white steer calls to mind similar unusual cattle in Welsh folk tales such as that of the 'Lady of Llyn y Fan Fach', endowing the story with a magical timbre.[49] At the same time, it is utterly down-to-earth, for Rosie's mother, while amazed and 'pleased to have him back', nevertheless sends the steer straight back down the road to the farmer in St Clears.[50] Echoing the precariousness indicated at the end of 'Fox', the fate of this white steer remains uncertain, despite its heroic determination to stay – and live.

Elsewhere in these Seven Stories there is a focus on the domestic hearth rather than the animals in the fields. As in 'Poem from Llanybri', the hearth is evoked as a distinctively female space, one that is literally decorated and made homely by the woman who presides there; in the story 'Tiles', for instance, Rosie tells the story of the old woman who drew patterns all over her tiled kitchen floor with a dock leaf, creating an effect 'like linoleum'.[51] Though this individual is now long dead, Rosie's narration of the story has succeeded in cheering her friend, Roberts herself, who had been 'doubled up with pain' but by the end of the story is able to lie 'back in peace.'[52] Rosie is actively scrubbing the floor of her friend's house and conjuring up an ideal image of female domestic creativity, both of which work together to bring her outsider friend into the warmth of her own hearth.

In the best known of these short prose pieces, 'Swansea Raid', the two female friends are again together, outside, watching the catastrophic bombing raid on Swansea from their vantage point on a hill overlooking the River Towy.[53] Jocularly, Roberts refers to the two of them by their wartime identity numbers, Xebo7011 and Xebn559162, but here Rosie's garrulous voice, with its frequent literal translations from the Welsh, gives way to Roberts's experimental high modernism. The raid is a riot of chemicals, which bathe them and the cows they are fetching, in unnatural, lurid colours – cyanite, puce and opal. Dismayed and alarmed, Roberts returns to her hearth, where the 'quiet clayfire with blue flames rising . . . bring solace to any heart.'[54]

These short pieces are vividly impressionistic. Although 'impressionism' is not widely used as a literary term, it is one that seems singularly appropriate to describe the work of Lynette Roberts and, to a degree, her female literary grandmothers, including Anne Beale, with her subjective travel sketches and Roberts's modernist precursors, including Katherine Mansfield and Virginia Woolf. Like the late nineteenth-century Impressionist painters, these writers sought to capture the 'transitory, subjective impressions' of the world around them, often foregrounding distinctively female experiences, spaces and relationships.[55] As Woolf put it in her essay 'Modern Fiction':

> The mind receives a myriad impressions – trivial, fantastic, evanescent, or engraved with the sharpness of steel. From all sides they come, an incessant shower of innumerable atoms; and as they fall, as they shape themselves into the life of Monday or Tuesday, the accent falls differently from of old; the moment of importance came not here but there; so that, if a writer were a free man and not a slave, if he could write what he chose, not what he must, if he could base his work upon his own feeling and not upon convention, there would be no plot, no comedy, no tragedy, no love interest or catastrophe in the accepted style, and perhaps not a single button sewn on as the Bond Street tailors would have it.[56]

Woolf of course put this theory of modern fiction into practice in her own work, both in the fully-fledged stream of consciousness of novels such as *The Waves* and in her short stories, one of which is entitled 'Monday or Tuesday'.[57] Lynette Roberts's stories bear an even more striking resemblance in technique to Woolf's short sketches than to Mansfield's: the lack of plot, the sensory vividness and the intense female subjectivity, for instance, are common features. Yet Roberts's elective Welsh identity and her concern to explore that identity in her work set her apart from Woolf, who often expressed distaste for national allegiances.[58]

The period of Lynette Roberts's literary production is relatively brief, and it largely coincides with the time she spent in rural west Wales. As Patrick McGuinness points out: '[i]t was in Llanybri that [she] produced her most original and characteristic work'.[59] In 1948 she left Llanybri with her two young children, her marriage to Keidrych Rhys over; in the mid 1950s she had a mental breakdown and, soon after, became a Jehovah's Witness. This spelled the end of her writing life; interestingly, however, she chose to return to west Wales in 1970 and remained there until her death in 1994, suggesting that the Welsh identity she elected and elaborated from 1939 onwards was not abandoned in later life. In much the same way as Anne Beale continued to be referred to as 'Miss Beale of Llandeilo'[60] throughout her life, so we could aptly refer to Roberts as 'Lynette Roberts of Llanybri'.[61]

In the political climate of 2018, at a time when immigrants to all parts of the British Isles are feeling increasingly threatened and unwelcome, it is instructive to look back to the 1940s in Wales, when a remote and relatively poor rural society offered hospitality to an eccentric Argentine in the midst of a world war. In return, that talented immigrant embraced Welsh culture and a Welsh identity, and produced an enduring body of literary work that is utterly distinctive. Whether such a mutual exchange will be possible in the brave new Wales of the future remains to be seen.

Notes

[1] Lynette Roberts, 'Notes for an Autobiography', in *Diaries, Letters and Recollections*, ed. Patrick McGuinness (Manchester: Carcanet, 2008), pp. 205–6.
[2] Roberts, 'Notes for an Autobiography', p. 205.
[3] The 'Notes' are included as an appendix to the book and come with a caveat from the editor, Patrick McGuinness, who reminds the reader of the circumstances under which these fragmentary notes were written: 'Roberts had just been sectioned under the Mental Health Act for the third time'. See *Diaries, Letters and Recollections*, p. 228. Nevertheless, the evidence of Roberts's very different upbringing and social/familial relations is internally consistent within the text as it stands.
[4] Roberts, 'Notes for an Autobiography', pp. 194, 192.
[5] Roberts, 'Notes for an Autobiography', p. 199.
[6] Roberts, 'Notes for an Autobiography', p. 198.
[7] Lynette Roberts, Letter to Robert Graves, *c*.7 May 1944, in *Diaries, Letters and Recollections*, p. 176. A similar complaint against the 'professors' is voiced in her 'Carmarthenshire Diary' entry for 2 May 1947, in *Diaries, Letters and Recollections*, pp. 79–80.
[8] Examples include 'Poem', which begins 'We must uprise O my people', in Lynette Roberts, *Collected Poems*, ed. Patrick McGuinness (Manchester: Carcanet, 2005), p. 13, which is repeated in Part II of *Gods with Stainless Ears*, in *Collected Poems*, p. 53; and the essay 'Simplicity of the Welsh Village', which uses 'we' for the Welsh throughout, as in 'We are worse off than our Welsh Colony in Patagonia', in *Diaries, Letters and Recollections*, pp. 127–32 (p. 131).
[9] Roberts, 'A Carmarthenshire Diary', in *Diaries, Letters and Recollections*, ed. Patrick McGuinness (Manchester: Carcanet, 2008), pp. 78, 68–9.
[10] See 'A Carmarthenshire Diary', in *Diaries, Letters and Recollections*, p. 47, and 'Raw Salt on Eye' in *Collected Poems*, pp. 6–7.
[11] Lynette Roberts, 'Notes for an Autobiography', p. 212.
[12] Lynette Roberts, *Gods with Stainless Ears*, in *Collected Poems*, pp. 60–1.

13 See 'A Carmarthenshire Diary', p. 37; see also the poems written at this time about the remembered landscapes of Argentina, for example 'The New World', 'Xaquixaguana', 'Argentine Railways', 'Blood and Scarlet Thorns', and 'Royal Mail', in *Collected Poems*, pp. 25–31.
14 For example, in the 17 June 1940 entry in 'A Carmarthenshire Diary' Roberts writes: 'The dignity and pride of the craftsmen and farm labourers should be permitted to prevail . . . The people I have met here in Llanybri seem to me to retain all the natural and true qualities of an aristocrat' (p. 17).
15 See *Diaries, Letters and Recollections*, p. 178.
16 See letters from Ernest Rhys to Roberts, 1 July and 3 September 1940, in *Diaries, Letters and Recollections*, pp. 25, 31.
17 See, for example, Benedict Anderson, *Imagined Communities: Reflection on the Origin and Spread of Nationalism* (London: Verso, 1983; rev. edn 2006); Eric Hobsbawm and Terence Ranger (eds), *The Invention of Tradition* (Cambridge: Cambridge University Press, 1983); Eric Hobsbawm, *Nations and Nationalism since 1780: Programme Myth, Reality* (Cambridge: Cambridge University Press, 1990).
18 Mike Savage, Gaynor Bagnall and Brian Longhurst, *Globalization and Belonging* (London and Thousand Oaks: Sage, 2005), p. 29.
19 William Williams, *Dictionary of Welsh Biography*: *http://yba.llgc.org.uk/en/s-BEAL-ANN-1816.html?query=anne+beale&field=name* (last accessed 17 September 2018).
20 Anne Beale, *The Vale of the Towey* (London: Longman, Brown, Green and Longmans, 1844), pp. vii, 2, 9. The river is nowadays spelt 'Towy' and this is also how Lynette Roberts spells it.
21 See Lynette Roberts's poem, 'Lamentation': 'To the village of lace and stone / Came strangers. I was one of these', in *Collected Poems*, p. 8.
22 Moira Dearnley, '"I Came Hither, A Stranger": A View of Wales in the Novels of Anne Beale (1815–1900)', *The New Welsh Review*, 1/4 (1989), 27–32 (29).
23 Anne Beale, *Traits and Stories of the Welsh Peasantry* (London: George Routledge and Company, 1849), p. 10.
24 Beale, *Stories of the Welsh Peasantry*, p. 22.
25 Beale, *Stories of the Welsh Peasantry*, pp. 50, 63; Roberts, 'A Carmarthenshire Diary', entry for 10 December 1939, p. 5.
26 Savage et al., *Globalization and Belonging*, p. 29.
27 Beale, *Stories of the Welsh Peasantry*, p. 111.
28 Beale, *Stories of the Welsh Peasantry*, p. 75.
29 See Lynette Roberts, 'Coracles of the Towy' and 'Simplicity of the Welsh Village', in *Diaries, Letters and Recollections*, pp. 133–8 and pp. 127–32. Originally published in *The Field*, 5 January 1945 and 7 July 1945 respectively.
30 Lynette Roberts, 'Plasnewydd', in *Collected Poems*, p. 5. The basis of the poem are Rosie Davies's words, recorded in the entry for 17 June 1940 in 'A Carmarthenshire Diary', p. 16.
31 Roberts, 'A Carmarthenshire Diary', pp. 78, 68–9.
32 Roberts, quoting the vicar's wife in 'A Carmarthenshire Diary', p. 5.
33 Roberts notes that in her picture of 'Llanybri Old Chapel' Rosie is seen 'wearing her best harvest apron when I painted her as an angel'. See Roberts, 'A Carmarthenshire Diary', p. 35.

[34] Photograph of 'Rosie and her family' by Douglas Glass reproduced in *Diaries, Letters and Recollections*, p. 11.
[35] Tricia Lootens, 'Hemans and Home: Victorianism, Feminine "Internal Enemies," and the Domestication of National Identity', *PMLA*, 109/2 (1994), 238–53 (249). See also: Felicia Hemans, *'The Domestic Affections' and Other Poems* (London: T. Cadell and W. Davies, 1812); 'The Homes of England', *Blackwood's*, 21 (April 1827), 392; *A Selection of Welsh Melodies* (London: J. Power, 1822).
[36] Roberts's discussion of the village *teulu* (family) in 'An Introduction to Village Dialect' provides another example of her sense of the communal structure of Welsh village life; she notes that 'the foundations of the *teulu* remain somewhat unchanged'. See 'An Introduction to Village Dialect', in *Diaries, Letters and Recollections*, p. 113. She also represents herself taking a full part in the communal village haymaking: 'Before sundown we had managed to take in 3½ gambos of hay'. See Roberts, 'A Carmarthenshire Diary', p. 15.
[37] 'Milltir sgwâr' – square mile, in Welsh. This phrase is often used to describe one's local patch – the places that are familiar and constitute 'home'.
[38] Siriol McAvoy, 'The Presence of the Past: Medieval Encounters in the Writing of Virginia Woolf and Lynette Roberts' (unpublished PhD thesis, Cardiff University, 2016), p. 27.
[39] Lynette Roberts, 'An Introduction to Village Dialect', p. 124.
[40] Katherine Mansfield, *The Collected Letters of Katherine Mansfield*, ed. Vincent O' Sullivan and Margaret Scott, (Oxford: Oxford University Press, 1996), p. 333.
[41] Mansfield, *Collected Letters*, vol. 1, pp. 330–1.
[42] Lynette Roberts, 'Fox', in *Diaries, Letters and Recollections*, p. 94.
[43] Katherine Mansfield, 'At the Bay', in *The Collected Stories of Katherine Mansfield* (London: Penguin, 2001), p. 205; first published in *The Garden-Party and Other Stories* (1922; written 1921).
[44] Lynette Roberts, 'Fox', in *Diaries, Letters and Recollections*, pp. 94–5.
[45] 'Here to Cwmcelyn I walked so many times. Nearly always in my scarlet cloak.' See Roberts, 'A Carmarthenshire Diary', entry for 3 January 1942, in *Diaries, Letters and Recollections*, p. 41; see also the poem 'The Circle of C' in *Collected Poems*, which mentions 'my cloak' and 'Fever as red as your cloak', p. 7.
[46] Alun Lewis, 'All Day it has Rained . . .', in *Selected Poems of Alun Lewis*, ed. Jeremy Hooker and Gweno Lewis (London: Unwin, 1981), p. 23.
[47] Lynette Roberts, 'Poem from Llanybri', in *Collected Poems*, p. 3.
[48] Anthony Conran, 'Lynette Roberts: The Lyric Pieces', *Poetry Wales* (special issue on Lynette Roberts), 19/2 (1983), 125–33 (132); also cited in Patrick McGuinness's 'Notes' to *Collected Poems*, p. 137.
[49] The Lady of Llyn y Fan Fach in Carmarthenshire emerged from the lake with her magical herd of white cattle; she eventually returns to the lake with all her herds when her human husband is cruel to her. The tale is retold in many forms; see, for example, John Rhŷs, *Celtic Folklore: Welsh and Manx* (Oxford: The Clarendon Press, 1901).
[50] Lynette Roberts, 'Steer', in *Diaries, Letters and Recollections*, p. 98.

51 Lynette Roberts, 'Tiles', in *Diaries, Letters and Recollections*, p. 96.
52 Roberts, 'Tiles', p. 97.
53 This occurred on the nights of 19, 20 and 21 February 1941, and is alluded to in several places in Roberts's work. The aftermath of those nights is also poignantly evoked in Dylan Thomas's 1947 broadcast, 'Return Journey', in *A Dylan Thomas Treasury: Poems, Stories and Broadcasts* (London: Phoenix, 2001), pp. 171–86.
54 Lynette Roberts, 'Swansea Raid', in *Diaries, Letters and Recollections*, p. 103.
55 *The Bedford Glossary of Critical and Literary Terms*, ed. R. Murfin and S. M. Ray (Boston: Bedford/St Martin's, 2009), defines 'impressionism' as 'writing that seeks to capture transitory, subjective impressions of characters, settings and events', p. 243.
56 Virginia Woolf, 'Modern Fiction', in *Collected Essays*, ed. Leonard Woolf, vol. 2 (London: Hogarth, 1966; originally published in 1919), p. 105.
57 Virginia Woolf, *The Waves* (Oxford: Oxford University Press, 2014; first published 1931); 'Monday or Tuesday', in Virginia Woolf, *Selected Short Stories* (London: Penguin Classics, 2000; first published 1921).
58 For example, her assertion in *Three Guineas* that 'as a woman I have no country. As a woman I want no country. As a woman my country is the whole world', in *A Room of One's Own and Three Guineas*, ed. Anna Snaith (Oxford: Oxford University Press, 2008), p. 185. For an extended and revealing comparison of Virginia Woolf and Lynette Roberts, see McAvoy, 'Presence of the Past'.
59 McGuinness, 'Introduction', in *Collected Poems*, p. xv.
60 See, for example, the review of Beale's novel *Country Courtships*, under the heading 'A New Novel by Miss Beale of Llandeilo', in *The Welshman*, 22 October 1869, 6.
61 Roberts's gravestone in the churchyard of Llanybri is simply inscribed with the words 'Lynette Roberts, Poet'.

3

'I REMEMBER THESE THINGS': MEMORY, MISREPRESENTATION AND CULTURAL TRADITION IN LYNETTE ROBERTS'S 'SEVEN STORIES'

Michelle Deininger

For women writers in Wales, the English-language short story was slow to flourish in a distinctly modernist mode. The supposedly romantic, idealized portraits of Welsh life explored by writers such as Allen Raine (1836–1908) in *All in a Month* (1908) and, to a certain extent, Bertha Thomas (1845–1918) in *Picture Tales from Welsh Hills* (1912) were infamously challenged by Caradoc Evans's vilification of rural, Welsh communities in *My People* (1915). While stories that are closer to Raine's style continued to appear, particularly in the periodical press, it seems almost as if Evans's work interrupts the relationship that should have emerged between modernism, robust cultural exploration and the outsider form of the female-authored short story in Wales. An early example of modernist experimentation can be seen in the work of Dorothy Edwards (1902–1934) whose stories of the 1920s continually play with language and identity, often embodying a male narrative voice and refusing to be pinned to a particular nationality or place. In Edwards, as Claire Flay notes, 'the moment of epiphany is not a stimulus for change . . . but rather serves to reinforce the static nature of [characters'] lives.'[1] In Lynette Roberts's short fiction, there is not so much an epiphany as an attempt to create a direct moment of connection between the narrative voice and a past that is about to be lost or forgotten. While Edwards utilizes the short story form to explore the 'soul-destroying isolation of the individual, and the inability of people to make meaningful contact with one another', Roberts enmeshes Welsh cultural recovery, community networks and vital interpersonal connections to imbue her fictions with a distinct sense of time and place, while maintaining the subtleties and suggestiveness of modernist fiction.[2]

Short-story collections by women from Wales are relatively rare in the 1920s and 1930s. Writing in 1933, in *The Bookman*, Glyn Roberts comments that he has 'never seen collected volumes of short stories by Welsh writers, or heard of their gay comings-together in the flat or the cellar of the leader of a Welsh coterie.'[3] While there were collections from male writers such as Rhys Davies (1901–1978) and Glyn Jones (1905–1995) in the 1930s, they were published in the second half of the decade. Aside from Edwards's *Rhapsody*, there were only a handful of collections published in the 1920s by women writers, including *The Nationalists and Other Goluth Studies* (1921) by Lily Tobias (1887–1984), *The Intruder and Other Stories* (1926) by Kathleen Freeman (1897–1959), and several collections by the now forgotten Clara I. Martin (1874–1958), including *Bearing Gifts* (1926) and *Fairy Tales for Grown Ups* (1927). During these two decades it was Welsh-language writer Kate Roberts (1891–1985) who published the most prolifically in the genre, including several collections, although this work was not made available in English until Storm Jameson's edition of *A Summer's Day* (1946). In many ways, Lynette Roberts's short fiction marks the beginning of a new wave of writing about Wales, challenging stereotypes, unpicking the representation of place and exploding the traditional format of the short story in and about Wales.

One of the pressing questions for many Welsh women writers of the first half of the twentieth century was how best to preserve cultural traditions that were on the verge of being lost or dying out through increased industrialization. One of the ways in which these traditions were preserved was through practical means, including institutions such as the National Museum of Wales and the National Library of Wales, which were both granted royal charters in 1907. Writing in 1937, Eiluned Lewis eloquently underlines the valuable role of such institutions in the survival of Welsh culture:

> We may picture the Welsh of the present and past generations as labouring to build a chain of fortresses to defend their ancient heritage of

culture from the forces of opposition and decay. Their most modern and impregnable bulwarks are the combined watchtowers and store-houses, the twin creations of Museum and Library ... [T]hese arsenals give immense satisfaction to those who regard as somewhat insufficient the achievements of earlier engineers.[4]

Lynette Roberts's 'Seven Stories', published as *An Introduction to Village Dialect With Seven Stories* (1944), form part of a literary 'store-house' of cultural heritage, detailing how women have lived in Wales, what their homes were like and exploring their relationship with the natural world around them. In parallel to the labour required for this endeavour, as identified by Lewis, Roberts's husband, Keidrych Rhys, writes of the work needed, in his journal *Wales* (1937–59):

> Before Welsh readers can enter fully into the aspirations of our coming writers of fiction, who are wisely discarding the conventions of dialogue and dialect of their predecessors, there will have to be some critical spade work. No doubt Lynette Roberts' stories collected over a period of four years, will have an invigorating effect in this direction.[5]

This chapter argues that Lynette Roberts's collection of short stories embodies the desire to preserve cultural traditions, especially through the mode of recounting memory through direct speech. At the same time, it also argues that her choice of form is especially well situated to act as a repository for a wealth of cultural knowledge that is in danger of marginalization and neglect. The short story has the potential to capture a snapshot of Welsh heritage in a way parallel to the photograph or the museum artefact, which can revitalize and recover elements of culture that would otherwise be lost, even with the advent of institutional practices of preservation.

As with the popular genres of the episodic sketch or the travel narrative of the nineteenth century, the 'Seven Stories' provide a sustained focus on the details that give a place and its people a unique identity. The stories are a series of closely observed yet structurally disconnected vignettes that seek to capture the moment at which cultural traditions seep back into modern life, often through the direct speech of characters who remember what rural life in Llanybri was like before the onset of the Second World War. The stories are snapshots of liminal moments – when the narrator reaches the outer walls of a nearby farm ('Fox'), sets foot inside a graveyard with freshly dug graves ('Graveyard'), or a visitor enters the narrator's domestic space ('Tiles' and 'Steer'). The stories' titles suggest a fragmented evocation of elements of rural life, from floor tiles to common animals, yet they also point towards war ('Swansea Raid') and the ways in which war threatens to jeopardize cultural memories through widespread destruction. This is no idealized portrait of a Welsh rural community, which is emphasized by the inclusion of large extracts of local dialect, unframed by conversation markers, such as 'she said'. Roberts refuses to prioritize the narrative perspective over the authenticity of the experience or memories that the stories explore. In doing so, she unsettles the power relations between writer and subject, the narrator and the narrated.

WRITING BACK: CHALLENGING THE NEW APOCALYPSE SCHOOL

Lynette Roberts's seven short stories form a preface to 'An Introduction to Village Dialect', an essay in which she 'endeavour[ed] to prove that [contemporary Welsh dialect] has both a tradition and a root' and traced a variety of sayings and folkloric traditions through texts from various periods of Welsh history.[6] As Patrick McGuinness notes, the essay is 'passionate and piecemeal, and is unlikely to satisfy the scholar'[7] as it looks to demonstrate 'the essence of all languages of the soil' (*DLR*, 119). Despite this dubiously essentialist position, Roberts's concluding remarks are especially significant as they suggest a desire to 'write back' to the models of Welsh identity she has encountered in contemporary literature, in a manner akin to postcolonial resistance. She hoped, specifically, to 'dispel the false misinterpretations used by both radio and amateur writers to represent the Welsh-speaking peoples' (*DLR*, 124). In a letter to the poet Robert Graves, she reiterates these same words, 'false misinterpretations' (*DLR*, 167), adding that these representations need 'correct[ing]', especially those found in 'short stories written by foolish pimps such as Henry Treece' (*DLR*, 167), of the New Apocalypse school. In many ways, then, we can read the 'seven stories' as a direct challenge to the models of Welsh speech and culture circulating in New Apocalypse writing.

A brief look at one of the stories Treece wrote entitled 'Two at the table' (1940–1) provides ample evidence for Roberts's claims. Originally published in the New Apocalypse journal *Kingdom Come*, the opening alone gives a flavour of the way Treece describes Welsh life: 'The day before yesterday Blodwen grinned along the alpine edge of the knife and sliced the rye-bread carelessly, thick as the tombstones outside the Wesleyan Chapel.'[8] The story focuses on Blodwen's affair with her lodger, Twm, the 'broad-shouldered caveman' from Swansea with 'gold hair that swung in the mountain air like a piper's sporran, and hands as big as a dinner-plate' (*HT*, 111). Much of the story's clumsy comic effect lies in the other characters' knowledge of the affair, which results in much sniggering behind the back of Blodwen's unwitting husband, Evan. Racial stereotypes abound, from Blodwen and Evan's 'dark' hair and features (*HT*, 114), to sexual licentiousness (including most of the widowed population of the village), lying, thieving and general stupidity. Characters' speech (and song) is rendered in a particularly condescending fashion, from Evan's claim that Twm has said he sings 'like a toad with a belly full of rusty nails – that was too much, look you' (*HT*, 118) to Twm's 'Celtic frenzy' (*HT*, 113) as he spots some dandelions and breaks into song. Even in a moment of free indirect discourse, when the text presents Blodwen's fear about her parents discovering her pregnancy (by Twm), the language is transcribed as stereotypically 'Welsh', with repeated exclamations of 'look you' (*HT*, 112). Considering these one-dimensional caricatures, it is no wonder that Lynette Roberts felt the need to write something more authentic and true to the Welsh life and culture that she observed around her.

'SEVEN STORIES': ETHNOGRAPHY AND AUTOETHNOGRAPHY

An important context for Roberts's writing can be found in the ethnographic work of St Fagans National Museum of History, situated at St Fagans castle, near Cardiff, which first opened in 1948. Roberts was obviously aware of Dr Iorwerth C. Peate, the first curator of the museum, as she refers specifically to his work in setting up the project in her essays, and makes mention of his book, *The Welsh House* (1940). The museum's purpose was to 'record and study the culture of Wales, including its crafts, architecture, costume, agriculture, folklore and dialects'.[9] In her essays, Roberts is particularly interested not just in recording, but also preserving Welsh architecture, especially that of rural communities, arguing in 'Simplicity of the Welsh Village' (1945) that it is 'far more urgent' to have the 'support of valuable persons like Dr Peate to help preserve and repair the numerous farms and cottages' than it is to put examples 'in a museum behind glass'.[10] While Roberts's short stories may have analogies with the project at St Fagans in their 'authentic' representation of Welsh dialect, they are far more than simple reproductions of culture or picturesque tableaux for consumption by tourists. The stories themselves, which I will discuss in depth later in the essay, are threaded through with details about domestic interiors that capture both the beauty and the drudgery of aspects of female cultural practices.

It is worth pausing for a moment to consider the relationship between the project of ethnography and how this relates to Roberts's writing. McGuinness suggests that her interest in recording daily life was influenced by the Mass Observation movement, and it is this fascination with the fabric of everyday life that aligns her work with ethnography.[11] Modern ethnography can be defined as a discipline that 'takes the position that human behaviour and the ways in which people construct and make meaning of their worlds and their lives are highly variable and locally specific.'[12] Within this discipline, itself a branch of anthropology, we find the term 'thick description', which can be defined as dense descriptions of social life from observation, through which broader cultural interpretations can be made. Clifford Geertz has drawn attention to the constructed nature of 'thick description' in ethnography, arguing that 'what we call our data are really our own constructions of other people's constructions of what they and their compatriots are up to'.[13] It is this layering of construction that Roberts seems to play with in 'Seven Stories', incorporating detailed discussion of cultural traditions drawn from the memories of a recurring Welsh character, Rosie, into conversations with an unnamed narrator.

An important feature of ethnography is the role of the participant/observer, who immerses themselves in the culture they attempt to describe while remaining, to a degree, detached and distant. Ethnography has traditionally been associated with colonial endeavours, especially the cataloguing of different cultures, and the participant/observer figure is not without political, and often troubling, undertones. An offshoot of this figure is traced in fiction in Sandra A. Zagarell's definition of a literary sub-genre known as 'narrative of community'. This genre, Zagarell argues, features a participant/observer narrator who often 'seeks to represent what gives the community its identity, what enables it to remain itself', and explores, amongst other things, 'values, practices, and lore that are threatened by time and change'.[14] It is a genre, Zagarell argues, that is focused predominantly on process, rather than progress, which is highly significant to our understanding of the 'seven stories'. Roberts is continually looking to memory to show how the present is shaped by processes that knit the community together, such as farming, domestic work and traditional methods of producing essential commodities.

There is another form of ethnography known as autoethnography, which draws together ethnographic observations with autobiography, and in which 'the realist conventions and objective observer position of standard ethnography have been called into question'.[15] This questioning of realist conventions is something that Roberts engages with at the level of the sentence in 'Seven Stories', breaking away from an authoritative narrative perspective by enabling characters from the community to speak directly and at length. At the same time, the stories are threaded through with details and anecdotes that relate to Roberts's experiences in Llanybri. Mary Louise Pratt argues that: 'If ethnographic texts are a means by which Europeans represent to themselves their (usually subjugated) others, autoethnographic texts are those the others construct in response to or in dialogue with those metropolitan representations.'[16] Here Pratt could almost be referring to Roberts's relationship with the representations put forward by Treece and the New Apocalypse school. Welsh cultural traditions seem to resonate for her, perhaps because of her own family's life as settlers of Welsh descent in Buenos Aires. The relevance of otherness is also important as Roberts was writing from *within* Welsh culture, while still being, intrinsically, an outsider. Reed-Danahay comments on the 'cultural displacement or situation of exile characteristic of the themes expressed by autoethnographers', noting that the figure of the autoethnographer is 'not completely "at home" '.[17] The sense of exile that Reed-Danahay identifies manifests in the 'seven stories' as the insistent desire to connect, either to the other characters who feature or with the memories that they share.

'FOX'

In the first of the stories, 'Fox', Roberts explores the experiences of a family of foxes who once lived in the middle of a cornfield. The story is framed by the narrator's perceptions of the landscape around her, specifically an area that would now be identified as Pembrokeshire, the county where Roberts's mother's family came from. The story opens, however, in a register that integrates the language of poetry with the knowing voice of the traveller, demarcating space that is in the process of being mapped by the narrator's eye. The opening paragraph flits between the wide vistas of 'green and transparent' sky (*DLR*, 94) and the detail of the foreground, with trees that 'appear blacker than usual under this astringent light' (*DLR*, 94). The language is that of the painter, or perhaps photographer, assessing the landscape as an outsider would a landscape painting or picture.

In 'Fox', the narrator emphasizes the separate details that make up the picture presented, such as the sunlight that 'threads through every crevice of the Prescelly Mountains . . . cutting out the outline of each wave and leaf as they sparkle with a million separate lights' (*DLR*, 94). Here the description leans toward a more modernist vocabulary of shape and outline, or even the French post-impressionist vogue for cloisonnism, which depicted objects in two dimensions with black outlines. The 'million separate lights' give the scene an almost pointillist aspect, suggesting an image made up entirely of glimmering points of light. Given Roberts's artistic training at the Central School of Arts and Crafts, these influences are perhaps unsurprising. Yet they also mark her movement away from the staunchly realist depictions of the Welsh landscape and its flora and fauna that would have featured heavily in travellers' accounts of Wales in the previous century.

In 'Fox', the speaker locates herself both within this landscape, in a specific valley, and as separate from the wider vista. The valley is 'hidden' from the 'surrounding mirror of pristine clearness' (*DLR*, 94). There is something primordial and almost threatening about this landscape, especially in an image of vapour forming the shape of dinosaurs, ghostly outlines sketched upon the landscape of a past now long gone. The sky at the beginning of the story is 'green and transparent' but this has 'no tie' with the 'living green of the soil . . . a green impaled by age, that knew the pagans stretched before their gods' (*DLR*, 94). The land and the sky are separate, distinct, unknowable to each other, mirroring the relation of the narrator to the people among whom she has inserted herself.

The second half of the story explores loss, again through the lens of natural processes. Rosie, the character who reappears most frequently throughout the seven stories, comments on how the farm's ducks have been taken by foxes. This loss is juxtaposed with the loss of other resources, such as timber stores and milk supplies, which have been depleted because of the recent air raids. Rosie switches from the present to a moment in her past when another family of foxes made their home in the same cornfield. There is something both audacious and playful about this occupation of farmland as the foxes create a 'little playground *right around* their home (*DLR*, 94). It is this audacity that Rosie respects – 'they're such smart fellows [she] can't be cross' (*DLR*, 94).

The foxes' stealing of birds, recounted by Rosie in the present, is part of an ongoing process of survival that is echoed in the past. In her childhood memory, Rosie recounts how her mother instructed her to chase one of the foxes for stealing the duck they had fattened especially for Christmas. Rosie remembers, however, how her mother relents, saying: 'Whist, I expect the young ones could do with it!' (*DLR*, 95). There is an understanding that this loss of this duck, meant for the family's festive meal, has enabled the foxes' survival. The story concludes, however, with two of the young foxes being taken for the hunt, leaving the reader with a disquieting sense of unnecessary violence. The beauty and latent volatility of the primeval landscape that is explored at the beginning of the story, coupled with a lamentation for the fate of these foxes in Rosie's past, potentially aligns Roberts with an ecocritical perspective, where the supposedly hierarchical position of humans within the natural world is undermined.

'TILES'

'Tiles', the second of the 'Seven Stories', begins in the middle of a conversation between the narrator, who is unwell, and her neighbour, Rosie. Rosie lights a fire, using a fuel made of traditional materials (called 'pele'), and then attempts to scrub the floor, prompting the narrator to complain about having floorboards instead of tiles, as 'almost every cottage has them but mine'.[18] This leads Rosie to tell of her experiences when she was a young woman:

> 'I'm telling you right, there was an old lady living just below our farm in Plasnewydd and mother used to send me down with a piece of bacon or some milk. She was very old and doubled up, and you could see the pleats and bows on her back as she bent over her stick. She wore a cap with frills and loops, and a flannel apron . . . Once a week she would do her floor over with a burdock – no dock-leaf, I mean – with the point. She'd go like this.' And Rosie stood to make the circle and placed a dot in the centre. 'She'd do like this, until when you came to look at it from

the door, it looked like linoleum. Sometimes she did other designs such as triangles, or small circles like trefoil, or squares. Round the hearth she would do stoning in another design. Under the grate was also white. She's dead now, I know; and I remember these things when I was 14, now I'm 46. It must be on cement and it comes off a dark green'. (*DLR*, 96–7)

The details contained in this extract could pass as ethnographic descriptions of rural Welsh traditions – from the style of female dress to the way homes were decorated by women. Iorwerth Peate's *The Welsh House* also includes some fascinating examples of these floor patterns, a practice that seems to belong to a different era by the time of publication of Roberts's short story. A similar image also appears in Charles Dickens's *Household Words*, in an article on rural practices in Cheshire from the 1840s:

> Inside the house, the first thing that catches the eye is the Welsh carpet not in the parlours, but the passage-rooms, pantries, and kitchen. This Welsh carpet is a pattern produced on the brick floor by staining the brick squares in figures with dockleaf juice. The prettiest pattern is perhaps produced by rubbing half of each square diagonally with dock-leaves. The diced appearance is really very pretty.[19]

In Roberts's story, the use of dialogue, coupled with the fact that she provides very little context regarding character or setting in the story's opening, complicates the participant/observer narrative model that Zagarell notes in earlier narratives of community. The patterns the old woman decorates her floor with may have parallels with the tradition of the *kolam*, which is found in ancient southern Indian culture, and is known by different names dependent on the region.[20] In ancient India, 'womenfolk specialized in line drawing, being trained in drawing patterns . . . and exquisite, unswerving line work was associated with the dexterity of the female hand.'[21] It has been described as 'the most important kind of female artistic expression', suggesting that, in Indian culture, it is recognized as a female-oriented but highly valued skill.[22] Roberts's story reflects a context in which the knowledge and skill needed to execute these comparatively complex designs is fast disappearing in an increasingly anglicized Wales; Roberts's story captures the existence of the designs, and some idea of their shape, but not how they are executed. The short story does the work of the ephemeral floor pattern; by reinscribing these designs into an account of Welsh cultural traditions, Roberts ensures that the memory of the practice cannot be easily effaced, even if the knowledge of its execution might be lost. Roberts's story also draws attention to the fragility of an oral tradition that saw lore handed down from mother to daughter. 'Tiles' tries to mimic that female-to-female link, extending from the old woman to Rosie, and from Rosie to the narrator. There are various gaps in the account that emphasize the impossibility of fully recreating the cultural tradition within prose. First, there is a generational time lag between Rosie's original experience and her *telling* of that experience, underlined by phrases such as 'I remember these things when I was 14, now I'm 46' (*DLR*, 97). There are also gaps in the description of completing the designs themselves, as Rosie describes 'another [circle], and another, all around it' (*DLR*, 96) without pinpointing where exactly these circles are placed. Perhaps most importantly, the designs themselves are ambivalent – they could be an expression of artistic autonomy, or a symbol for the repetitive, unending labour of women in the domestic sphere. As Gwyneth Tyson Roberts notes in *The Language of the Blue Books* (1988), making a 'Welsh carpet' involved 'stain[ing] a brick floor with patterns which imitated the design of a real carpet', which could perhaps indicate a longing for a higher social class and its associated financial stability, or even a kind of inauthenticity.[23] In the stories as a whole, there is a tension between the representation of the class position of the narrator compared to local inhabitant Rosie, who always appears in some kind of subservient role – offering to light the fire, picking the narrator's vegetables or feeling unfit to enter the narrator's cottage because of her working clothes. Yet Rosie has access to a range of cultural traditions that the narrator can only observe. What might have once been a sign of social aspiration is now an emblem of authenticity.

'STEER'

The third story, 'Steer', is about the natural cycles that underpin rural communities, and particularly the idea of return. Having been ill, the narrator has been presented with several gifts, ranging from 'two-thirds of an apple pie' to 'a white kitten from Plasnewydd' (*DLR*, 98). As with many of the stories, a small animal or simple object – in this case a kitten – is deployed as a catalyst to the main narrative turn of the story. Rosie comments that the kitten might run back to Plasnewydd, and then 'to stress her point' she tells the narrator a story of a steer that was sold at market and then escaped. Again, this is a narrative that is passed down from Rosie's mother to Rosie and then to the narrator. As Rosie's mother did not want to fatten the steer herself, he was bought by a farmer who lived six miles away. In Rosie's narrative, the steer then escaped, swam down the river, and survived despite the strong currents. He returns home, 'straight back by the shortest route, a way he had never travelled before' (*DLR*, 98). Rosie's mother is pleased he has returned but their reunion is cut short when the farmer arrives to take him back to his farm. The story seems to be commenting on the power of a sense of home, and belonging, suggesting that this relationship between animals and their place of origin is almost innate. At the same time, it highlights the futility of trying to escape fate – that liberation from social destiny will only be temporary. The use of the term 'steer' also suggests a deeper meaning, as it is usually used to denote a castrated bull calf. Castration ensures that steers are less aggressive than bull calves and produce better quality cuts of meat. The term 'steer' reminds the reader that there is only one possible outcome for this animal – the fattening process that will lead to it being slaughtered.

There is some real subtlety at work in this story, in that it could be read as a straightforward picture of what rural life is like, yet at the same time, it suggests a certain level of empathy for the plight of the creature and aligns Roberts with ecocriticism or zoocriticism. That the steer has the desire to escape in the first place suggests a level of consciousness far beyond what we might normally associate with a farm animal. The motif of escape is bound up in the very fabric of her writing, often imagined through the image of birds. This story suggests that escape from the natural rhythms and cycles of rural life is impossible and the steer's swift removal underlines the necessary, if sometimes brutal, processes that ensure communities do not go hungry. The extent to which this might also be a comment on Roberts's perceptions of the hardships within a rural community is left unexplored.

'GRAVEYARD'

'Graveyard' is, in many ways, a lament for cultural practices surrounding death that have altered in the wake of an increasingly capitalist society. The narrator describes a variety of funeral practices, and describes the different styles of headstone found in the village graveyard. She mourns the 'thick headstones of slate . . . sinking to the level of their neglected trades' while the 'engraved symbols of carpenter, mason, blacksmith, farmer, were beginning to dissolve' (*DLR*, 99). Here Roberts is referring to the use of slate for headstones, a tradition that lasted roughly until the turn of the twentieth century. Slate weathers relatively quickly, so the engravings on this material would be swiftly effaced. In comparison to the slate, the narrator comments that the 'heavy granite and deeply polished face of the red and black "chessmen" should be abolished' (*DLR*, 99). This refers to the obelisk style of headstone, often designed in red or black granite, which, though far more ostentatious and expensive, is long-lasting: granite is one of the hardiest types of stone, and for this reason it replaced white marble as the material of choice in the Victorian period.[24] The simple graves of the now long-dead craftsmen become markers of a past swiftly fading, while the showy obelisks represent 'commerce . . . stood at the head of the grave' (*DLR*, 99). In Europe, more generally, the cemetery 'became a locus for reactions against the encroachment of modernity on customs and values', especially as modern techniques for cutting stone meant that mass production, rather than handcrafted design, was the norm.[25] However, the use of slate, one of Wales's major exports in the nineteenth and early twentieth centuries, is itself a marker of the rise of industrialization, rather than a straightforward connection with an artisan past. The gravestones represent the physical labour of working men who hewed slate out of slate quarries — a form of manual work that is also in danger of being forgotten.

'PUB' AND 'SWANSEA RAID'

It is in 'Pub' and 'Swansea Raid' that the modernity Roberts laments in 'Graveyard' particularly comes to the fore. While 'Fox' makes passing reference to the impact of air raids, these two stories in the series repeatedly draw attention to Hitler, World War II and the threat to rural life from an increasingly mechanized style of warfare. In 'Pub', a short story that captures snippets of conversation around the bar, Roberts underlines the extent to which warfare has changed the community's consciousness, not necessarily for the better. A character called Williams, for example, has become 'attached to a land girl evacuated to a neighbouring village who spent most of her time going places in corduroy trousers' (*DLR*, 101) and has taken up residence in a stable. Land girls were a common feature in Wales during the

Second World War, as food supplies were running short, and young, single women were drafted in to farm the land. The men's talk in 'Pub' oscillates from large-scale political issues, such as the 'fate of Hitler' (*DLR*, 101), to the sexual possibilities represented by the land girl, and her living quarters in the converted barn. The men talk about her as if she were an animal: one comments that 'it's a pity to use good straw, all you need is a white sheet to lay her on', while another suggests that Williams should 'Shove her against a rick, mun' (*DLR*, 101). Williams refuses to become embroiled in this kind of talk, instead drawing attention to the unfairness of inflation on ordinary working people. He complains: 'I bought a pig tidy before the war for 30 bob apiece, now they're asking three to four pounds' (*DLR*, 101). By juxtaposing the discussion of the land girl with Williams's complaint about the price of animals, Roberts highlights a growing sense of dissatisfaction and dispossession among rural working people, suggesting that the men are unable to have control over their own lives and therefore seek to gain it through sexual aggression. The female body, possibly because it defies social norms when clothed in trousers, symbolizes a site of potential control. At the same time, the land girl is also a symbol of new ways of living. Unencumbered by family ties to the area, and situated in the village for work, she represents the social and economic shifts and changes that will come about as a result of the war. In Roberts's experience of living in Llanybri, the village was already neglected by the government. It was suffering due to the lack of running water and the wells running dry during the 1940s, conditions that Roberts wrote at length about in her 'A Carmarthenshire Diary' and are referred to directly in 'Pub'. Despite the lack of basic resources for the size of the population, the government has proposed to 'send [them] 40 more' (*DLR*, 102) evacuees. This lack of water means that when a hen roost catches fire in 'Pub', there is no way to put it out and the hens are 'roasted' (*DLR*, 102) by the time the fire is brought under control. This senseless death is a symbol of wider concerns about powerlessness within the community. The story concludes with an anecdote about Jack Vaughan who has found employment at Pendine. Pendine Sands were acquired during the war as a firing range, which is why Vaughan is paid 'Four pound ten for cleaning out the barrel of a gun' (*DLR*, 102). The parallel that emerges between the wages that Vaughan receives and the increased cost of buying a pig lamented by Williams earlier in the story is not accidental, not least because Vaughan, in his role as gun cleaner, can buy his breakfast for sixpence with 'bacon as much as you like' (*DLR*, 102). Here Roberts cleverly unpicks the impact of jobs that are tied to violence and the ramifications of an increasingly capitalist mindset, divorced from the land.

In 'Swansea Raid', the mechanization that is shown to underpin changing employments in west Wales is spelt out through the use of Roberts's wartime identity number, Xebo7011, and Rosie's, Xebn559162. This story was originally called 'From a New Perception of Colour: And I shall take as my example the Raid on Swansea' when it was published in 1941 in *Life and Letters Today*, and explores the 'three-day blitz' that Swansea endured from 19 to 21 February 1941. The organic shapes and colours found in 'Fox' give way to a Swansea described as a 'glade of magnesium' that 'flares like a swarm of orange bees' (*DLR*, 103). The oxymoronic use of imagery, in which fire and explosives interweave the natural and the manmade, makes the devastation all the more horrific – suggesting that this is a destruction of mankind's making. Leo Mellor argues in his study of the effect of bombing on the wartime imagination, *Reading the Ruins*, that 'no moral position of condemnation emerges' in 'Swansea Raid' – that Roberts 'revels in the scene as one of the transformative sublime.'[26] While there are moments of revelry in the alien beauty of the scene, I would argue that the recurring focus on the chemical compounds used, coupled with the whole collection's lament for man's impact on an increasingly fragile ecosystem, tells a different story.

'Swansea Raid' ends with Rosie fetching in the cows, in full knowledge that 'all copper compounds are poisonous' (*DLR*, 103) and that the cattle may well have been exposed to chemicals from the aerial combat. The narrator returns home, to the 'quiet clayfire with the blue flames rising' (*DLR*, 103). In contrast to the spectacular colours that have been fired across the sky, the blue of the fire 'bring[s] solace to any heart' (*DLR*, 103). Yet a sense of vulnerability remains, implying that the people inside their houses are equally at risk as the cows in the field.

'FISHERMAN'

'Fisherman' is marginally longer than the other stories, and pulls together much of the imagery, snippets of conversation and sense of community that defines 'Seven Stories' as a whole. The opening draws once again on the use of colour to suggest mood through the image of the 'irritating iron blue sky, that lifts the green from out of the leaves so that they are reduced in hue to a yellow fragility' (*DLR*, 104). Though the time of year is not specified, there is a sense that this is autumn or late summer, for swallows fly past towards the end of the story. T. S. Eliot's *The Waste Land* (1922) haunts the text, including the mythic figure suggested by John Roberts, the fisherman of the title who comes calling: 'Fish-alive. Fish alive, Alive-o' (*DLR*, 104), a Charon-like figure who ferries people across the estuary. His 'burnished flesh glowing like coals of fire' (*DLR*, 105) echoes the 'burnished throne' that 'Glowed on the marble' at the beginning of 'A Game of Chess' in Eliot's poem.[27] There is also a recurrent focus on bones and skeletons, from the 'skeleton rafters' of an abandoned chapel to the 'inner ribs' of the fisherman's boat (*DLR*, 105), images that echo Eliot's poem but also recall Coleridge's ship of death in the *Rime of the Ancient Mariner*. We are in mythic territory in this last story, a space in which Roberts attempts to merge fragments of stories and phrases, including the fisherman's repeated call, to create meaning in a world that is increasingly devoid of meaning. When the narrator asks the fisherman if he will return, he suggests not, referring to the 'soldiers camped near us [who] will be taking more than I can find' (*DLR*, 105). The coming of the soldiers means that the time-honoured tradition of coracle fishing is almost at an end; the villagers will no longer be able to rely on this journeying fisherman to meet their needs. The final image of the story is ambivalent. The narrator is left holding 'two fish bouncing as vigorously to free themselves from the willow, as a young calf tied and pulling to free himself from the mart' (*DLR*, 106). This image of life, fiercely fighting in the moment of certain death, is a metonym for 'Seven Stories' as a whole. As much as Roberts repeatedly brings to life rural traditions and practices through her stories, she also recognizes that they are on the very point of extinction.

CONCLUSION

Lynette Roberts's 'Seven Stories' marks a particularly important moment not just in the history of the modernist short story in Wales, but the history of the form as a whole. By imbuing the everyday with the language of poetry, she draws attention to the beauty to be found in the ordinary processes that make up rural life. At the same time, her exploration of the community's stories and memories, retold in their own speech patterns, breaks away from the humiliating representations found in works such as Henry Treece's. Reed-Danahay notes: 'The ability to transcend everyday conceptions of selfhood and social life is related to the ability to write or do autoethnography. This is a postmodern condition. It involves a rewriting of the self and the social.'[28] It is this rewriting that is key to understanding and appreciating the significance of Roberts's work. Not only does she rewrite Welsh rural identity as something authentic and rooted in tradition, rather than a caricature, but she elevates the work of women in the home and on the land. This rewriting is not just of the experience of the 1940s, but throughout generations long dead, ensuring that women's vital role in underpinning the continued existence of the community can be recognized, and perhaps even celebrated. At the same time, she is alive to the pressures that everyone will face in the wake of huge changes to employment, housing and social life. Her writing stands on the fault line between a past that is rapidly being forgotten and a future that is yet to be written and deserves to be recognized at long last.

Notes

[1] Claire Flay, *Dorothy Edwards* (Cardiff: University of Wales Press, 2011), p. 31.
[2] Flay, *Dorothy Edwards*, p. 19.
[3] Glyn Roberts, 'The Welsh School of Writers', *The Bookman*, 84 (1933), 248–9 (248).
[4] Eiluned and Peter Lewis, *The Land of Wales* (London: Batsford, 1937), p. 110.
[5] Keidrych Rhys, 'Editorial', *Wales*, 3/3 (1944), 4–6 (5).
[6] Lynette Roberts, 'An Introduction to Village Dialect', in *Diaries, Letters and Recollections*, ed. Patrick McGuinness (Manchester: Carcanet, 2008), pp. 107–24 (p. 107). Hereafter *DLR*. All further references are to this edition and are given in the body of the text.
[7] Patrick McGuinness, 'Introduction', in Lynette Roberts, *Diaries, Letters and Recollections*, ed. Patrick McGuinness (Manchester: Carcanet, 2008), pp. vii–xvii (p. xiv).
[8] Henry Treece, 'Two at the Table', in *I Cannot Go Hunting Tomorrow* (London: Grey Walls Press, 1946), p. 111. Hereafter *HT*. All further references are to this edition and are given in the body of the text.
[9] See 'The Museum of Welsh Life', in *The New Companion to the Literature of Wales*, ed. Meic Stephens (Cardiff: University of Wales Press, 1998), p. 519.
[10] Lynette Roberts, 'Simplicity of the Welsh Village', in *Diaries, Letters and Recollections*, pp. 127–32 (p. 128).
[11] McGuinness, 'Introduction', in *Diaries, Letters and Recollections*, p. xv.

12 J. J. Schensul and M. D. Lecompte, *Designing and Conducting Ethnographic Research* (Walnut Creek: AltaMira, 1999), p. 1.
13 Clifford Geertz, *The Interpretation of Cultures* (New York: Basic Books, 1973), p. 8.
14 Sandra A. Zagarell, 'Narrative of Community: The Identification of a Genre', *Signs: Journal of Women in Culture and Society*, 13/3 (1988), 498–527 (520).
15 Deborah Reed-Danahay, 'Introduction', in *Auto/ethnography: Rewriting the Self and the Social* (Oxford: Berg, 1997), pp. 1–17 (p. 2).
16 Mary Louise Pratt, *Imperial Eyes* (London: Routledge, 1992), p. 7.
17 Reed-Danahay, *Auto/ethnography*, p. 4.
18 Lynette Roberts, 'Tiles', in *Diaries, Letters and Recollections*, pp. 96–7 (p. 96). All further references are to this edition and are given in the body of the text.
19 Harriet Martineau, 'Cheshire Cheese', *Household Words* (2 September 1854), 52–6 (53).
20 According to Nicoletta Sala, the *kolam* is known as *Muggulu* in Andrapradesh, *Hase* in Karnataka, *Chowkpurna* in Uttar Pradesh, *Rangoli* in Gujarat and Maharashtra, and *Alpana* in Bengal and Assam. See Nicoletta Sala, 'Fractal Geometry in the Arts: An Overview across the Different Cultures', in *Thinking in Patterns: Fractals and Related Phenomena in Nature*, ed. Miroslav M. Novak (Singapore, River Edge, New Jersey, and London: World Scientific, 2004), pp. 177–88 (p. 184).
21 C. Sivaramamurhi, *The Painter in Ancient India* (New Delhi: Abhinav Publications, 1978), p. 8.
22 Sala, 'Fractal Geometry in the Arts', p. 184.
23 Gwyneth Tyson Roberts, *The Language of the Blue Books: The Perfect Instrument of Empire* (Cardiff: University of Wales Press, 1998), p. 13.
24 White marble ceased to be used as it was particularly susceptible to the effects of industrial pollution, including acid rain, which damaged the finish and made the inscriptions unreadable.
25 Felix Robin Schulz, *Death in East Germany, 1945–1990* (New York: Berghahn Books, 2013), p. 203.
26 Leo Mellor, *Reading the Ruins: Modernism, Bombsites and British Culture* (Cambridge: Cambridge University Press, 2011), p. 112.
27 T. S. Eliot, 'The Waste Land', in *The Waste Land and Other Poems* (London: Faber, 1990), ll. 77–8.
28 Reed-Danahay, *Auto/ethnography*, p. 4.

4

'WHAT CHANGES BREAK BEFORE US': SEMI-PERIPHERAL MODERNITY IN LYNETTE ROBERTS'S POETRY AND PROSE

Andrew Webb

Lynette Roberts's poetry and prose represent the Llansteffan peninsula as a synecdochal space in which tensions are played out between capitalist modernization, accelerated through the transformations wrought by the Second World War, and an indigenous Welsh culture, experienced in daily village life. *Poems* (1944) and *Gods with Stainless Ears* (1951) depict the penetration of this part of south Carmarthenshire by the forces of global warfare, experienced at their most devastating in aerial bombardment, but also in the changes to everyday life that followed the establishment of military bases and armaments factories across the region, and major shifts in population and employment patterns. In this way, Roberts's work registers the threat to the continuity of Welsh culture, questions the meaning of an Allied victory, and stands as a record of Welsh resistance to the globalizing forces made manifest in the British war effort.

In order to deepen our understanding of Roberts's representation of south Carmarthenshire, this essay will employ the concept of the 'semi-periphery', a term recently employed by Franco Moretti as part of his attempt to account for the cultural changes that are experienced through the nineteenth and twentieth centuries as capitalist modernity spreads into new geographical spaces.[1] Moretti nuances Immanuel Wallerstein's idea of the 'periphery' and the 'centre' in order to argue that social experience within a third kind of space – the semi-periphery – is critical to our understanding of cultural transmission when globalizing capitalist modernity expands its sphere of influence. Even more recently, a group of scholars called the Warwick Research Collective (WReC) have developed Moretti's somewhat speculative hypotheses into a literary-critical paradigm that successfully draws attention to the ways in which work by a range of writers from different times and cultures share formal features and subject matter typical of work from the semi-periphery. WReC's work challenges the conventional division of literary studies into periods or national/linguistic spaces. It suggests that the semi-periphery is not merely an interstice between the global and the local, between the periphery and centre, but is a distinctive kind of space in its own right in which attention is repeatedly drawn to conflicts between a globalizing capitalist modernity and a surviving, or reinvented, indigenous culture. Cultural expression from the semi-periphery is often marked by a negotiation of these forces – which are registered at the levels of both form and content – and by the way it records the synchronous co-existence of different historical times, the modern and the premodern, within the same space.

This definition of the semi-periphery offers a useful critical paradigm through which to consider Roberts's representation of south Carmarthenshire. In her work, customs from a pre-capitalist society co-exist with a globalizing capitalist modernity that, under the auspices of the British war effort, reorganizes patterns of population and employment in the area. Her work repeatedly returns to its central theme of Llansteffan as a space in which the forces of a global modernity, which are usually malign, rub up against a residual, or reawakened, Welsh culture. In her 1945 essay 'Coracles of the Towy', Roberts depicts pre-capitalist ways of life existing side-by-side with the latest features of modernity. A line of coracle fishermen set their net across the river's width and then 'with the net subsiding into position, they travelled downstream rapidly out of sight'.[2] The essay then takes in '[p]astoral meadows on the one bank grazing cattle and sheep; butterflies flitting among the agrimony and soft rush at the water's edge; the hard line of the Roman Hills; further distant, the limestone ridge of Llangyndeyrn' before asking: 'But near? What changes break before us. The Cow and Gate milk factory, railway signals. Harries' Towy works, galvanised sheds, Joseph Rank, flour merchants, the new Carmarthen bridge.'[3] This passage exemplifies Roberts's habit of juxtaposing the co-existence of realities from very different moments of history. The practice of coracle fishing is a surviving remnant of an earlier, pre-capitalist age, a practice dating from an older subsistence economy, and yet it co-exists with industrial-scale food production intrinsic to modernity – 'the Cow and Gate milk factory' and 'Joseph Rank, flour merchants'. Also registered in this extract is the transport network – the 'railway signals' and 'the new Carmarthen bridge' – that enables the incorporation of the area's agricultural economy into larger markets. Capitalist modernity, this passage suggests, is always in flux; it is a set of relentless 'changes' that constantly 'break before us' like a storm.

We can see a similar pattern elsewhere in Roberts's prose. In her 1944 essay, 'An Introduction to Village Dialect', she describes ancient '[farming] customs which prevail to this day', juxtaposed alongside newer, modern practices: 'The hand plough is used down at Cwmcelyn [near Llanybri, on the Llansteffan peninsula], and on the hills sowing of corn by hand, the toilers work side by side with modern agricultural machines.'[4] Again, Roberts's writing draws attention to the co-existence of traditional and modern agricultural practices. This is also evident in the testimony of George Woodcock, a London-based Canadian anarchist and poetry editor who visited Roberts in 1940. He describes Llanybri as 'the nearest thing to a genuine peasant community that I had ever experienced in Britain'.[5] While this might be an exaggeration, Woodcock certainly describes a land 'worked by primitive methods' and 'a field of barley being cut with sickles'.[6] He also reports that Llanybri is a place where 'the pattern of life in the village [that had existed] since medieval times' had recently been interrupted by 'the storms of the outside world' in the form of 'the bombs of the Luftwaffe'.[7]

Although modernity had long effected change in this part of south Carmarthenshire, the change was particularly marked in the late 1930s and early 1940s as a result of the preparations for, and onset of, war. The railhead at Ferryside had facilitated commerce and tourism since 1852; the subsequent development of the south Wales coalfield brought holidaying miners into the area in their thousands from the late nineteenth century; national agro-businesses, in the shape of a Cow and Gate factory and a Rank flour mill, had arrived in the years following World War I. But through the 1930s and into the 1940s, when Roberts was writing, the transformative power of globalizing forces was particularly evident. The early 1930s witnessed the spread of the national electricity grid, and the establishment of the Milk

Marketing Board, a national network of processing and distribution plants, which integrated Carmarthenshire dairy farmers into a British market. The final years of the 1930s saw the establishment of armaments factories and military bases that, as we shall see, had already transformed employment and population patterns across the region long before the area suffered heavy bombing raids in 1941.

Roberts first registers the entry of war into south Carmarthenshire in 'Swansea Raid', an account of the February 1941 Swansea Blitz:

> I, that is Xebo7011, pass out into the chill-blue air and join Xebn559162, her sack apron greening by the light of the moon. I read around her hips: 'BEST CWT: CLARK'S COW-CAKES, H.T.5.' I do not laugh because I love my peasant friend . . .
> A blasting flash impels Swansea to riot! Higher, absurdly higher, the sulphuric clouds roll with their stench of ore, we breathe naphthalene air, the pillars of smoke writhe, and the astringent sky lies pale at her sides. A Jerry overhead drops two flares; the cows returning to their sheds wear hides of cyanite blue, their eyes GLINTING OPALS! We, alarmed, stand puce beneath another flare, our blood distilled, cylindricals of glass . . . High explosives splash up blue, white, and green . . . Bleached, Rosie turns to fetch in the cows. I lonely, return to my hearth, there is a quiet clayfire with blue flames rising that would bring solace to any heart.[8]

This account shares some of the characteristics of writing from the semi-periphery. In one moment, Rosie has a pre-capitalist identity as a 'peasant' who wears 'sack aprons' to 'fetch in the cows'; in the next moment, she has a modern identity based on the number on her wartime identification card – 'Xebn559162'. War transforms the speaker and Rosie into 'cylindricals of glass', their 'blood distilled', a description that registers their vulnerability to the flares and bombs being dropped from above. The Welsh domestic space, the symbolic home of Welsh identity, is similarly invoked in the closing image of the 'quiet clayfire' of the 'hearth'. It remains a place that 'would bring solace to any heart', thereby retaining its pre-modern role. However, it is now also a space in which world war is uncannily present. The hearth's 'blue flames rising', given what the speaker has just witnessed, cannot but recall the '[h]igh explosive[s] splash[ing] up blue, white, and green' in Swansea, as well as the 'cyanite blue' of the cows under the bombers' flares. In this sense, the 'blue flame' of the 'quiet clayfire' becomes an image that simultaneously represents the pre-capitalist mode of the Welsh farmhouse, a place of solace and home, and the sudden intrusion into this space of the latest modern forms of aerial warfare. Even the 'hearth' – the traditional heart of Welsh culture – can no longer be seen as a place beyond the reach of these global forces.

Roberts's most sustained portrayal of the impact of World War II on south Carmarthenshire occurs in *Gods with Stainless Ears*, published in 1951 but written in the 1940s.[9] While it registers the impact of war as a further penetration of south Carmarthenshire by capitalist modernity, it focuses less on the bombardment of the area, and more on the transformations wrought by the British war effort. Despite occasional glimpses of a possible future in which technology is harnessed for local benefit, such moments are ultimately subsumed under the apocalyptic vision of a future in which technologically advanced global forces obliterate Welsh culture. The poem calls for a reawakening of Welsh culture as an act of resistance to these forces.

The preface to the poem registers the local and the global forces that define the space around the bay of Cwmcelyn, where the poem is set, and records Roberts's search for a poetic form adequate to the task of capturing the two poles of this historical context. The Carmarthenshire 'rural village' context has its own 'localised folklore' (*CP*, 43). It is a place that resonates with Welsh myths, poems from the Welsh-language tradition, and customs. Yet it is also global in the sense that it is a synecdochal location – first, its 'background is similar to any rural village' and, secondly, it has been transformed by the dictates of the industrial war machine: the 'Factory hands' and 'lines' of mass production typical of life on the Home Front (*CP*, 43). It has also been reached by 'newsreel' and 'film', globalizing modernity's latest forms of cultural expression (*CP*, 43). Roberts decides against 'varied metre forms' or 'heroic couplet[s]', instead alighting on the long modernist poem, written in mainly regular, five-line stanzas, as the form through which this breadth of material could best be conveyed (*CP*, 43).

In its opening section, the poem employs what Roberts describes in the preface as 'congested words [and] images' to register the fusing together of the 'timeless' natural world of the Llansteffan peninsula with industry and military activity: 'the same tide leans back' to reveal 'Saline mud / Siltering, wet with marshpinks' while the estuary's 'ironing edge' is 'a railway line washed flat' (*CP*, 44). There is an allusion to the tin industry, still then one of the area's major employers, in the depiction of the sea as 'tin splintered from a crab-green cave' (*CP*, 44). But the most radical fusing of imagery describes the latest forms of industrial warfare: the 'new beaks scissoring the air' suggests the military planes in training over the bay (*CP*, 44). Even domestic space is invaded by the RAF: 'to rattle of boiling buckets, / Sleeve of plane rippling over hedge' (*CP*, 47). Such imagery registers how, thanks to significant changes in employment and population, the area had become transformed by the war. RAF Pembrey opened along the coast in 1936, and in 1941 an air gunnery school was established with almost 2,000 personnel.[10] From the start of the war, Carmarthen was home to more than 10,000 evacuees from south-east England. In 1945, these newcomers were joined by American airmen, part of the 100,000-strong group of Americans in south Wales.[11] There were also three prisoner-of-war camps in Carmarthenshire alone.[12] As her poem 'Lamentation' shows, Roberts's move to Llanybri in 1939, albeit to marry the Welsh-speaking Keidrych Rhys, enabled her to identify with these new arrivals:

> To the village of lace and stone
> Came strangers. I was one of these
> Always observant and slightly obscure.[13]

As these opening lines suggest, Roberts the incomer is an embodiment of the wider forces that were driving population changes in that part of south Wales, while her relationship to Rhys also provides her with an 'insider' status. This unusual position provides her with the material for *Gods with Stainless Ears*.

The poem registers the rapid change to gender roles brought about by the war. Part I depicts a shipbuilders' yard or steel plant in which workers are 'spidering each man stark / On steelweb, hammering in rivets ambuscade / Interrupted by sirens screaming tirade' – presumably the air raid warnings or the factory hooters (*CP*, 47). This industrial scene, with its 'blast and red-hot ingots; clatch / Of ricocheting wheels', is in stark contrast to the pastoral, even bucolic, imagery employed to describe the inhabitants' 'daily . . . water trudge' to the village pump (*CP*, 47). But it is now the women who work the fields – 'to each striped tidy plot aproned women work' – and tend the animals – 'Women titans are weathervanes who fetch / In the cows' (*CP*, 47). From its opening section onwards, then, *Gods with Stainless Ears* registers the wartime shift in gender roles and employment patterns that had taken place in this part of south Wales, a change that Deirdre Beddoe characterizes as unprecedented and transformative.[14] While men of working age were conscripted, and sent all over the world on military service, women were increasingly employed in agricultural and industrial work.[15] Many travelled up to thirty miles to work in the recently constructed armaments factory in Bridgend, or the new TNT explosives factory down the coast at Pembrey. The former employed 35,000 workers, the overwhelming majority of whom were women. The change in gender roles was particularly marked in south Wales, which, prior to the war, had a low level of female paid employment, having been a principal source of the Home Counties' female domestic labour force. While this transformation of gender roles is registered most explicitly in *Gods with Stainless Ears*, particularly through the image of 'women titans', it is also present in the poem 'Plasnewydd' in which the speaker describes how 'The women – that's the men, / Pull their aprons over their heads' to carry out the agricultural labour.[16]

Gods with Stainless Ears registers the many ways in which the British war effort changed south Carmarthenshire. Part I suggests that the whole area around Llansteffan has been taken over by 'Soldiers, tanks, lorry' that 'make siege on the bay' (*CP*, 45). Here the term 'siege' suggests an occupation or a war of attrition against a local stronghold. In this sense, it alludes to a more widespread change: the commandeering of land by the War Office. By 1945, 10 per cent of Welsh land had been appropriated in this way.[17] The better-known example of this is Epynt in Breconshire, a Welsh-speaking upland area, whose people were forced to move to make way for the permanent establishment of a firing range. But the appropriation of land for military purposes was a rolling process that also occurred in south Carmarthenshire. In July 1943, the entire Carmarthen bay area, from Tenby to Laugharne, and inland to six miles, was commandeered by the War Office in order to carry out Operation Jantzen, a practice run for the D-Day landings. This is the event that takes centre stage in *Gods with Stainless Ears*.[18] The poem includes a description of the soldiers in manoeuvres on the shore:

> Men nettled with pie-powdered feet, angry
> As rooks on their pernickety beds 'training
> For another Cattraeth' said Evans shop. (*CP*, 46)

As others in this volume have pointed out, 'Cattraeth' refers to a legendary seventh-century battle that took place in modern-day Catterick, Yorkshire, in which the old Welsh kingdom in that part of Britain suffered a heroic defeat at the hands of the Saxons. It is famously described in the medieval Welsh poem *Y Gododdin*. Roberts's use of the term suggests that the 'siege' of the Carmarthen bay area by Allied forces represents not only preparation for Allied victory, but in one sense another defeat for Wales.

The idea that the British war effort is a threat to Welsh culture is developed elsewhere in the poem. Even the most fanciful aspects of the poem can be read as attempts to register the extraordinary, phantasmagoric transformation of Welsh space presaged by these events. For example, a 'ten-toed woodpecker' seems to be a machine gun, the sound of which hammers out the sequence 1620B6, the wartime ID of the speaker's lover – incidentally the ID number of Keidrych Rhys (*CP*, 45). A similar transformation of perception can be observed in the text's 'cut' from the Carmarthen bay shore to the 'frame' of 'Soldier lonely whistling in full corridor train' (*CP*, 45). Here, the speaker's reference to 'frame' and 'cut' suggest the cinematic form from which the poetic technique is derived, as do the poem's sudden shifts from one locale to another. The radio is another case in point. The war accelerated the importance of the radio, and thereby contributed to the situation described in the poem in which the Welsh-speaking village of Llanybri has been inundated with the English language. Its 'culture' is being 'entombed', and the speaker registers this: 'engrave the village Llanybri '42 / For OK saltates [leaps] the cymric hearth and / BBC blares from Bermondsey tongue' (*CP*, 48). The BBC, via radio, invades the centre of Welsh domestic space, the symbolic heart of Welsh culture. This is a new technology of cultural modernity that is changing long-accepted demarcations of space and national culture, enabling the English language to penetrate into spaces where it would previously not have been heard. There is an allusion to a Churchill speech that would have been disseminated into Llanybri's homes via radio: 'COMPUNCTION. / Kom-pungk'-shun: discomforts of the mind deride / Their mood' (*CP*, 45). Churchill's speech, delivered in July 1941 in the context of German bombing of British cities, prepared the way for Allied reprisals, and uses the word 'compunction':

> We ask no favours of the enemy. We seek from them no compunction. On the contrary, if tonight the people of London were asked to cast their vote whether a convention should be entered into to stop the bombing of all cities, the overwhelming majority would cry, 'No, we will mete out

to the Germans the measure, and more than the measure, that they have meted out to us.'[19]

Roberts's poem suggests that this powerful political rhetoric, disseminated by radio, is one of the means by which citizens are inured to violence in their name, one of the 'discomforts of the mind' that 'deride' – with its connotations of insult and derange – the soldiers' 'mood'. We learn that 'Men [are] purred to fight – each other', a line that suggests that men have been persuaded and cajoled by rhetoric to take part in the war effort (*CP*, 46). The speaker identifies a repeating pattern – 'Men' who 'slave, spit and spade' for a 'Gerontocracy', an officer class 'yellow with argyria' for whom 'silver / . . . smoothed their palm', who fight in the interests of 'the money-goaders' (*CP*, 46). Also yellow, but not metaphorically, are the munitions workers ('you / Of acetated minds, workers with xantheine / Faces'), their hair and faces yellowed by the chemicals they worked with, a reference to those who laboured in the huge Royal Ordnance factories at Pembrey and Bridgend (*CP*, 46). Later lines assert that the war is being fought in the interest of 'TAWDRY LAIRDS AND JUGGLERS OF MINT' (*CP*, 61). This phrase explicitly connects the war effort, and the reorganization of labour conditions that it entailed, to those in charge of a capitalist system in whose interests – the poem suggests – the war is waged, and from which there are profits to be made. Incidentally, it also echoes the pacifist discourse of Woodcock who describes the war as one fought for the 'vested interests of the Tory moneybags'.[20]

In Roberts's poem, the speaker's anger is directed away from the distant German and Japanese 'enemy', for example in the allusions to both these nations at the start of Part III:

> Embrowns himmel hokushai. Manure seeps
> In long rags, pavilions hut, camouflages
> Arsenical veins. (*CP*, 56)

Here, 'himmel' is German for sky, while 'hokushai' refers to the nineteenth-century Japanese print maker, famous for his vivid depictions of elemental landscape of mountain, wave and sky. The language that describes the insistently local – even the soil surrounding the soldiers' 'hut' – invokes a global context. Whether it is manure from the surrounding fields, or faeces from the camp toilets is ambiguous. The point is that soldiers everywhere are bodily the same, living under the same sky; war poisons the culture of every nation. It is in this context that we should read the speaker's call for the various groups in the poem – soldiers, munitions workers, the Welsh – to rebel against the conditions in which they find themselves. In Part I, munitions workers are urged to 'revolutionise your land' (*CP*, 46). Part II begins, after a Welsh-language epigraph by the fourteenth-century bard Dafydd ap Gwilym, with a revolutionary, if wishful, call to arms: 'We must uprise O my people' (*CP*, 53). But in the absence of the speaker's calls for revolution being heeded, readers witness instead the subsequent physical and mental breakdown of the speaker, her soldier-lover, the soldiers and the munitions workers, and the wider demise of Welsh culture.

The latter stages of the poem describe the debilitating physical and spiritual effects of the war on the speaker, her lover and the people of the area. In Part II, the soldiers suffer from 'Food chyles constricted in their stomach' (*CP*, 54). In Part III, the soldiers' 'maladjustment of mind and spirit' (*CP*, 56) continues, and the speaker's soldier-lover, 'gunner / 1620B64', is depicted 'sending death / To no other than the girl he loves' in the form of a letter rescinding his love for her (*CP*, 57). The speaker blames her lover's change of heart on his role as a soldier, and the military regime imposed on him: 'He nearest to the heart stands dead in his / One and a half round the battle-waist suit' (*CP*, 58). It is at this point that the speaker suffers a miscarriage that she puts down to the lack of medical care ('no near doctor for six days') and skewed state financial priorities during wartime ('Razed for lack of / Incomputable finance') (*CP*, 61). She implores her readers to 'REMEMBER AGAIN / BLOOD IS HUMAN. BORN AT COST. REMEMBER THIS / ESPECIALLY YOU TAWDRY LAIRDS AND JUGGLERS OF MINT' (*CP*, 61). With these lines, Roberts links the loss of the unborn child, and the breakdown of her relationship, to the pursuit of a war that, as she repeats elsewhere, is fought in the interests of those who hold the economic reins. This section ends with formal breakdown as well: the five-line stanza is reduced to a single line – 'The night sky is braille in a rock of frost' – in which there is no longer sight, speech or sound, only a cold, dark, unreadable world (*CP*, 61). Another line suggests that all the calls to 'upprise' have fallen on deaf ears: 'O my people here / With labour illused and minds deranged' (*CP*, 63). Here, the word 'labour' connects the labour of producing a child, with the work in the shipyards, the army camps and the munitions factories depicted elsewhere in the poem. The image of 'minds deranged' recalls the earlier image of the harmful effect of ideological propaganda on the soldiers' minds. War, it seems, has conditioned all spheres of everyday life – causing miscarriages and personal grief, physical and mental breakdown of the individual, and the death of Welsh culture.

At this point, the beginning of Part V, the poem takes a supernatural, magical turn that Anthony Conran dismisses as a 'grave mistake'.[21] He suggests that Roberts should have finished the poem at the end of Part IV with that powerful image of the loss of an unborn child and a people broken on the wheel of an industrial war machine. Yet if Roberts had finished there, the poem would have avoided what could be described as its magical realist turn: the point at which the speaker and her lover are reunited and 'rise through the strata of the sky to seek peace and solace from the sun' (*CP*, 64). They ascend on a 'steel escalator', an 'aluminium / Rail' on which they climb 'at gradient / 42°' on to a 'trauma stratus' above the clouds and then 'out of gravity and territorial / Sight on to a far outer belt muscling-in / The Earth's curve' (*CP*, 65–6). The lovers exist 'contented in this fourth dimensional state' (*CP*, 66) until 'compelled to descend . . . / [b]y the State. By will of those hankering / After pig standards of gold' (*CP*, 67). It seems that even a magical, metaphysical realm beyond the pull of gravity is not beyond the reach of the wartime state. The couple return to a dystopian vision of a

> Network of rails: pylons and steel installations
> The only landmarks of our territory . . .
> Down, to this bleak telegraphic planet and its solid
> Pyramids of canvas. (*CP*, 68)

This reference to the 'pylons' and 'steel installations' recalls the spread of the national electricity grid through the 1930s, as well as the huge radar installations that had sprung up in coastal areas during the course of the war. This is a land in which any remnant of the local is subsumed within a 'network' in which the local associations of place have disappeared. The 'Bay known before' is now without any sign of human life; rather, it is covered in 'Barbed wire', full of 'wellshafts / Of putrid flesh sunk deep in desert sands' and a sign '*Mental Home for Poets*' into which, after 'Free[ing] dragon from the glacier glade', the speaker's lover disappears (*CP*, 69). The speaker is left alone to face 'a hard and new chemical dawn': a 'tangerine and hard line of rind on the / Astringent sky' (*CP*, 69). This is a surreal, post-apocalyptic landscape, a hyper-accelerated version of the present in which all distinctive local culture has been erased by an all-powerful military-industrial complex, a reference to the cold war threat of nuclear apocalypse that had begun by the time of the poem's publication in 1951. In this sense, the text is a powerful record of the threat posed by new forms of globalized industrial warfare to any continuation of local identity.

Through its depiction of an awakened Welsh consciousness, *Gods with Stainless Ears* contests the concept of an Allied victory. The 'dragon' freed 'from the glacier glade' is an image of emancipation that suggests that a revitalized Welsh identity offers a way of challenging the forces that have all but erased Carmarthen bay. But the image of the dragon is not restricted to the close of the poem. Readers are invited, in the introductory 'Argument' of Part V, to consider the 'dragon' as a 'symbol' that has 'been already introduced' (*CP*, 64). Indeed, at the end of Part I, the dragon does make an appearance. The speaker describes an incident in which the Welsh flag was torn down by a group of English soldiers who had been drafted into a Welsh regiment: ' "Pull down the bastard." "Pull down the flag" ' (*CP*, 49). It is after this act by English soldiers that the dragon on the flag 'without sound crept back like myth / Into folds of earth: grew greener shafts of resilience' (*CP*, 49). It is significant that it is not German bombs, but the British war effort that leads to this symbolic erasure of Welsh culture. What is being insisted upon here is the distinctiveness of Welsh culture in the face of the British war effort. Indeed, seen through this long historical lens, the war effort is simply the latest form taken by a British imperialism that threatens to erase Welshness.

Raising Welsh consciousness, the poem suggests, is a way of building resistance to the globalizing forces that have taken the form of the British war effort. The Welsh-language epigraphs, as well as the references to the Welsh-language literary tradition, draw attention to the text's Welshness. *The Red Book of Hergest*, *The Black Book of Carmarthen*, the poems of Llywarch Hen, and the 'white starling' sent by Branwen from her imprisonment in Ireland back to Wales are all explicitly mentioned. But the allusions to Welsh-language culture are not simply there to register cultural difference. In particular, Roberts's use of Welsh myth draws on a supernatural resource that aims to counter the prevailing mode of power. As we have seen with her turn to magical realism, this is one of the tools available to the writer who sees her culture faced with such overwhelming odds. While the dragon is freed only at the end of Part V by the poet who is then admitted into the '*Mental Home for Poets*', myth plays a more active role of resistance earlier in the poem. At several points, the speaker uses Welsh myth as a means of magically countering the seemingly all-powerful military complex. At the end of Part II, the speaker notes that her lover and the 'allergic, / Gunners', are 'cough[ing] . . . in midsummer lanes', 'the ghosts of ulcer / Hover[ing] in front of their paths', their minds 'deride[d]' by their enlistment (*CP*, 54). The speaker then takes on the role of medicinal healer, steeped in the Welsh folk tradition of the physicians of Myddfai, the historical family line of doctors who trace their knowledge of the medicinal qualities of plants back to an ancestor – one of the Tylwyth Teg or fairy folk – who married into the human race. Roberts's speaker comes 'To their aid. To his aid. To my lover. / Under tincture of Myddfai Hills' with a 'mixture' that she has 'made' (*CP*, 54–5). To cure her lover's 'eyestrain', she then prepares 'collyrium of well water / From the Ffyn-on-ol-bri springs', still at that point the main source of fresh water for those who lived in Llanybri (*CP*, 55). This would be an apt metaphor for Roberts's own work in *Gods with Stainless Ears*: a Welsh poetic 'admixture' as a tonic for magically healing the ills caused by a globalizing modernity that has no place for Wales.

There are occasional points when the poem looks forward beyond the war to a world in which globalizing forces are harnessed for the benefit of these local traditions and customs. In Part V, the speaker dreams of a world in which there is 'Work and pay for all', and where global passenger air travel is a reality: 'aerodromes', instead of being used for military ends, 'lift planes where ships once crawled, over / Baleful continents to the Caribbean Crane, / Down, to the Southern Christ of Palms' (*CP*, 65). This techno-primitivism, a benevolently technological future in which technology is used to sustain an indigenous culture, is echoed elsewhere in Roberts's work. 'Coracles of the Towy', for example, imagines 'a coracle covered with synthetic textile made from the cellulose of reeds, and machine-sprayed with ICI plastics'.[22] But these are occasional visions in Roberts's work; more usually, the annihilating forces of war predominate.

Roberts's writing on the Llansteffan peninsula, then, draws attention to its position as a semi-peripheral space, an area in which different historical times seem to be synchronous, and in which a long-standing Welsh culture co-exists with a globalizing capitalist modernity. War is represented in Roberts's poetry as an intrusion into every aspect of daily life, one that serves as a catalyst for globalizing, capitalizing forces that now threaten the very survival of Welsh culture. Her wartime writing registers this threat, occasionally envisioning a world in which these forces are no longer put to military ends, but are harnessed for local benefit. But in the final analysis, such visions are subsumed under the present reality of a war that threatens to erase the distinctiveness of all local cultures. In this sense, by registering the extent of the threat, *Gods with Stainless Ears* can be read as a record of Welsh resistance to the cultural imperialism made manifest in the British war effort.

Notes

[1] Franco Moretti in 'Conjectures on World Literature' and 'More Conjectures on World Literature' extends Immanuel Wallerstein's idea of the periphery and the centre into the literary field, and introduces the concept of the semi-periphery. See Franco Moretti, 'Conjectures on World Literature', *New Left Review*, 1 (2000), 54–68, and Franco Moretti, 'More Conjectures on World Literature', *New Left Review*, 20 (2003), 73–81. More recently, the Warwick Research Collective (WReC), in *Combined and Uneven Development: Towards a New Theory of World-Literature*, have developed Moretti's ideas by building on the work of Frederic Jameson. WReC's work deserves a full treatment elsewhere. The definition of the semi-periphery that follows builds on WReC's work, but is my own.

[2] Lynette Roberts, 'Coracles of the Towy', in *Diaries, Letters and Recollections*, ed. Patrick McGuinness (Manchester: Carcanet, 2008), pp. 133–8 (p. 135).

[3] Roberts, 'Coracles of the Towy', p. 135.

[4] Lynette Roberts, 'An Introduction to Village Dialect', in *Diaries, Letters and Recollections*, pp. 107–24 (p. 110).

[5] George Woodcock, *Letter to the Past* (Toronto: Fitzhenry and Whiteside, 1982), p. 218. Woodcock would later return to Canada, where he became a prominent writer and critic.

[6] Woodcock, *Letter to the Past*, p. 219.

[7] Woodcock, *Letter to the Past*, p. 223.

[8] Lynette Roberts, 'Swansea Raid', in *Diaries, Letters and Recollections*, p. 103.

[9] Lynette Roberts, *Gods with Stainless Ears*, in *Collected Poems*, ed. Patrick McGuinness (Manchester: Carcanet, 2005), pp. 41–78. Hereafter *CP*. All further references are to this edition and are given in the body of the text.

[10] Dylan Rees, *Carmarthenshire: the Concise History* (Cardiff: University of Wales Press, 2006), p. 144.

[11] Stuart Broomfield, *Wales at War: the Experience of the Second World War in Wales* (Stroud: The History Press, 2009), p. 119.

[12] Broomfield, *Wales at War*, p. 132.

13 Lynette Roberts, 'Lamentation', in *Collected Poems*, p. 8.
14 Deirdre Beddoe, *Out of the Shadows: a History of Women in Twentieth-Century Wales* (Cardiff: University of Wales Press, 2000), p. 117.
15 Martin Johnes, *Wales Since 1939* (Manchester: Manchester University Press, 2012), p. 13.
16 Lynette Roberts, 'Plasnewydd', in *Collected Poems*, p. 4.
17 Johnes, *Wales Since 1939*, p. 26.
18 Broomfield, *Wales at War*, p. 139.
19 Winston Churchill, speech at County Hall on 14 July 1941. See *https://www.nationalchurchillmuseum.org/do-your-worst-well-do-our-best.html* (last accessed 20 February 2018). See also *https://www.youtube.com/watch?v=cRBGfYVOELk* (last accessed 20 February 2018).
20 Woodcock, *Letter to the Past*, p. 201.
21 Anthony Conran, *The Cost of Strangeness: Essays on the English Poets of Wales* (Llandysul: Gomer, 1982), p. 198.
22 Roberts, 'Coracles of the Tywy', p. 136.

5

Welsh Literary Modernism, Lynette Roberts and David Jones: Unearthing 'a huge and very important culture'

Daniel Hughes

In March 1934, two young writers began corresponding with one another, and after several letters back and forth, in the autumn of 1934, they travelled to Aberystwyth, where they met with Caradoc Evans.[1] In the two decades following the explosive publication of his book *My People*, famed for its grotesque, satirical depictions of Welsh life, Evans had remained one of the most divisive, and hated, figures in Wales.[2] Yet, Dylan Thomas and Glyn Jones travelled to Aberystwyth not as critics of Evans, but as pupils and pilgrims. Evans, after all, had written what can 'perhaps best be seen as the first modernist work to have been produced by a Welshman'.[3] In doing so, he set off a cultural 'big bang' that while in some ways destructive also prefigured decades of modernist anglophone literary activity in Wales. As the 1930s got under way, the literary explosion and cultural chaos *My People* had sparked took on a new, exciting shape: that of a Welsh modernist formation. Two members of this formation – Lynette Roberts, and the half-Welsh, London-based artist and writer David Jones – shared a particular interest in old forms of Welsh culture, and both writers, in typical modernist fashion, adapted this material into a new, experimental, modern(ist) Welsh literature, which opened up 'a huge and very important culture.'[4]

The term 'formation' comes from Raymond Williams's *Culture*, and is the most fitting term to conceptualize the development of modernism in anglophone Welsh writing following *My People*.[5] Williams holds that different kinds of formation have enabled and precipitated cultural production throughout history. As cultural production developed in the late nineteenth and early twentieth centuries, so too did the formations that enabled cultural production, becoming less formal, less rigidly organized than they had been before.[6] Characteristic of the twentieth century in particular, Williams suggests, are groups 'in which there was no constitution, or lesser formality of organization. Here the break is more explicitly toward a particular style or a more general cultural position.' He goes on to argue that in such groups 'immediate social relations are often not easy to distinguish from those of a group of friends who share common interests.'[7] Glyn Jones and Dylan Thomas thus became part of a larger, more flexible literary grouping, the most notable members of which were poet and editor Keidrych Rhys, the Englishwoman Peggy Whistler, who used the pen name Margiad Evans; the London-based, half-Welsh poet and illustrator David Jones; and the Argentina-born poet of Welsh descent, Lynette Roberts. Rhys, who was married to Lynette Roberts, edited and published the work of all of these authors through his magazine *Wales*, which launched in 1937, and in his anthology *Modern Welsh Poetry* (1944). David Jones was not only a contributor to *Wales* and to *Modern Welsh Poetry*, but was also a friend of Lynette Roberts, and both writers were edited and published by T. S. Eliot at Faber and Faber.

The social and literary connections between Jones and Roberts are documented in Roberts's published diaries, as well as in fragments of surviving correspondence.[8] These suggest that the two began corresponding at some point prior to the summer of 1943. The first letter from Roberts to Jones, dated 30 August 1943, demonstrates that not only were the pair discussing *Wales*, but they were also communicating over broader matters of ethnic, national and cultural identity within the context of Welsh history, literature and legend. Roberts seems to have been contacted by Jones for assistance in researching early Welsh ancestry, and although she professes she may not be much help, she does offer to share with him *The Lives of the Cambro-British Saints*, which she cites in both *Gods with Stainless Ears* and her unpublished novel, 'Book of Nesta'.[9] Roberts's diaries and letters to Robert Graves also provide evidence of direct meetings between her and Jones, as well as a further exchange of books between the pair. She sent Jones two books on 'Celtic Inscriptions on Gaul' prior to May 1944, and visited Jones in October of the same year.[10] The only other piece of surviving correspondence takes on a much more personal tone, with Roberts again writing to Jones, telling him of her domestic life, offering to give him a kitten, and signing off with 'My love to you David. I have often thought about you. All my love, Lynette.' Though this letter is undated, based on the facts within the letter – Roberts and Rhys are still married, their son, Prydein has turned one, T. S. Eliot's brother has recently died – I would estimate that it was written between November 1947 and July 1948. This implies that after their initial 1943 correspondence, Roberts and Jones became fairly close friends, and remained as such for several years.

This friendship, as I have suggested, formed one thread of a larger group, which, at first glance, appears to conform to Williams's definition of a modern formation: a group of friends connected by a common interest, 'organized by some collective public manifestation such as an exhibition, a group press or a periodical.'[11] In this instance, the 'common interest' was a desire to write experimental literature in the English language that was yet shaped by Welsh cultural paradigms. However, during the period in which anglophone writers collaborated on *Wales* and published modernist texts, many also entertained other interests. Dylan Thomas moved from Wales and stood at the heart of literary circles in London and New York, for example, while David Jones pursued engraving and illustration. The links that connected the Welsh modernist formation, then, were contingent and time-bound: in existence from the 1930s to the 1950s, it came to an end when Dylan Thomas's death in 1953 and Lynette Roberts's mental breakdown in 1956 prematurely ended the careers of two of the most talented members of their generation. Yet, as the Jones/Roberts correspondence demonstrates, the formation that took shape after Caradoc Evans's 'big bang' ensured that modernist writing and writers in Wales had both outlets for publication and a community of writers in which they could write, work and live.[12]

The first issue of *Wales* began not with an editorial, but with Dylan Thomas's bewildering, surreal 'Prologue to an Adventure', a clear statement of modernist intent signalling a break from old writers, old publishing models, and the old relationship between the English-language literature of Wales and the nation to which it belonged.[13] The name *Wales* demonstrates the magazine's explicit interest in national and cultural identity. It was a natural home, then, for writers such as Lynette Roberts and David Jones, for cultural and national identity are fundamental issues in the writings of each author. In his essay 'Welsh Culture', Raymond Williams argues that there are seemingly paradoxical forces at play in the formation of Welsh culture: 'There is the proud and dignified withdrawal to Fortress Wales: the old times, the old culture; the still living culture. There is the moving out from the enclave; the new work, the new teaching, the sense and in places the reality of a modern Welsh culture.'[14] I would contend that Jones's and Roberts's literature embodies both of these impulses, and that their modernist experiment – the reality of their modern Welsh culture – is reliant upon a withdrawal to 'Fortress Wales'. In a related sense, Williams suggests that there are dual pressures on Welsh identity. First, people 'knowing the past is the past', whilst also demonstrating 'a fixation on the past', part real, part mythicized, because the past, in one form, is one thing they can't take away from us.' As Williams notes, this 'complexity is so difficult to separate, because they live, often, in the same bodies, the same minds.'[15] In *Marxism and Literature* (1977), Williams again illustrates this concept, but does so in a broader theoretical context. The tendency of 'knowing the past is the past' becomes the archaic, and the 'fixation on the past' becomes the residual. Williams defines residual culture as that which 'has been effectively formed in the past, but is still active in the cultural process . . . as an effective element of the present.' Residual culture includes elements excluded from the dominant cultural identity, which can in turn be reactivated, reshaped, into the emergent, defined by Williams as 'new meanings and . . . new practices, new relationships and kinds of relationship'. Emergent culture 'depends crucially on finding new forms or adaptations of form', as Roberts and Jones do in their poetry.[16] In their correspondence, then, we have evidence of Roberts and Jones engaging with past expressions of Welsh culture (the texts Roberts offers to share with Jones) that are still active in their present time. Williams's theorization of the interplay of these cultural forces, his identification of modern formations, and his concept of 'Fortress Wales' – the site of residual culture and emergent culture – provides a fluid yet cogent theoretical lens through which to formulate a comparison of David Jones and Lynette Roberts.

The shared features of their two epic war poems – Jones's *In Parenthesis* (1937) and Roberts's *Gods with Stainless Ears* (1951)

– makes these texts the most logical point of comparison. In addition to being edited by T. S. Eliot and published at Faber, both texts include key formal and thematic elements largely considered to be hallmarks of literary modernism: explanatory notes in addition to a formal, fragmented structure; linguistic experimentalism within a mythic-historic paradigm; explorations of modern, mechanical war. *In Parenthesis* is, obviously, a First World War text, about a battalion of infantrymen, with much of the poem's narrative taking place on the Western Front. Conversely, *Gods with Stainless Ears* is a text about a woman's Home Front experience of the Second World War, intensely rooted in the locality of a rural west Wales village. Yet both texts are rooted in an exploration of national and cultural identity, with *Gods* being more obviously Welsh-centric, featuring recurrent *Cymraeg* (Welsh-language) paratexts and a strong stand of cultural nationalism throughout the poem. In the preface to *In Parenthesis*, Jones suggests that his poem is, at least partially, an attempt to reconfigure what he calls 'the genuine tradition' of Britain, with his mixture of soldiers from London and Wales as representative of this.[17] This does not necessarily signal acceptance of the unitary (and political) identity offered in the term 'Britain'. Instead, Jones offers a reimagining of British national identity, one which relies on relocating Welsh culture at the heart of both Britain and a Christian European tradition. As Jones argues, 'that elder element [that is, Welsh culture] is integral to our tradition' (*IP*, xiii).

Rather than reconfiguring British identity, Roberts's poem is more overtly concerned with Welsh cultural identity. *Gods with Stainless Ears* is a 'heroic' poem, and, in modernist fashion, its fragmented structure draws attention to its constructed textuality. Structurally, Roberts uses a variety of paratexts, including her preface, *Cymraeg* epigraphs, a prose 'Argument' preceding each section of her poem, and notes after the end of the poem's narrative to control the shape and meaning of the text. Linguistically, the diversity of *Gods* can be baffling. The unconventional, experimental English of the poem is framed by *Cymraeg*, and informed by the Bible, classical and Welsh myth, local legend, geology, flora and fauna. This radical linguistic and stylistic experimentation within a tightly controlled paratextual structure is not only a modernist attempt to express the experience of modern, mechanized war; it is also an exploration of conflicting and complementary poles of experience. Roberts juxtaposes and combines the rural and the urban, the traditional and the modern, the 'English' (British) and the Welsh, masculinity and femininity, and universality and locality throughout the poem. Her preface establishes that while the structure of the poem is the same throughout, the 'rhythm, texture, and tone' are subject to change.[18] These fluctuations mean I will discuss *Gods* with attention to its temporal narrative in order to highlight the points of flux, whilst making comparisons with *In Parenthesis* where appropriate.

In their prefaces both authors mount a pre-emptive defence of the stylistic methods of their poem. Jones deems it necessary 'to say something of the punctuation', explaining how and why he has flouted conventional forms of typography and punctuation (*IP*, xi). Roberts, more succinct in her preface than Jones, is also more straightforward in her explanation of stylistic choices, stating that '[t]he use of congested words, images, and certain hard metallic lines are introduced with deliberate emphasis to represent a period of muddled and intense thought' (*CP*, 43). Both poets paradoxically relate and distance their poems to/from their own lived experience. Jones states at the start of his preface: '[t]his writing has to do with some things I saw, felt, & was part of', yet further down the same page he insists that '[n]one of the characters in this writing are real persons, nor is any sequence of events historically accurate' (*IP*, ix). This is partially a defence of 'minor anachronisms' (*IP*, ix) within the text, yet it also serves to distance the poem from Jones's lived and actual experience, despite Jones's initial introduction informing the reader that *In Parenthesis* is at least in some part formed from this experience. Similarly, Roberts states that her own tragedy 'though part may be expressed, is outside the page' of *Gods* (*CP*, 43). This paradoxical impression of authorial closeness and distance may be explained by each author's professed struggle to control and shape the disparate fragmentary materials and experience that comprise their texts. Jones admits that '[t]here are passages which I would exclude, as not having the form I desire' (*IP*, x), while Roberts conveys a similar perfectionism, informing the reader: 'I have tried to control the stanzas in the fifth part of this poem' (*CP*, 43). There are, in these prefaces, clear stylistic and structural similarities to their composition, and both authors confess that their attempt to control, reform and shape experience of modern mechanical warfare – experience that is both theirs and *not* theirs – has, by their own standards, not been entirely successful. This, I would suggest, is the true *difficulty* of modernist poetry, which lies in the struggle to compose subjective, chaotic, non-unitary experiences into a new, universal whole.

Roberts's *Gods with Stainless Ears* demonstrates an attempted universality both at odds with, and inextricably linked to, its historic and geographic cultural specificity. She suggests in her preface that *Gods* could feature 'any rural village' (*CP*, 43), yet the *Cymraeg* epigraph that precedes the preface immediately introduces a sense of cultural specificity and difference. This difference in identity is then reinforced in Part I, where national-cultural paradigms are used to introduce and define the key figures and themes of the poem. One of the key figures of *Gods*, the 'gunner', belongs to a Welsh regiment and is introduced as 'a dragon of wings'. This Welsh paradigm is reinforced both temporally and spatially, as the speaker informs us that it is 'Saint Cadoc's Day', and that we are near 'Llanstephan, Llangain, and Llanybri' (*CP*, 44–5). While this temporally and spatially specific moment is defined by Welsh culture, a gendered interplay (again defined through reference to a specific Welsh geography) is also introduced: '*Father Precipice of Denbigh Rock, / Mother Mild of Pembroke Streams*' (*CP*, 46), counterposing paradigms of fixed, masculine solidity with a fluid, flowing femininity. Finally, this Welsh rural space is defined as 'natural', 'wild with birds and somewhat secluded from man' (*CP*, 44), and the mention of 'Homeric hills' infers that this is an ancient, near mythical natural haven.[19] These interplaying oppositions and unities are juxtaposed against the mechanical invaders of the bay, as 'Soldiers, tanks, lorry make siege on the bay' and planes fly overhead ('new beaks'). Roberts strengthens these juxtapositions (between the organic and mechanical, the feminine and the masculine, imprisonment and escape) with language steeped in notions of opposition, violence and conflict, as 'Machine sets against clay' and soldiers 'Drill new hearts and hearths' (*CP*, 44–6). The technological assault is, like the rural space being invaded, rooted in a particular national-cultural identity: 'For OK saltates the cymric hearth and / BBC blares from Bermondsey tongue' (*CP*, 48). In these two lines, Anglo-American jargon ('OK') is transferred into ('saltates' refers to the process of transferring particles via water and wind) the formerly private, and domestic, Welsh living space ('cymric hearth') via British broadcasts ('BBC blares'). This alludes to radio technology enabling the invasion of the domestic, Welsh space by its attempted standardization of language, dialect and accent into an ideal English ('Bermondsey tongue' being received pronunciation). As the poem moves on, the

English soldiers show disrespect toward a native Welsh culture and pull down 'the bastard' Welsh flag (*CP*, 48–9). But despite 'their culture / entombed' (*CP*, 48), the lowered flag bleeds into the ground and 'without sound crept back like myth / Into folds of earth: grew greener shafts of resilience' (*CP*, 49). The ancient cultural inheritance rooted in this locality will endure despite the imposition of a mechanized, English-British invading force, suggesting that the Welsh cultural inheritance of Roberts's west Wales bay is ultimately the more resilient.

In contrast to the fluctuating oppositions identified by Roberts, Jones's preface suggests that more fixed (though not entirely fixed) tensions are key to *In Parenthesis*. Whereas Roberts begins her poem by depicting a Welsh domestic locality being invaded by mechanized English forces, Jones refers several times to Welsh soldiers and Londoners being representative of what he terms the 'genuine tradition'. He qualifies this by stating that 'no two groups could well be more dissimilar' before asserting that both groups 'react to the few things that unite' them, such as their shared distrust of the military hierarchy (*IP*, x). In his preface, Jones is attempting to reconcile what he describes as a 'hotch-potch' with what must become 'our tradition' – in other words, his 'genuine tradition' (*IP*, xi–xiii). These tensions, embodied by the 'hotch-potch' of English and Welsh soldiers, and the class conflict inherent in the idea of soldiers united against their military superiors, are established in the first two sections of the poem, and form part of a recurring motif of unity and disunity.

In the opening part of the poem, names, as signifiers of identity, are crucial in shaping the rank, personality and nationality of the soldiers. John Ball's relatively simple name, for example, contains several meanings. Like Roberts's gunner, who is similarly referred to by his army number, 1620B64, Ball is dehumanized through his ID number, 25201. His name is both a play on John Bull – the national personification of Britain, though more often England – and an allusion to the English Lollard priest who was one of the leaders of the fourteenth-century peasants' revolt. John Ball, then, is an allegoric English everyman. Similarly, Welsh soldiers in Ball's battalion are easily identified by their names, such as Captain Gwyn, Mr Jenkins and, most importantly, Lance Corporal Aneirin Merddyn Lewis. Lewis's rank evokes a past age of chivalry ('Lance' implying medieval knights), suggesting a nobility of character but also linking the soldiers as a group with past conflicts, while his Welsh names root him in a mythic complex associated with a specific culture. Aneirin is the name of a Welsh bard and the presumed author of *Y Gododdin*, a medieval Welsh poem that recounts the disastrous defeat of the Gododdin (a Brythonic people) at Catraeth (perhaps Catterick in North Yorkshire). This links Corporal Lewis – and by extension the battalion on its way to the Somme – not only with a centuries-old poetic culture, but also with a catastrophic, final defeat. The name Merddyn positions Lewis as a figure of knowledge and power, after the Arthurian magician, Merlin. Lewis is described as having 'Welsh depths', a deep mythic, historical and cultural grounding that (in contrast to the common John Ball) 'brings in a manner, baptism, and metaphysical order to the bankruptcy of the occasion', according to the speaker (*IP*, 2). Lewis's Welshness, therefore, elevates the men heading to the trenches, positioning Lewis himself as a microcosm of Welsh culture throughout the poem, and a vehicle for Jones's elevation and reconstruction of the depravity of modern warfare through the prism of Welsh mythology. Lewis is shown to have access to a spiritual, metaphysically transcendent culture denied to English soldiers such as Quilter, who 'knew nothing of these things' (*IP*, 2). Quilter's name evokes fragmentation, and the process of patching together fragments into a greater whole. The pluralistic mention of 'the Quilters and the Snells' (*IP*, 7) implies that like John Ball, Quilter is a symbolic everyman, indicative of the whole battalion: Quilter is one fragment of the 'genuine tradition' that Jones's soldiers embody.

In the early sections of Roberts's poem, however, the suggestion is that of two incommensurate cultures in conflict, rather than as fragments of a larger whole. This is strengthened by her own mention of Catraeth, the disastrous defeat of 'Welsh' forces fighting Angle kingdoms recounted in *Y Gododdin* (*CP*, 46). As already noted, Jones also makes use of Catraeth in *In Parenthesis*, yet rather than locating his battalion on one side of a specific cultural conflict, he stresses instead a motif of temporally unified military defeats, linking Catraeth with the final defeat of Arthur at Camlann, as well as the battle of the Somme.[20] The binary oppositions established in the opening pages of Roberts's *Gods* – the invading, mechanized English/British soldiers versus the Welsh, natural, mythic and civilian locality of the bay – are complicated by the figuration of the Welsh gunner, who is both a compound of these opposing binaries and a personification of Wales. The personified Wales is subsumed by the war effort: 'Poor called / Cymru; unquestioning, unanswering, / Remaining just the same . . . / . . . till the lurid sun spills across / The sky like a shot Indian' (*CP*, 49). It is suggested here that by being complicit in the British war effort, the passive Welsh personification will speed the destruction of the native culture, as inferred by the 'shot Indian' – a clear and powerful invocation of the slaughter wrought on colonized peoples.[21] This suggestion is rather different to Jones's poem, which, through its portrayal of figures such as Corporal Lewis, positions a mythical Welsh culture and the figure of the Welshman as central to the war effort. If Jones uses war to reposition Welsh culture in relation to Britishness, then Roberts sees war and everything it represents as antagonistic to Welsh culture.

The sense of complication conveyed by the binary oppositions personified by the gunner is strengthened in Part II of *Gods*. The opening 'Argument' of the second section issues an appeal to 'all people to discard their sorrow, break through destruction', indicative of a universal appeal to pacifism. The opening stanza begins 'We must upprise O my people', which, in light of the prose 'Argument' could be read as an appeal against war towards pacifism, or as a call by the speaker to people of the Welsh national culture (*CP*, 52–3). This ambiguity emphasizes the complication and shifting of binary oppositions within the poem. The speaker's people are 'trenched in sorrel' (*CP*, 53), and the 'Argument' states that the 'flowers of the field contrast sharply with the clouding dispiritedness of the soldiers' (*CP*, 52), suggesting that the Welsh people of the bay are fortified – 'trenched' a conscious allusion to the terminology of warfare – in their connection to the natural world, which contrasts strongly with the homesick –and therefore rootless, or uprooted – soldiers. Welsh images of home and domesticity reinforce a rooted, secure identity – recalling the idea of the 'Cymric hearth' of the opening section – and are used to comfort the homesick gunner. The speaker evokes particular parts of the locality, such as the 'Myddfai Hills' and 'Ffyn-on-ol-bri springs', as well as mythologized aspects of daily life, such as the 'seiriol cat' and the 'Sloe-gin from Merlin's desk' (*CP*, 54–5). Alongside the particularities of the local, Merlin, of Arthurian mythology, and Sant Seiriol (of Penmon priory and later Ynys Seiriol, Anglesey) are invoked, a mythic/historic overlay that relates the complex gunner figure back to his national culture. This, in turn, separates him from the other homesick soldiers (who are, presumably, homesick for England) and adds a cultural-nationalist dimension to the relationship between the gunner and the girl, indicating that they, and their relationship, are also rooted, 'trenched', in this particular locality.

The fluctuation of opposing binaries continues in the third part of the poem. The speaker now draws attention to the wider opposition of the war – that of the Allies versus the Axis powers – with the phrase 'Embrowns himmel hokushai' (*CP*, 56). *Himmel* is the German word for 'sky' or 'heaven', and *hokushai* is presumably a reference to Katsushika Hokusai, a Japanese artist most famous for 'The Great Wave off Kanagawa'. 'Embrowns' links to the subsequent imagery of poisoned manure and soil ('Arsenical veins', 'sedimentary hate'), suggesting that the Axis powers have now become the biggest threat to the west Wales bay. The international/intranational conflict of Welsh versus English has fluctuated into the international conflict of Allies versus Axis, and, similarly, the conflicts occurring within the bay itself shift. The fifth and sixth stanzas of this section indicate an inter-service conflict between the Navy and the Army, and a domestic conflict between the gunner and the girl also breaks out (*CP*, 57–8). The girl's anger is also directed *at* conflict itself, suggesting a strengthening of the appeal to pacifism in Part II. The final two stanzas indicate her disdain for the ahistorical, mechanized and meaningless existence of the gunner, particularly because she feels there are 'battles [which] should be / fought at Home: as trencher companions' (*CP*, 59). This is a further evocation of the national-cultural 'Cymric hearth', the private, domestic space, while the phrase 'trencher companions' – an evolution of the 'trenched' from Part II – domesticates the language of war. Recalling the juxtaposition of the solid 'Father Rock' and the fluid 'Mother Stream' earlier in the poem, Roberts now allows traditional gender roles to fluctuate. The traditionally male space of the trench becomes a trencher, a domestic item. Roberts repeats this rhetorical trick throughout the poem, filtering the experience of war through a traditionally feminine, domestic lens. The sky is 'the washing line of blue' (*CP*, 49), the bay is also a 'dishwater tributary' (*CP*, 57), and just as the gunner is encouraged to become a 'trencher companion', the English soldiers that have entered the bay are domesticized: at the outset of the poem, they 'Shell and peel pods and spuds' (*CP*, 47). This gendered, feminine lens is a marked point of difference with *In Parenthesis*, the central concern of which is trench-companions, rather than trencher-companions.

The fourth part of *Gods* continues the shift away from the cultural-nationalist paradigms with which the poem opened toward a more universal, humanist tone, as the girl's miscarriage is linked into the broader bloodshed of war.[22] The speaker moves from 'the foetal fall' to the 'BLOOD OF ALL MEN', and in the fourth stanza entreats her readers to 'REMEMBER AGAIN / BLOOD IS HUMAN. BORN AT COST', a statement that combines the trauma of birth and miscarriage with the death of soldiers on every side of the war (*CP*, 60–1). This fourth, capitalized stanza is boldly pacifistic, railing against 'TAWDRY LAIRDS' and 'JUGGLERS OF MINT', against nobility, hierarchy and finance (*CP*, 61). By directing the pacifistic message at nobility and finance, the speaker is continuing a motif introduced in the opening section of *Gods* with the mention of the BBC: that of a developing centralized, mechanized 'State', which will only become fully apparent in the final section of the poem. Finally, the speaker confirms the shift away from a cultural-nationalist paradigm by distancing herself from 'Callous Cymru', the gunner and personification of Welsh culture. Whereas the gunner was earlier 'callid' – that is, crafty or cunning – he is now cold and uncaring, demonstrating the strains on his relationship with the girl.

Roberts's association of personal, maternal loss with the death of soldiers of every nationality is worth comparing with a similar motif of maternal loss and infanticide in *In Parenthesis*. The title of the final seventh part of Jones's poem 'The Five Unmistakable Marks', is an allusion to Lewis Carroll's *Hunting of the Snark* (*IP*, 220), yet, as Dilworth argues, it is also evocative of the five wounds of Jesus at his crucifixion.[23] Such an allusion would suggest an element of redemptive sacrifice in this final section of the poem, yet this is undermined in the opening lines of Part VII as Thomas Dilworth explains:

> The single, unannotated, English phrase, 'and under every green tree' (153), may be the most powerful allusion in the poem – to the sacrifice by the Israelites of their children to Moloch and Baal (II Kings 12:10), an act traditionally seen as the cause of the Babylonian Captivity and the dispersal of the Twelve Tribes. Metaphorically, war is bloody, meaningless sacrifice of children. Infantrymen are implicitly victims.[24]

Jones's allusion to infanticide plays on the similarity between 'infantry' and 'infant', and as Dilworth argues, equates the death of infantrymen with the 'meaningless sacrifice of children', just as Roberts does by equating the girl's loss of a baby with the continuing slaughter of war.

In its final section, Jones's poem is increasingly fragmented, struggling (as Jones himself suggests in his preface) to convey the chaos of modern warfare. The soldiers' helplessness is filtered through a recurrent maternal prism: 'Ball pressed his body / to the earth and the white chalk womb to mother him' (*IP*, 154); the speaker imagines a soldier's birth when 'wet-nurse cocked a suspicious eye' (*IP*, 159); 'Heirs . . . from the Gower peninsula' are described as 'detailed from the womb', and a soldier named C. S. M. Taylor is mentioned 'whose mother sang for him' (*IP*, 161). Finally, an appeal to all mothers is pluralistic in its use of languages – Welsh, Germanic, English – and evolves into a Christian plea: '*Mam*, moder, mother of me / Mother of Christ under the tree' (*IP*, 176–7).[25] The theme of maternal loss has also previously been explored in Part 5 of the poem, when 'Rachels' across Wales and London – the two strongest locations of national and cultural identity in the poem – mourn their lost sons (*IP*, 131). While the link between biblical loss, maternal loss and different national losses are suggestive of a united Christian sacrifice, the allusion to infanticide renders this sacrifice meaningless. Jones and Roberts use different fragments to explore these themes – Jones uses biblical allusions, while Roberts draws on her own lived experience – yet this modernist poetic practice demonstrates the way in which differing experiences are reconstructed into a new whole.

The allusion to shared sacrifice sees both poems at their most universal. Yet the modernistic practice essential to these poems also undermines and exposes the constructed nature of universality in each poem. Despite Roberts's suggestion in her preface that the poem's events could take place 'in any rural village', the use of fragments and linguistic experiment in *Gods* draws conscious attention to internal cultural difference in a way other, less experimental forms would not. Her use of *Cymraeg* paratexts, for example, is designed to, in her words, 'give the conscious compact and culture of another nation' (*CP*, 76). In contrast to Roberts, Jones uses English-language translations of Welsh material in his poem, and his paratexts (those preceding each part of the poem, at least) are a combination of national English literature and an English translation of an excerpt from *Y Gododdin*.[26] Rather than evoking the culture of another (separate) nation, Jones uses his paratexts to construct a microcosm of the 'genuine tradition' that he introduces in his preface. The first paratext of the poem – in part through its all-capitalized typography – positions the text as a memorial to 'my friends in mind of all common & hidden men', including 'the enemy front-fighters who shared our pains' (*IP*, unpaginated). Again, the link with Roberts's preface and her suggestion of universality is clear. Jones's second paratext is from the *Mabinogion*, and features soldiers opening an enchanted door, and consequently reopening the pain and chaos of war: as the reader does by turning the page, and as the writer has done by creating the text. These paratexts (in both poems) are not only indicative of the constructedness of each author's cultural conceptions – whether Jones's 'genuine tradition' or Roberts's 'conscious compact and culture of another nation' – but are also, in their repeated use, and the fragmentation such repetition results in, indicative of the density of the modernist dilemma. Not only are Jones and Roberts attempting to 'make sense of' their lived and actual experience of war, they are also attempting to make sense of their national culture. There is a need in much modernist literature to respond to the various crises of modernity – such as mechanized war and social fragmentation – and to reimpose a coherent narrative upon this chaos. Roberts and Jones choose to do so through paratextual prisms and their collaging of cultural, historical and religious fragments, which refract and reconstruct their lived wartime experiences into a paradoxically ahistorical whole.

The final section of *Gods* adopts an apocalyptic tone, similar to the chaotic and increasingly fragmented finale of *In Parenthesis*. The epigraph to this concluding part is a *Cymraeg* passage from the book of Revelations, and in his final section, Jones too evokes Revelations with images such as 'Riders on pale horses loosed' (*IP*, 160). Roberts's final 'Argument' suggests a pessimistic, ruinous climax to the poem, as the gunner and the girl fail to achieve a better future: he, the gunner, 'walks meekly into the Mental Home' (*CP*, 64). The girl, though, turns towards 'a hard and new chemical dawn, breaking up the traditional skyline', suggesting a simultaneous ending and beginning: a reordering of the world into a postwar order. Crucially, a final opposition forms in this section – that of the girl and the gunner reunited against 'the State'. As they return from their heavenly ascent, they are '*Disendowed,* / By the State' (*CP*, 67).[27] This first overt conceptualization of the state has formed steadily from fluctuating, threatening fragments of authority over the course of the poem: the 'Jerrymandering / Gerontocracy' and the BBC's 'Bermondsey tongue' (*CP*, 46, 48); the answered appeal to parliament, which is seemingly a continuation of the medieval Marcher Lords in Part III ('Would the Warden of the Marches send us telegrams?' (*CP*, 57)); and, in the fourth part of the poem, the 'TAWDRY LAIRDS' and 'JUGGLERS OF MINT' (*CP*, 61). By the final page of the poem the gunner stands alone, 'against a jingle of Generals / and Cabinet Directors' (*CP*, 69); the military and civilian spheres are no longer oppositional to one another but are now united against the lone gunner. Similarly, the peripheral coastal railway from the opening stanzas of the poem (evoked in the 'ironing edge', *CP*, 44) has become a 'stronger / Network of rails: pylons and steel installations / The only landmarks of our territory' (*CP*, 68). A once nebulous, spatially peripheral state has used the conflict to strengthen itself and subdue the bay.

However, I would argue that the final stanza of the poem undermines the pessimism suggested by the 'Argument':

> Salt spring from frosted sea filters palea light
> Raising tangerine and hard line of rind on the
> Astringent sky. Catoptric on waterice he of deep love
> Frees dragon from the glacier glade
> Sights death fading into chilblain ears. (*CP*, 69)

The poem ends with the bay – frozen since the third part of the poem – thawing under a new dawn, described in organic, and not mechanic, terms: 'rind', 'palea' and 'tangerine'. The now 'astringent' – 'astringent' can describe a liquid used to heal cuts – sky is also 'iconic', offering promise. The sun is reflecting off melting ice – 'Catoptric' suggesting the reflection or focusing of light, 'waterice' suggesting ice melting from its solid state – as the bay thaws, which in turn frees the dragon, the symbol of Welsh cultural nationalism (and the gunner). Previously, in the 'Argument' to this section, it had been suggested that the gunner would '[walk] meekly into the Mental Home', yet he now 'Sights death fading into chilblain ears', a reference to the title of poem. The previously 'Stainless Ears' are now 'chilblain', suggesting a fluctuation from mechanical – stainless steel – into the organic, and while the ears are damaged, the damage is peripheral and death is fading. The penultimate image of the Welsh dragon emerging from underneath the bay engages a recurrent motif – that of a subterranean Welsh culture hidden throughout the poem. For example, in the landscape 'where past / Is not dead but comes uphot suddenly sharp as / Drakestone' (*CP*, 48); the Welsh flag creeping 'like myth' into the earth (*CP*, 49), or the offer of '*cambric joy*', playing off the Latinization – Cambria – of Cymru (Wales), but also implying the geologic Cambrian period, suggesting age, density and subterraneanism (*CP*, 50).[28] In another example, planes fly over 'Cambrian caves where xylophone reeds hide / Menhir glaciers'; again suggesting an ancient, frozen, subterranean Welsh culture is thawing at the end of the poem (*CP*, 65).[29] The final stanza, therefore, culminates in a hitherto residual Welsh culture becoming emergent, as the dormant Welsh culture contained within the landscape awakens to face the simultaneously promising and threatening postwar dawn. Welsh culture, so often under the surface of this poem and the world it constructs, also paradoxically confronts the reader paratextually at the start of every section of the poem. The structural, modernist experimentation used by Roberts again draws particular attention to a residual and finally emergent national-cultural paradigm.

Jones arguably does something similar when utilizing Welsh myth and history throughout *In Parenthesis*, most obviously during Dai Greatcoat's 'boast' (*IP*, 79–84). Thomas Dilworth recalls Jones telling him that this boast corrects the typical 'Englishman's view of history – 'that of Churchill, extending from the Renaissance to himself.'[30] Dai's boast might end with the refrain 'Old soljers never die' (*IP*, 84), but Dai's first name reveals the fate of these soldiers: they are sent to the front to die. The rest of the boast is comprised of historic, mythic and biblical fragments. Through associations with émigré – but never invading – armies, Dai's boast also strengthens the temporal unity created by Jones during the second section of the poem and Dai himself assumes an archetypal position.[31] He claims to belong to a trio of emigrant hosts; in the first he 'marched, sixty thousand and one thousand marched, because of the brightness of Fflur'; in the second 'I marched, sixty thousand who marched for Kynan and Elen because of foreign machinations' (*IP*, 82). The identity of the final, third host is left ambiguous, yet, as Dilworth suggests, 'By implication, the third emigrant host is the current British Expeditionary Force, of which Dai and his listeners are members.'[32] Dai, a member of all three hosts and thus an archetypal figure present throughout historical and mythical conflicts, opens and closes the temporal unity that links this battalion with all common soldiers through history. Morally, Dai uses biblical allusions to position himself in the redemptive Christian tradition. The archetypal soldier is therefore recreated as a witness to the death of Abel ('I was with Abel when his brother found him') (*IP*, 79); as David against Goliath, the noble underdog ('I took the smooth stones of the brook, / I was with Saul / playing before him') (*IP*, 80); and as a member of the escort of Jesus at the crucifixion, complicit in his redemptive death ('I served Longinius that Dux bat-blind and bent . . . I saw Him die') (*IP*, 83); finally, Dai sides with heaven against hell: 'I was in Michael's trench when bright Lucifer bulged his primal salient out' (*IP*, 84). The soldiers of the battalion are now made part of a temporal unity that places them within an ongoing Christian tradition, emphasizing the justness of their position.

The subterranean Welshness that emerges at the end of Roberts's poem is located in the middle of Jones's poem. This formative Welshness is evident not only in Dai's name, but also in *how* he speaks and structures his boast: Dai 'articulates his English with an alien care' (*IP*, 79), and as Jones makes clear through his notes with repeated references to 'the Welsh tradition' (*IP*, 207–10), Welsh cultural fragments – as with *Gods* – are integrated throughout his boast. As Dilworth argues, both the content and the structure of the boast is reliant on the Welsh Triads. Jones expresses Dai's monologue as a series of triadic boasts –'a triad being a Welsh bardic mnemonic grouping of three related figures, objects or events.'[33] Dai, the archetype centre of the central section of Jones's poem, speaks in a Welsh voice, and his words are organized (through the triadic structure) in a Welsh way. Welsh culture is threaded throughout the myths and histories of France, Rome, Greece, and the Bible, relocating and reconstructing this culture as a pillar of Western civilization, and suggesting a cross-cultural mythic-historic unification of which these soldiers are the latest manifestation. The 'conscious compact and culture of another nation' thus emerges through Dai and reshapes the Christian European tradition. *Gods with Stainless Ears* ends with the emergence of a subterranean Welsh culture that is always paradoxically present, in the geologic imagery of the bay, in the *Cymraeg* epigraphs of each section, and through recurring allusions to Welsh literary culture; the structurally central section of *In Parenthesis* sees Dai Greatcoat weave Welsh culture into the roots of Western, Christian, British canon; drawing attention to, boasting of, and relocating that which has always been there.

* * *

In her 1943 letter to Jones, Lynette Roberts states: 'I *believe*, but this is 50% faith 50% intuition that soon within 500 years a huge & very important culture will be opened up in Wales: and that will be from underneath the earth rather than from the surface.'[34] Similarly, in his preface to *In Parenthesis*, Jones envisages the 'Celtic cycle' as 'a subterranean influence as a deep water troubling, under every tump in this Island' (*IP*, xi). These beliefs are obviously articulated poetically within each text, and by extension I would argue that Jones and Roberts open up 'a huge and very important culture'. The culture that they mine for their modernist experimentation is not just subterranean; in Raymond Williams's terms, it is also residual, and made emergent by Jones and Roberts. Their use of the old culture to create new culture represents the 'moving out', the departure from what Williams called 'Fortress Wales', yet without 'Fortress Wales', these poems could not function, or exist. Their modernistic poetics are informed and structured – spatially, linguistically, mythically – by Welsh cultural paradigms. It is their literary modernism, identified in their use of textual fragments and residual culture, their linguistic experiment informed by *Cymraeg*, that represents *both* aspects of 'Fortress Wales': the return to an old culture that makes possible the creation of a genuinely new – in content and form –Welsh culture. Across both texts, the residual is reconfigured, reconstructed and made emergent. As Roberts says, she and Jones open up 'a huge and very important culture', in more ways than one.

Notes

[1] Paul Ferris, *Dylan Thomas: The Biography* (London: Dent, 1999), p. 115.
[2] On this point, see Keiron Smith, '"Constructing the Map": Welsh Criticism of Caradoc Evans', *Almanac*, 16 (2012), 89–120.
[3] M. Wynn Thomas, '*My People* and the Revenge of the Novel', *New Welsh Review*, 1 (1988), 20.
[4] In a 1943 letter to David Jones, Roberts seems to be indicating that archaeological discoveries will discover new information about Wales's past, including legendary links to Troy (Brutus of Troy was the first legendary king of Britain, according to the *Historia Britonum* and Geoffrey of Monmouth's *Historia Regum Brittaniae*). In the present chapter, the phrase is used to define Roberts's and Jones's own contributions to Welsh culture. See Lynette Roberts, 'Letter from Lynette Rhys', National Library of Wales, David Jones Papers CT7/2 (MS: 1943).
[5] Raymond Williams, *Culture* (London: Fontana, 1981).
[6] Williams, *Culture*, pp. 57–8.
[7] Williams, *Culture*, pp. 65–6.
[8] Lynette Roberts, *Diaries, Letters and Recollections*, ed. Patrick McGuinness (Manchester: Carcanet, 2008); Roberts, 'Letter from Lynette Rhys', National Library of Wales, David Jones Papers CT7/2 (MS: 1943); Lynette Roberts, 'Undated Correspondence', National Library of Wales, David Jones Papers CT3/6, 149–50.

9   W. J. Rees, *The Lives of the Cambro-British Saints* (Llandovery: William Rees; London: Longman; Abergavenny: J. H. Morgan, 1853). Roberts mentions another text in the letter, which she also cites in both *Gods with Stainless Ears* and 'Book of Nesta': Thomas Stephens, *The Literature of the Kymry* (London: Longmans, Green and Co., 1876).
10 Roberts, *Diaries, Letters and Recollections*, pp. 175–7, pp. 179–80.
11 Williams, *Culture*, p. 66.
12 Lynette Roberts and Keidrych Rhys lived in Llanybri, Carmarthenshire, from late 1939, and various members of the formation (such as Dylan Thomas and Nigel Heseltine) attended their wedding in Llansteffan and visited them in their Llanybri cottage. Thomas, of course, had moved to nearby Laugharne in 1938. Jones never visited Roberts in her home, though she recorded her 1944 visit to Jones in London in her diary (see n.10).
13 Alongside the work of Welsh modernists such as Dylan Thomas, Glyn Jones, Lynette Roberts, Margiad Evans and Nigel Heseltine, *Wales* featured work from writers such as Hugh MacDiarmid, Robert Graves and (posthumously, of course) Franz Kafka.
14 Raymond Williams, 'Welsh Culture', in *Who Speaks for Wales? Nation, Culture, Identity*, ed. Daniel Williams (Cardiff: University of Wales Press, 2003), p. 10.
15 Williams, 'Welsh Culture', pp. 5–11.
16 Raymond Williams, *Marxism and Literature* (Oxford: Oxford University Press, 1977), pp. 121–8.
17 David Jones, *In Parenthesis* (London: Faber and Faber, 1961), p. x. All further references are to this edition and are given in the body of the text, using the abbreviation *IP*.
18 Lynette Roberts, *Gods with Stainless Ears*, in *Collected Poems*, ed. Patrick McGuinness (Manchester: Carcanet, 2005), p. 43. All further references are to this edition and are given in the body of the text, using the abbreviation *CP*.
19 In her notes, Roberts states that the mention of 'Homeric hills' is an allusion to 'legends in the locality' (*CP*, 71), an indication of Roberts's anthropological gaze that is present throughout the poem.
20 On this point, see Thomas Dilworth, *Reading David Jones* (Cardiff: University of Wales Press, 2008), pp. 25, 77. See also pp. 137–8 of *In Parenthesis*, as well as Jones's notes accompanying the poem (*IP*, 219).
21 This could be a reference both to the wars fought against the Native Americans and the British Raj's massacres of its Indian subjects. In both cases, the pacifistic, anti-imperialist implications of this image are clear.
22 Roberts suffered a miscarriage in March 1940.
23 Dilworth, *Reading David Jones*, p. 80.
24 Dilworth, *Reading David Jones*, p. 80.
25 *Moder* is the Limburgish word for mother, guardian.
26 In order from Part I to VII, extracts from *Y Gododdin* are paired with *Rime of the Ancient Mariner*, *Henry V*, Gerald Manley Hopkins's *Bugler's First Communion*, *Le Morte D'Arthur*, *Alice Through the Looking Glass*, *Le Morte D'Arthur*, and Lewis Carroll's *Hunting of the Snark*.
27 For further discussion of the gunner and the girl's ascent through the 'various outer strata', see the comparisons with contemporary cinema made in Nigel

Wheale's 'Beyond the Trauma Stratus: Lynette Roberts' *Gods with Stainless Ears* and the Post-War Cultural Landscape', *Welsh Writing in English: A Yearbook of Critical Essays*, 3 (1997), 98–117.

[28] A reference to trees as 'paleozoic sentinels' (*CP*, 56) also alludes to the Cambrian era. The broader paleozoic era includes the Cambrian era.

[29] 'Menhirs' are a type of standing stone, suggesting standing stones hidden beneath ice.

[30] Dilworth, *Reading David Jones*, p. 56.

[31] For more details, see Jones's accompanying notes in *In Parenthesis*, pp. 208–9.

[32] Dilworth, *Reading David Jones*, p. 57. For more specific information on each host, see Dilworth, *Reading David Jones*, pp. 56–7, and Jones, *In Parenthesis*, pp. 208–9.

[33] Dilworth, *Reading David Jones*, p. 56.

[34] Roberts, 'Letter from Lynette Rhys', National Library of Wales, David Jones Papers, CT7/2 (MS: 1943).

6

'CRUSADERS UNCROSS LIMBS BY THE GREEN LIGHT OF FLARES': LYNETTE ROBERTS'S AVANT-GARDE MEDIEVALISM

Siriol McAvoy

Lynette Roberts is usually seen as a distinctively 'non-nostalgic' modernist, committed to recording the 'now' of everyday life during wartime and looking forward to change in a postwar world.[1] Her poems take aesthetic pleasure in the flight lines of air traffic, for example, the chemical compounds of modern industry, the 'galvanised sheds' that punctuate the west Wales landscape. Roberts's private writings indicate her commitment to developing new forms capable of addressing the demands of her contemporary moment: see her emphasis, in her letters to Robert Graves, on meanings 'transferred & *brought up to date*'; on using words only 'in relation to today – both with regard to sound (i.e.: discords ugly grating words) & meaning' – even if that meant stretching the formal cohesion and coherence of her texts to breaking point.[2]

And yet, her poetry and prose are fundamentally shaped by her fascination with the medieval past. An omnivorous reader of literary histories and historical textbooks, she studied medieval Welsh and Anglo-Saxon poetry, and scrutinized early Welsh law. Her writing is suffused with references to a range of personages and texts associated with the British Middle Ages: twelfth-century writer Gerald of Wales, the narratives commonly known as the *Mabinogion*,[3] Chaucer's ballades and the plays of the Chester Mystery Cycle all make up the densely 'allusive substratum' to her work.[4] Roberts even wrote an (unpublished) historical novel, the 'Book of Nesta', a modernist 'potboiler' that imaginatively recreates the life of the twelfth-century Welsh princess, Nest ferch Rhys.[5] Such premodern interests did not limit themselves to Wales or England, either; her 'Heroic' poem *Gods with Stainless Ears* invokes Dante's *Divine Comedy*, and she was fascinated with Italian art of the Quattrocento period, publishing an article on Florentine artist Lorenzo da Monaco (*c.*1372–1424), one of the last great proponents of the Late Gothic style, in *Life and Letters Today* in 1940.

David Jones – a Welsh-affiliated poet with whom Roberts has often been compared – also used the Middle Ages as an imaginative framework in his search for transcendence in the battlefields of World War I. Similarly, T. S. Eliot – a personal friend of Roberts's, and her publisher at Faber – turned more and more to the Middle Ages after converting, like Jones, to Anglo-Catholicism in 1927; his verse play *Murder in the Cathedral* (1935) dramatizes the assassination of Archbishop Thomas Becket in 1170, while the poem *Little Gidding* (1942) cites an affirmation by fourteenth-century mystic Julian of Norwich in response to the destruction of war. Yet unlike Jones and Eliot, Roberts did not ascribe to any organized religion during the 1940s and early 1950s, when she was writing most actively.[6] Like other modernist women writers in Britain at the time, such as Storm Jameson and Naomi Mitchison, she instead espoused principles of social commitment and solidarity, insisting in a letter to Robert Graves that 'escapist, not socially conscious' were 'almost the last things which I want to be.'[7] Indeed, medievalism is often regarded as a conservative, nostalgic phenomenon, and modernist women writers seemingly had little to gain in returning to a past imagined by male writers like Eliot and Ezra Pound as distinctly masculine and hieratic. Why, then, at such a high point of political and social crisis, when contemporary events made demands of the poet almost more than ever before, did Lynette Roberts turn so persistently to the culture of the Middle Ages in her writing – particularly that of medieval Wales?

In this essay, I focus primarily on *Gods with Stainless Ears*, together with the lyric poems 'Earthbound', 'The Shadow Remains' and 'Poem from Llanybri', in order to explore the important medieval subtext to Roberts's poetics, and to demonstrate the centrality of the Middle Ages to her exploration of national identity. I argue that the medieval past functions in her work as an imaginative frame through which to engage with, and reimagine, national identity, from a liminal, gendered perspective. In Roberts's writing, as we shall see,

Welsh and female identity are frequently rooted in the premodern past. Medieval Wales thus comes to figure as a site of 'internal difference' – a half-historical, half-imagined space in which to challenge hegemonic narratives of British identity, and in which to navigate a way out of divisive, prescriptively masculinist models of nationhood.

Emphasizing the role of medievalism as a gendered response to conflict, I also suggest that rewriting the premodern past constitutes a central part of Roberts's attempt (shared by other modernist women writers in Britain at the time) to examine and reformulate all the national traditions that had led to war.[8] In this context, premodern Wales becomes in her work the locus for an alternative national tradition, identified not with 'a heroic past, great men, glory', but with touch, materiality and particularity.[9] As I shall argue, she uses this alternative tradition to challenge the universalizing myths and abstractions of nationalism, ultimately reformulating national identity as an ethically charged, locally oriented form of engagement, in which all genders play an equal part. In this sense, her writing demonstrates what Liedeke Plate terms 'a feminist approach to the past confident that change is possible and that it will be brought about by changing the stories which shape cultural foundation myths and thus human existence'.[10]

One way in which Roberts transforms the medieval past is by presenting medieval history as a spatialized landscape, embedded in the life of her locality. The first part of this essay therefore situates her poetics in relation to a broader neo-Romantic turn in British visual art of the 1930s and 1940s, suggesting that by directing the gaze of the woman artist at the landscape of medieval tradition, Roberts dislocates, unsettles and pluralizes fixed categories of identity and place. As we shall see, her representation of the medieval past as landscape allows her to recover local and popular counterhistories generally obscured by 'grand narratives' of national development. But if the Welsh landscape offers an alternative (and markedly spatialized) point of access to history for Roberts, so too does material culture. The second part of this essay will therefore consider Roberts's engagement with a Victorian tradition of medievalist design. The act of making craft offers a rhythmic and tactile connection with unrecorded spiritual and psychic histories, the 'inner world' of minority life. Vaunting the regenerative and therapeutic potential of creative labour, Roberts, as I show, harnesses a 'domestic' medieval craft in order to dissolve the bounds between the public and private in poetry.[11]

Roberts's medievalism can be seen to figure as part of the 'home anthropology' identified by Jed Esty in late modernist texts – a self-reflexive practice, where writers looked inward, to the archaic or 'primitive' traditions of Britain, in order to reconnect with the past and thus, in Esty's account, to '[translate] the end of empire into a resurgent concept of national culture.'[12] Esty's thesis, however, remains broadly Anglocentric, focused as it is on predominantly English writers and what he sees as the literary redefinition of a specifically 'Anglocentric culture paradigm'.[13] While Roberts's anthropologically inflected poetry certainly demonstrates how British modernists responded to the fact of 'becoming minor' in the wake of imperial decline, it also shows that certain writers in the British Isles interpreted 'the end of empire' as a moment of postcolonial awakening for Britain's own colonial peripheries. Engaging creatively with the Middle Ages and medieval tradition, I suggest, is a fundamental part of Roberts's participation in a Welsh cultural and nationalist project. Significantly, it allows her to adopt a public voice as a woman writer, to speak for and to a Welsh nation whose political cause she embraced yet from which she was partially estranged, by gender and by her Argentine birth.

Roberts's attitude to medieval culture, then, is defined both by survival – a concern with cultural connection and continuity – and subversion. Unlike modernists like Pound, Eliot and Yeats, she refuses to revere the authority of the Middle Ages, tending instead to conjure it in irreverent and playful terms, and is always careful to subordinate the claims of the past to the needs of the present. Placing medieval and modern(ist) forms in unexpected dialogue with each other, her work troubles the developmental chronology of the nation, thereby inviting her readers to actively draw new connections between past and present. Like Walter Benjamin, she lays emphasis on the power of forgotten or repressed histories to activate change in the present, opening out literature, self and society onto the future. In the section that follows, I outline some of the key texts and cultural contexts informing Roberts's medieval imagination, before moving on to interrogate the formal and thematic resonances of the premodern in her poems and essays.

ROBERTS'S MEDIEVALISM: TEXTS AND CONTEXTS

Medievalism – the imaginative engagement with medieval ideas and forms – is a literary and aesthetic phenomenon in Western culture that extends from the Renaissance to the present day.[14] A fluid formation, it shape-shifts in accordance with the changing preoccupations of its historical context; yet, as Alice Chandler has suggested, underlying its diverse forms is the desire 'to feel at home in an ordered yet organically vital universe.'[15] During the nineteenth century, the British Middle Ages were idealized as a time of 'faith, order, joy, munificence, and creativity' that stood in stark opposition to the 'satanic mills' of the modern present.[16] Portrayed as a time of social connectivity and cohesion, the medieval past was summoned in order to highlight the loss of 'organic community' in the modern, industrial world. If, then, medievalism can largely be seen as a cultural response to a moment of crisis – the spike in medieval Romanticism around the time of the French Revolution is a case in point[17] – it is perhaps no wonder that writers and artists in the British Isles returned in such significant numbers to the Middle Ages during the 1930s and early 1940s, marked as these years were by mass unemployment and class unrest at home, the rise of totalitarianism in Europe, and growing ecological anxieties linked to the development of technology, all of which generated new anxieties about the role of art and the artist. However, rather than offering a kind of imaginative escape route, as it sometimes did during the nineteenth century, the medieval is frequently used by modernist writers in order to clarify a moment of perceived cultural and psychosocial disorder, or to reflect on the historical conditions of modernity itself. From John Piper's photographic watercolours of medieval glass (1936) to David Jones's *In Parenthesis* (1937), from Virginia Woolf's representation of premodern folk culture in her essay 'Anon' (1941) to Michael Powell's and Emeric Pressburger's adaptation of Chaucer in their wartime film, *A Canterbury Tale* (1944), modernist writers and artists held up fragments of the medieval past as a kind of talisman against civilization's ruin.

Welsh-identified writers were, significantly, at the forefront of this development: Jones's *In Parenthesis* embroiders a web of connections relating to early medieval Welsh literature and King Arthur; John Cowper Powys's *A Glastonbury Romance* (1932) draws on Sir John Rhŷs's *Studies in the Arthurian Legend* (1891) to suggest the Welsh connections of the Grail myth, while Dorothy Edwards's *Winter Sonata* (1928) transposes narratives from the *Mabinogion*. There is a similarly Celtic orientation to Roberts's medieval imagination. Her poems contain a plethora of allusions to Welsh texts, including the *Mabinogion*, *Y Gododdin*, the heroic cycle of *englynion* (Welsh strict-metre poetry) associated with the early bard Llywarch Hen, the *Book of Taliesin*, and late-medieval gnomic poetry. *Gods with Stainless Ears* includes untranslated epigraphs from fourteenth-century court poet Dafydd ap Gwilym and Saint Cadoc (Cattwg), an early Welsh saint, and makes allusion to the two seminal codices of medieval Welsh literature, the *Black Book of Carmarthen*, and the *Red Book of Hergest*. Together, these writings make up what Tony Conran has called the *traddodiad*, the Welsh-language, bardic culture of Wales that developed out of the ruins of Celtic Christianity around the sixth century and flourished over the Middle Ages, reaching its apex in the fourteenth and fifteenth centuries.[18] As Conran has also observed, the Methodist revival of the eighteenth and nineteenth centuries occasioned a radical change in Wales's social structure, whereby '[t]he old culture – Celtic, tribal, hierarchical – was swept away', to be replaced by a more egalitarian religious culture marked by 'sobriety, hard work, cultivation of the soul'.[19] By the twentieth century, the *traddodiad* was regarded in Wales as a kind of 'buried treasure', and was seized upon by Welsh-language writers keen to break away from the strictures of their Nonconformist heritage.[20] Roberts did not speak Welsh, and was reliant instead on her Welsh-speaking husband and modern translations for her access to Welsh-language tradition. Undeterred, she set out to excavate the 'buried treasure' of a medieval Welsh past in order to innovate her own space of 'imaginative freedom' as a woman writer.[21]

Such preoccupation with a premodern Welsh 'civilization' demonstrates Roberts's susceptibility to the nationalist climate that witnessed the formation of Plaid Genedlaethol Cymru, the Welsh nationalist party, in 1925. Saunders Lewis, one of the party's founders, was an ardent medievalist who held that the project of Welsh self-definition and a 'return to the medieval principle' were one and the same.[22] The Middle Ages were for Lewis the last bastion of Welsh independence: in an essay entitled *Egwyddorion Cenedlaetholdeb (Principles of Nationalism)*, he argued that prior to the Act of Union with England in 1536, the unifying moral authority of the Catholic Church created a space in which minority cultures were permitted to flourish, as they never could within the modern nation state.[23] Strangely, though, Lewis's Romantic nationalism was also a sort of anti-nationalism: he presented the Christian, pan-European culture of the Middle Ages as a way of thinking beyond the modern, imperial nation state, which in his view had only ever had deleterious effects on Wales. Roberts's perception of nationhood and history, however, was shaped less by Lewis's conservatism than by the progressivist ethos of *Wales*, the groundbreaking magazine of anglophone Welsh writing that, running from 1937–9, 1943–9 and 1958–60, was edited by her husband Keidrych Rhys. Rhys was a firm supporter of the Welsh nationalist cause, and his political conviction had been intensified by the outbreak of World War II; in an editorial to the new series in 1943, he announced that 'henceforth the policy of *Wales* . . . if it needs defining will be a serious and responsible one *towards* Wales.'[24] Significantly, this development brought with it a new, historical consciousness. While previous issues of *Wales* had, to Rhys's admission, 'concentrated almost exclusively on new "experimental" writing', during the Second World War the magazine started to interpose medieval Welsh texts in English translation, or essays on premodern Welsh themes, among modernist, experimental ones – a technique that made ancient Welsh poetry appear suddenly avant-garde.[25]

While distrustful of modern democracy, Roberts shared *Wales*'s anti-fascist convictions and commitment to 'free expression'.[26] Travelling to Munich with her friend Kathleen Bellamy in the late 1930s, she had witnessed the fear and brutality of the Nazi regime at first hand, and was disturbed by the aggressive repression of Jewish people and artists that she witnessed there.[27] As suggested, her engagement with medieval culture often functions as part of her attempt to reconnect with lost or fragile roots, connected to a repressed maternal past.[28] Yet, for all its concern with rootedness, her writing constantly opposes the Fascist metaphorization of the Middle Ages as a site of 'pure' origins. Texts such as the 'Book of Nesta' and *Gods with Stainless Ears* present medieval Wales, not as a site of originary naturalness or ethnic/linguistic 'purity', but as a vibrant space of cultural hybridity and linguistic polyphony that mirrors and illuminates the present day, as we shall see. In this sense, her use of the medieval past affirms Elizabeth Bowen's contemporary speculation: 'I wonder whether in a sense all wartime writing is not resistance writing?'[29]

THE SPATIALIZATION OF HISTORY: MAKING THE PAST PRESENT

Most commentators on Roberts's work have remarked on the geographical dimensions of her literary imagination, and this spatialized perception extends to her representation of history.[30] The past emerges in her writing, not as a page in a book, but as a strange, shifting territory through which her speakers can wander at will. As Charles Mundye has observed, Roberts's use of medieval history and myth is almost always anchored in the immediate geography of Llanybri, Carmarthenshire, where she lived from 1939 to 1949.[31] The area constellating the village of Llanybri and the Taf and Tywi estuaries appears in her writing as a chronotope, a time-space unit in which 'time . . . thickens, takes on flesh', and medieval and modern, time and timelessness, intersect.[32]

Roberts's spatialized sense of history also speaks of women's gendered experience of time and space in war, as expressed, perhaps, in Elizabeth Bowen's claim that 'I see war (or should I say I feel war?) more as a territory than as a page of history'.[33] Bowen's perception of war as territory conveys a sense of immersion in the now, yet also signals a more expansive temporality spreading in different directions.[34] As Margaret and Patrice Higonnet argue: '[w]omen experience war over a different period from that which traditional history usually recognizes, a period which precedes and long outlasts formal hostilities'.[35] This suggestion resonates with Roberts's wartime texts: *Gods with Stainless Ears*, for example, concerns itself not only with the immediate events of the conflict, but with the emotional fallout in its aftermath and the long arcs of history leading up to it. Furthermore, because place is inherently multiple, capable of bringing together elements from disparate historical moments into sudden proximity, I argue that Roberts's identification of the past in (or as) a landscape therefore serves her aim – shared with other British women writers such as Naomi Mitchison and Virginia Woolf – to 'explore and challenge the boundaries of the temporal symbolic order'.[36]

GODS WITH STAINLESS EARS: REVISIONING THE HEROIC

Written over 1941–3, but not published until 1951, *Gods with Stainless Ears* is subtitled 'A Heroic Poem', and in it Roberts reaches for a radically new idiom capable of reflecting the experience of ordinary people – and particularly women – in total war. She achieves this partly by reformulating the structure of the classical epic, shifting the emphasis it places upon the individual male hero to focus instead on the experience of those ordinary people – again, particularly the women – left behind. Collapsing the binary model that associated the 'home' with stasis and the feminine, and the outside world with action and masculinity, she conjures a lived reality in which aerial bombing had transformed the 'home front' into the 'front line' of war.

The poem opens with a depiction of Cwmcelyn, the 'bay wild with birds', rendered strange and remote by the ruins that shadow it:

> ... the same tide leans back, blue rinsing bay,
> With new beaks scissoring the air, a care-away
> Cadence of sight and sound, poets and men
> Rediscovering them. Saline mud
> Siltering, wet with marshpinks, fresh as lime stud
> [...]
> This is Saint Cadoc's Day. All this Saint Cadoc's
> Estuary: and that bell tolling, Abbey paddock.
> Sunk. – Sad as ancient monument of stone.
> Trees vail, exhale cyprine shade, widowing
> Homeric hills, green pinnacles of bone.[37]

Roberts's poetry often takes the form of what Paul Robichaud terms a 'native cultural archaeology', where the premodern past is shown to exist primarily in the form of material traces, embedded in the local landscape.[38] Her south Carmarthenshire is in some ways a Romantic location, full of crumbling ruins and echoes from a distant, mythical past. But building up classical and medieval allusions in layers like a cubist collage, her poem also adopts an x-ray vision, penetrating through the different strata of the soil in order to discover a forgotten history beneath. The speaker presents the Welsh landscape as a text to be read, with the Middle Ages living on within the present, as in a palimpsest. The archaic past is brought to the surface by the 'Siltering' waters of the bay, 'siltering' being an archaic verb that here takes its sense from 'silt': 'to flow or drift in after the manner of silt' or 'to pass gradually away'.[39] In this context, it suggests both the erosion of the Welsh cultural past, and a history that is still in process, articulated in the eddying flows that signal a shifting relationship between past and present. The tolling bells, their sound mimicked in the incantatory rhythm of the stanza ('This is Saint Cadoc's Day. All this Saint Cadoc's / Estuary: and that bell tolling, Abbey paddock. Sunk'), provide a form of rhythmical connection with an early medieval past. Like Ezra Pound's Midi, west Wales emerges as a space of what Peter Nicholls terms 'intermingled temporalities' and 'visionary location[s]', anticipating and setting the scene for the visual/visionary narrative that is to ensue.[40]

The idyllic opening description of *Gods with Stainless Ears* is, as several critics have commented, markedly ekphrastic.[41] With its strange patchwork of forms and multiple perspectives, it is suggestive of contemporary paintings such as John Craxton's 'Welsh Estuary Foreshore' (1943) – a work that, inspired by the art of Picasso, was described by Craxton as 'a synthesis of ideas, objects and forms gathered during my visits to Pembrokeshire'.[42] This visual eclecticism is sustained throughout Roberts's poem:

> Trees crisp with Maeterlink blue, screen
> Submarine suns and baskets of bees: but
> Men nettled with pie-powdered feet, angry
> As rooks on their penickety beds 'training
> For another Cattraeth' said Evans shop. (*CP*, 46).

While the poem's opening conveys a sense of age and timelessness, accentuated by the cyclical rhythms of the natural world, this scene appears to be intensely modern, with trees taking on the bold primary colours and hard, geometric outlines of modernist art. 'Maeterlink blue', as Patrick McGuinness observes, is a reference to the Belgian Symbolist playwright Maurice Maeterlinck, author of the play *The Blue Bird*, or *L'oiseau bleu*.[43] Premiered at Konstantin Stanislavski's Moscow Art Theatre in 1908, this play is about a poor woodcutter's daughter, Mytyl, and her brother, Tytyl, who, aided by the good fairy Bérylune, go off in search of the Blue Bird of Happiness, which, after many adventures, they find in their back yard.[44] This allusion, then, places the rural environs of Llanybri within a cosmopolitan, European context, positioning them as a space for avant-garde art, while simultaneously affirming Roberts's localist aesthetic – the detailed, luminous attention to place that she imbues with redemptive qualities in the context of the war.[45]

The Carmarthenshire landscape is here inflected by a marked sense of unreality, or perhaps heightened reality: the 'Trees crisp with Maeterlinck blue, screen[ing] / Submarine suns' are two-dimensional, like a stage set in a play, while the presence of the war just off-stage exposes the peace of the bay as an artful sham or facade that 'screen[s]' the imperial violence hinted at in the 'submarine sun'. The 'screen' also introduces a cinematic quality to the scene, emphasizing a controlling sense of vision and distance that resonates with the 'lucid detachment' that scholars have noticed in the poetry of Keith Douglas and other writers of the Second World War.[46]

However, the enchanted self-containment of Llanybri-as-artwork is soon opened out onto history by the violent intrusion of the war, in a turn signified by the conjunction 'but'. The 'Men nettled with pie-powdered feet, angry / As rooks on their pernickety beds' allude to the irritated discontent of garrisoned soldiers, caught in the 'net' of history; 'piepowder' is an archaic term, derived from the Anglo-Norman *epoudrous* or *pié poudrous* ('dusty feet'), which was used during the Middle Ages to designate a traveller, wayfarer or vagabond. It also gives the name to the medieval piepowder court, 'the humble court of the market or fair in which the disputes of wayfaring merchants, the dusty-footed men, were settled'.[47] This connection signals Roberts's interest in local history: there are several fragmentary references to piepowder courts in south Wales in the Cardiff Records (1340), the Charters of Neath (1339) and the records of Newport in Wentloog (1385).[48] The men's 'pie-powdered' feet therefore locate the experiences of the deracinated soldiers (and other migrant 'aliens' into Wales in the war) within a deeper historical context, incorporating them into the patchwork of Wales's own past. Because the piepowder court was 'the lowest and most expeditious of the courts of justice' in the medieval common law system, the allusion evokes a long-standing history of ordinary people's attempt to seek legal redress, from the Chartist riots to the miners' struggle – as if to point out the simmering democratic potential inherent to 'war's aggregations of individuals'.[49] It also returns the narrative of *Gods* to the colonial tensions that attended the Norman incursion into Wales in the eleventh and twelfth centuries, by hinting at the imposition of Norman jurisdiction on an indigenous Welsh legal system – part of Roberts's strategy of holding up the premodern past as a mirror to the complexities of the present.[50]

Roberts's collaging technique means that, rather than existing as separate points on a temporal continuum, the past and present lie level, in the same time and spot. In this way, they are set in dialogue with each other: the medieval past is shown to be influenced by the art and technology of the present, just as the present continues to be affected by the past. This dialogic counterpointing of the medieval and the modern(ist) is sustained in the final two lines of the stanza: '"training / For another Cattraeth" said Evans shop.' Ventriloquized through a local villager, 'Evans shop', this statement invokes the oldest surviving Welsh poem, *Y Gododdin*. Ascribed to Aneirin, a Brythonic bard from the sixth century, but extant in a manuscript of much later date, *Y Goddoddin* records a disastrous battle fought by a tribe of Britons from the northern region of Manaw Gododdin against the Saxons at Catraeth (now Catterick in North Yorkshire). From one perspective, the allusion conveys a Nietzschean perception of war as endless repetition – suggesting that ordinary people are locked into rehearsing the same old national stories of violence, territorial dispute and defeat. Virginia Woolf made a similar point in *Three Guineas* when she cautioned that if women were to join public life without seeking to change it, they would only perpetuate a sequence of violence and acquisition:

> [S]hall we not be doing our best to stereotype the old tune which human nature, like a gramophone whose needle has stuck, is now grinding out with such disastrous unanimity? 'Here we go round the mulberry tree, the mulberry tree, the mulberry tree. Give it all to me, give it all to me, all to me. Three hundred millions spent upon war.'[51]

However, rather than explicitly serving the purpose of feminist satire (as does Woolf's use of the child's nursery rhyme here), Roberts's choice to voice the narrative of Catraeth through the homely figure of 'Evans shop' reflects her commitment to recording the everyday impressions and speech of those around her. Showing how literary tradition is assimilated and reused in the speech of ordinary people, the statement by 'Evans shop' thus gestures to Saunders Lewis's view that an ancient literary tradition had so impressed itself 'not only on the [Welsh] language but on all those who so use it that their use of it is seen to be literature.'[52] In this sense, then, the allusion to *Y Gododdin* enables the quirky, polyphonic chorus of Llanybri inhabitants that feature in *Gods*.[53]

Yet the speech marks enclosing the line 'training for another Cattraeth' also endow medieval tradition with a distinctly secondhand, quotational quality. Like Woolf's wartime novel *Between the Acts* (1941), which examines myths of Englishness through the conceit of a small-scale village pageant, it emphasizes a sense of history as masquerade and performance. Indeed, there is a staged 'campness' to Roberts's treatment of medieval Welsh tradition throughout *Gods with Stainless Ears*, often balanced delicately between homage and pastiche.[54] In Part I, for example, local mayors transform into medieval princes who 'Lift skirts and torques and wade out to sea' (*CP*, 50) after a plane crash, their heroic medieval costume (the 'torques', Roberts tells us in her notes, are a reference to a description of princes' headgear in the poetry of Llywarch Hen, found in the fourteenth-century *Red Book of Hergest* (*CP*, 72)), only emphasizing their powerlessness in the face of the human disaster. Incongruous images such as these indicate the gulf opened up between past and present by a new, technological warfare that has rendered all existing modes for describing war inadequate: 'to what age can this be compared?' (*CP*, 46) asks the narrator in Part I, and her question remains unanswered. Yet Roberts's cross-dressing Welsh mayors also signal her elaboration of a 'queer' national history that 'disregards temporal boundaries and somatic coherence' to reveal the multiplicity and fluidity of all identities.[55]

NEO-ROMANTICISM AND THE MEDIEVAL PAST: '"NOW" IS INCLUSIVE'

The interweaving of history, nature and place in Roberts's writing bespeaks her participation in the neo-Romantic impulse that rose to prominence in Britain during the late 1930s and 1940s, as mentioned above. Championed in the pages of *Axis*, one of Britain's foremost experimental art magazines, by the 1940s neo-Romanticism had radiated out to encompass many different forms, including literature, film and illustration. Proponents of the style fused a Romantic attention to the natural world with an aura of surreality, theatricality and apocalypse.[56] Neo-Romantics also presented the culture of the Middle Ages as something of a touchstone for their art, seeing in it the basis for a new avant-garde: as Alexandra Harris observes, 'their response to modern art was coloured by the brilliant hues of medieval stained-glass windows and the bold lines of early carvings'.[57] Indeed, in an article published in *Axis* in 1936, Geoffrey Grigson and John Piper disavowed the separation of premodern past from modern present implied by traditional concepts of history, arguing '[t]here is no "past", there are no pictures painted "in the past" . . . There is only a human instant, a *being*. "Now" is inclusive'.[58] This 'now', as Clare Morgan points out, included an art sensibility 'based in those "Middle ages" when . . . time did not exist in the way it does in modernity'.[59] Similarly, for Roberts the 'now' expands to include the 'strange' temporalities of medieval Wales (an amalgam of prophetic time, sacral time, genealogical time, historical time), which intersect in her writing to unsettle the secular chronology of modernity.[60]

Neo-Romanticism represented, in one sense, a rebellion against the 'peevish, pinched formalism' and abstract universalism of high modernism, through a renewed embrace of place, particularity and cultural groundedness.[61] This found expression in a visual remapping or 'retopographizing' of the British landscape, partly through an attention to the shadows of an ancient past. New technologies of transport aided this project by prompting new ways of seeing the landscape: the *Shell Travel Guides*, for instance, brought a modernist, neo-Romantic aesthetic to a growing readership of middle-class motoring enthusiasts.[62] However, the travel espoused in these guides was not the high-speed, technological transport of modernity; instead, their recommended movement was measured and meandering, so that the traveller might take in as many details of her surrounding environment as possible. Alexandra Harris sees the neo-Romantic impulse in late modernism as part of an 'imaginative [re]claiming' of a home country – an attempt, through art, to travel home,[63] suggesting that the 'Romantic Moderns', prevented from travelling in Europe, imagined themselves as 'pilgrims in their own country'.[64]

The concept of pilgrimage – closely identified in the interwar imagination with Geoffrey Chaucer, forgotten byways and a premodern, Catholic past – re-entered the popular and literary imagination during the 1940s, often serving as a metaphor for the reclamation of national culture in the shadow of war. In his 1942 essay 'On Pilgrimages in England: Voyages of Discovery', Edward Blunden describes what he sees as the new drive toward 'national self-discovery' in terms of a 'pilgrimage' toward the cultural shrines 'which . . . stand for the country we are now fighting for', an act rendered all the more urgent by the threat of invasion and destruction.[65] Roberts's poetry enacts her own 'pilgrimage' home to Wales, the country of her parents' families. However, as I show, the pilgrimage home also signals her desire to 'journey out' into other cultures, and is fundamental to her reconceptualization of 'home' as a mobile space.

This intention is laid out at the beginning of her first book of poetry, *Poems* (1944), with her 'Poem from Llanybri'. Written in 1941, the text is addressed to soldier poet Alun Lewis, whom Roberts had visited at his barracks at Longmore in Hampshire in the spring of that year.[66] Defined by McGuinness as the 'portal to the book',[67] it offers a 'way in' to her poetics of location:

> *If you come my way that is...*
> Between now and then, I will offer you
> A fist full of rock cress fresh from the bank
> The valley tips of garlic red with dew
> Cooler than shallots, a breath you can swank
>
> In the village when you come. At noon-day
> I will offer you a choice bowl of cawl
> Served with a 'lover's' spoon and a chopped spray
> Of leeks or savori fach, not used now,
>
> In the old way you'll understand. (*CP*, 3)

Rejecting the abstract concept of the 'nation', 'Poem from Llanybri' focuses instead on a sense of belonging conveyed through experiential knowledge of the local and particular. But while it has often been read as a celebration of 'a rooted culture that is also a culture of rootedness', the poem is also about journeying.[68] It was written as an 'invitation' for Alun Lewis to visit Llanybri, and it therefore represents, simultaneously, a traveller's 'voyage in' to Llanybri and a host's 'voyage out' to meet him. Tony Conran has observed that the text invokes a premodern Welsh bardic tradition of poetry as an interpersonal 'social ritual', suggesting that '[like the old bards], she is conscious that where two or three poets meet, there poetry is also'.[69] Thus, Llanybri – like the poem that reimagines it – emerges as a meeting place, a point of intersection and dialogue.

At the end of the poem, the act of travelling and writing poetry come together:

> You must come – start this pilgrimage
> Can you come? – send an ode or elegy
> In the old way and raise our heritage. (*CP*, 3)

Here, the ritualistic element of the poem observed by Conran is made evident in the call to 'raise our heritage', and the speaker's request that her interlocutor 'start this pilgrimage' suggests that the entire poem projects a form of pilgrimage. Victor and Edith Turner claim that during the European Middle Ages, the practice of pilgrimage precipitated the phenomenon of *communitas*: a restructuring of normal social relations along communal, egalitarian lines.[70] The Walsingham pilgrimage, revived in 1923 by Father Hope Pattern, may have provided a contemporary parallel to this.[71] Roberts's own interest in pilgrimage may have been derived from her fascination with early Celtic Christianity and the narratives of the Cambro-British saints; she would have been aware that many Welsh sites, such as Bardsey, St Davids and Pennant Melangell, became focal points for pilgrimages commemorating Welsh saints during the Middle Ages.[72] Importantly, pilgrimage practices were enmeshed in the local and the popular during the Middle Ages: 'spontaneously engendered' local pilgrimages broke out frequently all over Christendom, resisting the centralized control of Rome.[73] 'Poem from Llanybri' proffers a model of *communitas* as a mode of resistance to the centralized, administered state control that Roberts often critiques in her writings, as well as a means of structuring relations between poets. She asserted in a letter to Robert Graves: 'I do not believe in group, collective gatherings – this sort of thing is acceptable to craftsmen – but not to poets.'[74] But here she presents the *communitas* of premodern pilgrimage as an alternative to the 'groups' and 'movements' that had dominated the British poetry scene of the 1930s, allowing for a kind of unity-in-difference that is shaped and conditioned by the fact of sharing a common purpose. Like all rites, pilgrimage is a process. Thus, 'Poem from Llanybri' identifies national tradition – and the art that sustains it – as, in the words of Alex Davis and Lee Jenkins, 'something actively to be *made*, constructed, not something to be passively inherited'.[75]

Pilgrimage has to do with new vision. Victor and Edith Turner underline the idea that, moving out of 'the human experience of social structure', pilgrims go off in search of an 'extraordinary' sight.[76] 'Poem from Llanybri' is similarly structured around new ways of seeing, destabilizing fixed perceptions of the pastoral and of Wales by making strange that which should be homely or familiar. Although the poem appears to present itself as a homely, domestic 'offering', the vivid colours evoked by the 'garlic red with dew' and the 'lime-tree' (*CP*, 3) bring the bright colours of Argentina – the place of Roberts's birth and upbringing – into west Wales, while the untranslated Welsh terms and unusual syntax provide the slightly estranged effect of reading a text in another language, or from another time. The pointed references to local flora, geography and village customs in many of Roberts's poems evoke the observant gaze of the ethnographer upon a strange new culture. Here, however, the speaker also presents herself as part of the culture being perceived. Offering hospitality and warning about the danger posed by traversing the fen, she adopts the position of translator or guide to the 'native' culture of Llanybri, providing her reader a 'way in' to its way of life. Her role thus anticipates James Clifford's conception of the 'Ex-centric' or 'hybrid "native" ': a 'traveling "indigenous" culture-maker' who, first appearing as a 'native', later emerges as a traveller.[77] Described by Clifford as '[i]nsider-outsiders, good translators and explicators', the intermediary status of the 'hybrid "native"' mirrors Roberts's own ambivalent position vis-à-vis Welsh culture.[78] Additionally, while, as Clifford argues, traditional ethnography tends to obscure a culture's external relations through the practice of 'localization', the 'hybrid "native" ' reveals a culture's complex connections to, and relations with the wider world, pointing to the 'hybrid, cosmopolitan experiences', which, for Clifford, are as significant as its 'rooted' ones.[79]

Similarly, while 'Poem from Llanybri' may appear to ground itself in the 'timeless' folk traditions that were conventionally attributed to non-Western cultures, its temporality, like pilgrimage, is actually that of transition: the 'events' of the poem all occur in a conditional, imaginary time 'between now and then'.[80] While the transitional temporality of 'Poem from Llanybri' may reflect the experience of war as an interlude between a past and an uncertain future, it also replicates the experience of exile. For Mae Henderson, the anthropological model of liminality, identified with pilgrimage by Victor Turner, 'provides a handy conceptual model for the study of exile – or border crossing "betwixt and between" countries and/or cultures – as a processual rite.'[81] Thus, the pilgrimage 'over the threshold' of Llanybri also becomes evocative of the 'border-crossing' of exile. Indeed, as Judith Kegan Gardiner and Angela Ingram have observed, for the colonial woman writer, the journey homewards is also the outward path, for no place is fully 'home'.[82]

The act of pilgrimage also disrupts everyday temporality, in the words of Alexandra Peat giving rise to 'multiple layers of continually superimposed experience.'[83] The landscape of *Gods* is similarly comprised of 'multiple layers of continually superimposed experience'. The notes that Roberts provides to the poem, for example, reveal the distinctly medieval 'allusive substratum'[84] of the text: figures, encounters and events from medieval Welsh history and mythology frequently erupt in the modern landscape of her poem, contributing to what John Wilkinson refers to as its 'dreamwise' quality – that is, its capacity to attend to reality while exaggerating, distorting, overcondensing and diverting it.[85] While the dream-like nature of Roberts's text points to its status as an inner landscape (an evocation, perhaps, of Wales's national unconscious), it also functions as part of Roberts's manipulation of time in the poem, for as Jeremy Hooker suggests, in the dream world of the mind, 'history and myth are as "here and now" as "real" events'.[86]

Gods with Stainless Ears, like 'Poem from Llanybri', is also concerned with lost, mythical origins – both of Wales and the (poetic) self. Indeed, its concern with the 'uhr-texts' of Welsh culture becomes evident in the mythic coastal landscape featured at the beginning of the poem, with its 'Abbey paddock. / Sunk. Sad as ancient monument of stone' and 'widowing / Homeric hills, green pinnacles of bone' (*CP*, 44). Roberts localizes the reference to Homer in her notes by citing an extract from Gerald of Wales's *Itinerary through Wales* (1180): 'Maenor Pyrr . . . that is, Mansions of Pyrrhus, who also possessed the Island of Chaldey, which the Welsh call Inys Pyrr, or the Island of Pyrrhus . . . distant about three miles from Pembroch', adding her own aside: 'There are historians who believe the Trojans came and settled on this coast. In years to come archaeologists may discover both the Temples and City as Sir Arthur Evans and Schliemann discovered Knossos and Troy – by studying the legends in the locality.' (*CP*, 71) This picks up on the claim (first suggested by twelfth-century writer Geoffrey of Monmouth) that the Welsh were descended from the line of Aeneas of Troy, via Brutus, itself part of an ancient historical tradition linking Wales with the classical world.[87] However, Roberts's postulation of a direct, material link between Troy and Wales is complicated by the fact that it is mediated by Gerald of Wales, an idiosyncratic storyteller and purveyor of myth. Gerald's travelogue *The Itinerary Through Wales*, an account of his tour of Wales with Archbishop Baldwin in 1188, appears to have offered a kind of sourcebook for *Gods with Stainless Ears*; it is cited as an influence or source of information on three different occasions in her notes to the poem.[88] Gerald, too, had a liminal, hybrid identity, his mixed Norman-Welsh heritage affording him a distanced gaze on his home culture, and his journeys are full of digressions, diversions and wonder. It could be suggested that Roberts looks to Gerald of Wales as a model for the construction of a new, postmodern historiography that, crossing the divide between poetry, history, autobiography and myth, remakes all of these.[89]

The landscape of Part I yields another dream-like echo of medieval mythic origins:

> ... John Roberts covered with ligustrum,
> Always sanitary and discreet, rows to and fro from
> Bell house to fennel, floating quietly on the tide. (*CP*, 45)

John Roberts was the local coracleman at Llanybri: in her diary and short story 'Fisherman', Roberts emphasizes the heroic status attributed to him for his navigational skills and important role in ferrying villagers across the estuary to Laugharne.[90] Both hero and 'green man' of medieval folklore, he is adorned with ligustrum, which, as Roberts tells us in her notes, is the botanical name for privet, 'one of the sacred trees mentioned in Taliesin's Battle of the Trees' (*CP*, 71) – a connection she may have derived from Robert Graves's translation 'Câd Goddeu' ('Battle of the Trees'), published in the December 1945 edition of *Wales*.[91] These allusions convert the 'pastoral' scene of the poem's opening into a battlefield, or at least shows the latter as the hidden face of the former. The doubling of John Roberts with the poet Taliesin takes the poem back to the birth of the poet himself. A Brythonic poet associated with the period following the departure of the Romans, Taliesin has historically been identified with the origins of the Welsh poetic tradition. He lingers on the interstice between history and myth: no records of his life exist beyond his poetry, and his life has been subject to many legendary rewritings. Indeed, in a letter to Robert Graves, Roberts speculates on Taliesin's possible origins:

> What puzzles me is what does he mean by I was born 'Under the region of the summer stars'. As the legend carries the tale in various versions that he was shipwrecked & found in a coracle, or like Moses cradled in reeds, I have often wondered if it may have meant under the Southern Hemisphere or tropical stars.[92]

John Roberts and his coracle thus connects different times and spaces, just as his ferry service connects the villages dotted along the west Wales coast. Through his association with Taliesin, he offers a living link between Wales's present and its past, between the Welsh landscape and the 'tropical stars' (colonial or non-Western spaces), between Roberts's present existence in Llanybri and her childhood in the southern hemisphere, between everyday life and a spiritual, cosmic world. Weaving together Gerald of Wales, Homer and Taliesin, Roberts creates a new mythology of birth (or perhaps *re*birth), reformulating Wales's origins as mobile, travelling, rather than fixed.

A further preoccupation in Roberts's writing is the idea of survival and with what goes on after change and disaster. These existential concerns frequently find expression in her exploration of historical survivals. She often presents the Middle Ages as a form of living history, active within the fabric of the everyday. Specifically, her medievalism is often enfolded in her representation of Welsh village life. In an earlier letter to Robert Graves, for example, she explains that she chose to set her novel the 'Book of Nesta' in the twelfth century because 'rural villages in Wales are still so medieval in craft & manner', and because her upbringing 'in a French & Spanish convent' had afforded her an insight into the 'atmosphere & . . . conditions' of the period.[93] Roberts's perception of the Welsh village as a vital repository for a premodern material culture was influenced by Welsh anthropologist Iorwerth C. Peate, who presented the rural west as the harbour of '[f]olk songs, superstitions, crafts, the gentle bearing of the poor, and a host of other things which are like the fragments of a dream lost in the uproar of industry's juggernaut.'[94] However, far from appearing as a space in which to elude modernity, the Welsh village is portrayed by Roberts as one of those rural 'centres for the avant-garde' described by Alexandra Harris – a space where art and life coalesce, giving rise to the possibility for new cultural and social formations.[95]

Roberts's training was primarily in design: she studied at the Central School of Arts and Crafts, which, founded in 1896, was a product of the late nineteenth-century Arts and Crafts movement fronted by William Morris.[96] Fittingly, then, Morris's influence can be traced across Roberts's poetry.[97] He summoned the Middle Ages in order to project a utopian, socialist vision of 'the democracy of medieval institutions, the fraternity of guilds, [and] the creative freedom of the medieval craftsman'.[98] Reanimating Morris's ghost through a focus on domestic art and medieval craft, Roberts develops a 'naive' modernism that presents creative labour as a therapeutic response to the psychic violence of war, and that draws on the motif of medieval village craft in order to bridge the divide between 'high' and 'low' culture, the public and the private.[99]

In his comparative study of Wales and African American culture, *Black Skin, Blue Books* (2012), Daniel Williams observes that

Zora Neale Hurston drew on anthropological forms of culture to reveal what she perceived as 'the inner lives of rural folk'.[100] In a similar fashion, Roberts draws on a medieval craft tradition in order to speak up for her Welsh community, emphasizing the potential of material objects and practices to lend visibility to the inner, spiritual life of a minority culture. This project once again speaks of her desire to assume a public voice, to heal the historical rift between the woman writer and her community that had only been heightened under the pressures of war.[101] In her poem 'Earthbound', Roberts uses the trope of medieval village craft associated with Morris and his Pre-Raphaelite design aesthetic, fused with medieval Welsh culture, to explore and redefine the role of the modern woman writer in relation to her (national) community. The text's opening depicts a domestic environment marked by mimesis and reflection; the speaker sits at her dressing table 'Suggest[ing] my lips with accustomed air' like a heroine of contemporary cinema, when a 'reflected van like lipstick' arrives, bringing news of a man's death (*CP*, 10). The multiple mirrors refracting the speaker's gaze are suggestive of the mediated nature of death in an age of mass media and mechanized warfare, emphasizing its transformation into spectacle. However, the rest of the poem traces a movement away from this private experience of death and toward what Esty terms 'the public performance of civic rituals':[102]

We made the wreath standing on the white floor,
Bent each to our purpose wire to rose-wire;
Pinning each leaf smooth,
Polishing the outer edge with the warmth of our hands.

The circle finished and note thought out,
We carried the ring through the attentive eyes of the street:
Then slowly drove by Butcher's Van to the 'Union Hall'.

We walked the greaving room alone,
Saw him lying in his upholstered box,
Violet ribbon carefully crossed,
And about his side bunches of wild thyme.
No one stirred as we offered the gift. No one drank there again. (*CP*, 10)

The poem is based on an episode from Roberts's own life when she and an evacuee friend made a wreath in response to a death of a villager in Llanybri in 1941.[103] Here, as Tony Conran has suggested, the speaker becomes 'no longer a total outsider but capable of behavior which has social significance'.[104] The artists' bodies, infused into their craft through the warmth of their hands, become integrated, through their sacrificial gift, into the body of the community. Invoking the Welsh bardic model of the poet as 'a sort of craftsman, well integrated in the community of which he [sic] is a product',[105] Roberts presents her speaker-artist as a craftswoman whose 'wreath becomes a symbol of participation; almost a symbol of the poem that has been made of it'.[106]

Conran argues that in the case of Welsh-identified writers Lynette Roberts and Brenda Chamberlain, 'the boundaries between public and private are frequently transgressed'.[107] In 'Earthbound' this can be seen in the movement of the wreath from the 'white floor' of the cottage to the public, masculine space of the 'Union Hall'. Roberts posits the domestic sphere as a locus for an art that mediates between public and private experience, without subsuming one into the other.

It is, perhaps, no wonder that in war's 'complex climate of uncertainty and lost direction', Roberts should so long for simplicity.[108] Her poem 'The Shadow Remains' ('a good poem of my v. simple life'),[109] demonstrates her desire to return to basics so as to heal and begin again:

> To speak of everyday things with ease
> And arrest the mind to a simpler world
> Where living tables are stripped of a cloth;
>
> Of wood on which I washed, sat at peace:
> Cooked duck, shot on an evening in peacock cold:
> Studied awhile: wrote: baked bread for us both. (CP, 4)

The poem traces a search for a culture in which body, life-world and language are integrated, not fragmented. The speaker's participation in the domestic rhythms of her (female) community allow for a moment of psychic equilibrium or peace, her activities opening out a space for thought, hinted at in the pauses signalled by the punctuation. The presence of Morris haunts the text: the 'living tables . . . stripped of a cloth' are redolent of the small wooden tripod table, originally owned by Morris, on which the poet H.D. would hold her séances during the 1940s, for instance.[110] Several critics have noted how the material devastation wrought by aerial bombing raids led to a new awareness of the importance of matter during the war: as Gill Plain suggests, there was a sense of fighting not so much for ideals as for the material, tactile elements of culture.[111] Roberts draws on the legacy of Morris and the Pre-Raphaelite movement in order to assert the spiritual and psychological significance inherent to the material, tactile elements of a minority culture. In 'The Shadow Remains', ordinary activities are imbued with a sacramental, ritual dimension – the consumption of flesh, and the sharing of bread, gesture to pagan and Catholic rituals – while the parataxis and repeated use of the colon in the second stanza imbue the text with an incantatory rhythm suggestive of both chanting and enchantment. Here, the connections between medieval past and modern present take the form of what Marea Mitchell terms 'rhythms or pulses or waves that ripple over each other', which become folded into the 'flow' of writing.[112] The speaker's performance of homespun traditions is thus presented as a form of memory work that links the present day with a spiritual heritage.[113]

Medieval fascinations come to the forefront in other areas of Roberts's work. For example, like William Morris and Edward Burne-Jones, Roberts was attracted to medieval monasticism, aligning it with a 'domestic' counterhistory that becomes an inspiration for her modernist art. For example, in an article on fourteenth-century Florentine artist Lorenzo da Monaco ('Lorenzo the Monk') published in *Life and Letters Today* in 1940, she draws on her powers of artistic scene-making in order to reanimate everyday life in a Camaldolese monastery:

> We can imagine these monks hunched over a table, some working on powdered parchment lightly brushed over with a hare's foot. Their puckered faces too near their work, tracing drawings first with sinopia, then colouring the endless legends which surround their monastery. In one corner calligraphers reshape their quills or make a new brush from the tails of miniver; whilst others the lesser accomplished grind and mix various colours. There is a hum of bees and smell of herbs with the humdrum of voices and murmuring of prayers.[114]

Similarly, while the miniaturist technique that Roberts adopts in her poetry has invited comparison with Emily Dickinson (*Gods with Stainless Ears*, for instance, is 'hyperattuned to small detail', in Nigel Wheale's words,[115] homing in microscopically on soldiers 'Washing like flies to pin of elbow' (*CP*, 56) and geese whose 'Eyes and ears surrounded with orange cord / Detect and hear the running pads of spiders' (*CP*, 48)),[116] the strategy is, in fact, indebted to her fascination with the intricate manuscript illuminations of the medieval monks. Indeed, in the same article, she recounts how she consulted the Camaldolese Gradual, an illuminated twelfth-century choir book then held at the Kensington museum, every day for four months to detect signs of Lorenzo's hand.[117]

Roberts's unpublished historical novel the 'Book of Nesta' similarly insists upon the power of the creative imagination to restore a tangible sense of the past: in her introduction, she states that '[t]his book is to be read as it was written, as an imaginative work recollected around the hearth'.[118] The text eschews traditional, hero-centred narratives in favour of a history articulated in what Ben Highmore has called 'the details of life and the pulsings of affect',[119] as a more appropriate mode for capturing women's lives, pausing over such details as the plants in a herbarium at a monastery in St Davids, the 'quick rhythm' of Welsh craftsmen in the 'turn of their work', and the 'mattress [. . .] filled up with sweet yellow straw and head pillows from the pluckings of geese' made by Rhys ap Tewdwr for his wife.[120] The 'Book of Nesta' acknowledges the development of new forms of social history during the twentieth century, spearheaded by medievalist women scholars in particular, who were drawn to the Middle Ages due to the fact they offered 'a different view on the relations between communality and individuality, or the public and the private' to the modern model of the individual citizen in the nation state.[121] Eileen Power's influential *Medieval People* (1924), for instance, imaginatively recreated the life of ordinary figures 'unknown to fame', and was 'chiefly concerned with the kitchens of History'.[122] Welsh women modernists were cognizant of the political and feminist potential of this new historiography. Reviewing a book on *English Country Life* in *Wales* in 1939, Margiad Evans described it as 'a corner cupboard history . . . a summary of man's odd needs', and praised it for capturing a fleeting, unrecorded past, 'the wink and the bye-way [*sic*]'.[123] Like Roberts, Evans poses a subterranean connection between medieval monasticism and domestic culture; speculating on 'the effect of household life of the dispersal of the monasteries', she adds that 'Monks were sly housekeepers.'[124] Refracting the history of the monastery, a masculine centre of power and spirituality, through the lens of rural Welsh life, both Margiad Evans and Lynette Roberts point to the continued presence (or at least, continued potential) of monastic culture, with its legacy of creativity, autonomy and community, in Welsh women's lives.

CONCLUSION

While some critics see Roberts's medievalism as a strategy for rendering war more remote, from another perspective her work reveals how war brought history home: where once women had been excluded from history, now they were living it – immersed in it – in an immediate and tangible way. Although she was drawn to Romantic ideals of simplicity and 'unfeathered ways',[125] her writing refuses to support an unbroken cohesion of time and language. Roberts's perception of the medieval past as a 'mess' of traces and fragments that refuse to quite 'add up' – evident in *Gods with Stainless Ears*, but discernable throughout her writing – undermines nationalistic principles of order, hierarchy and unity. Gesturing to similar strategies associated with surrealism and the European avant-garde, it points instead to her 'valorisation of a culture's detritus and trivia as well as its strange and marginal practices'.[126]

Roberts's interest in the culture of the medieval past conveys her desire to anchor her writing 'in something solid', to coin Keidrych Rhys's phrase, to reach back to traditions that might offer a sense of purpose and connection.[127] But for all its concern with roots, her writing emphasizes the constructedness of all pasts in the present – including her own. Infusing her vision of medieval Wales with memories of her Catholic upbringing in Buenos Aires, she weaves the private threads of her own life into the national history of Wales. She thus uses the outsider's perspective of the 'colonial' woman writer in order to remake the literary landscape, 'traversing in order to dislocate – or unfix – the Wales in and out of which she writes.'[128] Moreover, drawing on the legacy of the medievalist Arts and Crafts Movement, she 'mak[es] the past . . . present' – to cite William Morris – in order to experience and thus, appropriate history as a woman.[129] Furthermore, she lays emphasis on the power of material artifacts to embody a collective, emotional history, connected to 'the internal life of minorities'.[130] Roberts's attitude to national culture, Welsh and British, can be summarized in terms of the wartime rhetoric of 'make do and mend': the Welsh Middle Ages appear as creative fragments that, in Walter Benjamin's words, 'flash up in a moment of danger',[131] and she repurposes these in order to facilitate broader cultural flourishing in an unknown postcolonial world.

Notes

1 John Goodby, 'Dylan Thomas and the Poetry of the 1940s', in *The Cambridge History of English Poetry*, ed. Michael O'Neill (Cambridge: Cambridge University Press, 2010), pp. 858–78 (p. 871).
2 Lynette Roberts, letters to Robert Graves, dated 13 December 1943 and 18 December 1944, in Lynette Roberts, *Diaries, Letters and Recollections*, ed. Patrick McGuinness (Manchester: Carcanet, 2008), pp. 168, 181.
3 As Sioned Davies notes, the *Mabinogion* is the collective name now given to eleven medieval Welsh tales found mainly in two manuscripts, the *White Book of Rhydderch* and the *Red Book of Hergest*. The term is a scribal error for *mabinogi* (derived from the Welsh *mab*, meaning 'son', 'boy'). It was Lady Charlotte Guest's translation (1838–49) that first popularized the term *Mabinogion*. See Sioned Davies's introduction to *The Mabinogion* (Oxford: Oxford University Press, 2007), p. ix.
4 The term is used by Paul Robichaud in *Making the Past Present: David Jones, the Middle Ages, and Modernism* (Washington DC: The Catholic University of America Press, 2007), p. 23.
5 With its playful splicing together of different temporal references and troubling of historical facticity, the 'Book of Nesta' anticipates trends in contemporary 'biofiction'.
6 In fact, Roberts could be rather negative about it: in her 'Carmarthenshire Diary', she denounces the 'puritan and stony religion' of the Welsh Nonconformists, and is critical of the hypocrisy of the vicar's wife when she refused to accommodate evacuees in her seven-bedroom vicarage in Llanybri. See Lynette Roberts, 'A Carmarthenshire Diary', entries for 7 May 1942 and 23 June 1940, in *Diaries, Letters and Recollections*, pp. 48, 22.
7 Lynette Roberts, letter to Robert Graves, dated 10 February 1944, in *Diaries, Letters and Recollections*, pp. 172–3.
8 For an extended exploration of this practice in relation to the writing of Virginia Woolf, see Siriol McAvoy, 'The Presence of the Past: Medieval Encounters in the Writing of Virginia Woolf and Lynette Roberts' (unpublished PhD thesis, Cardiff University, 2016).
9 Ernest Renan, 'What is a Nation?', trans. Martin Thom, in *Nation and Narration*, ed. Homi K. Bhabha (London and New York: Routledge, 1990), pp. 8–22, p. 19.
10 Liedeke Plate, *Transforming Memories in Contemporary Women's Rewriting* (Basingstoke and New York: Palgrave Macmillan, 2011), p. 8.
11 Ulla Wisherman and Ilze Klavina Mueller note that '[w]hether the debate was about characterizing the private as the political, creating alternative public spheres, or the disintegration of the private sphere under the influence of the mass media . . . the central question [in twentieth-century feminist debate] was always how boundaries could be dissolved'. See their 'Feminist Theories

on the Separation of the Private and the Public: Looking Back, Looking Forward', *Women in German Yearbook*, 20 (2004), 184–97 (184–5).
12 Jed Esty, *A Shrinking Island: Modernism and National Culture in England* (Princeton: Princeton University Press, 2003), p. 2.
13 Esty, *A Shrinking Island*, p. 2.
14 David Matthews, *Medievalism: A Critical History* (Cambridge: D. S. Brewer, 2015), pp. ix–x.
15 Alice Chandler, *A Dream of Order: The Medieval Ideal in Nineteenth-Century English Literature* (London: Routledge and Kegan Paul, 1971), p. 1. This longing to inhabit a holistic, 'organically vital universe' is also reflected in Roberts's embrace of rural culture and frequent emphasis on the concept of what she called the 'wholesome'.
16 Chandler, *A Dream of Order*, p. 1.
17 Chandler, *A Dream of Order*, pp. 2, 4. In this regard, medievalism finds common ground with modernism, which for scholars such as Andrzej Gasiorek can also be seen as 'respond[ing] to a sense of crisis'. See Andrzej Gasiorek, *A History of Modernism* (Chichester: Wiley and Blackwell, 2015) p. 7.
18 Anthony Conran, *Frontiers in Anglo-Welsh Poetry* (Cardiff: University of Wales Press, 1997), p. vii.
19 Conran, *Frontiers in Anglo-Welsh Poetry*, p. 2.
20 Conran, *Frontiers in Anglo-Welsh Poetry*, p. 67.
21 Conran, *Frontiers in Anglo-Welsh Poetry*, pp. 66–7.
22 Saunders Lewis, *Egwyddorion Cenedlaetholdeb ('Principles of Nationalism')* (Caerdydd: Cymdeithas Plaid Cymru Archive Society, 1975 [1926]), pp. 1–19 (p. 9).
23 Lewis, *Egwyddorion Cenedlaetholdeb ('Principles of Nationalism')*, p. 5.
24 Keidrych Rhys, 'Editorial', *Wales*, 3/1 (July 1943), 4–6 (4).
25 Rhys, 'Editorial' (July 1943), 5. In the July 1943 issue, for example, scholar H. Idris Bell's translation from *Canu Llywarch Hen* (collected in the fourteenth-century *Red Book of Hergest*, but dated by scholars to as early as the seventh or eighth centuries), and essay on the medieval 'Welsh poetic tradition' are found alongside contemporary texts by John Cowper Powys and William Empson.
26 Rhys, 'Editorial' (July 1943), 4.
27 Lynette Roberts, 'Notes for an Autobiography', in *Diaries, Letters and Recollections*, p. 203: 'It was some years before the War but in Munich the baiting of the Jews had started. The Nazis would search for them out of their homes and take them jeering into the middle of the road. Other shops with Jewish names would be broken down, the glass falling everywhere'. When the National Anthem was played in the park, she refused to stand up, in protest.
28 See, for example, her historical novel the 'Book of Nesta', which, based on the life of the grandmother of Gerald of Wales, is deliberately set up by Roberts in her preface as a maternal recuperation of Wales's colonial past under the Normans, or her allusion to the '*Mother Mild of Pembroke Streams*' to Part IV, *Gods with Stainless Ears*. She insists in her prose 'Argument' that the anguish of the Madonna becomes 'the nucleus and theme of the whole poem'. See Lynette Roberts, *Collected Poems*, ed. Patrick McGuinness (Manchester: Carcanet, 2005), pp. 46, 60.

29 Elizabeth Bowen, 'The Demon Lover (Preface to the American Edition)', in Collected Impressions (London: Longmans Green and Co., 1950), p. 50.
30 See, for example, Charles Mundye, 'Outside the Imaginary Museum: Mythology and Representation in the Poetry of Lynette Roberts and Keidrych Rhys', PN Review, 40/2 (2013), 23–8 (23); Laura Wainwright, 'New Territories in Modernism: Anglophone Welsh Writing, 1930–1949 (unpublished PhD thesis, Cardiff University, 2010), 66; McGuinness, 'Introduction', in Collected Poems, p. xxv.
31 Mundye, 'Outside the Imaginary Museum', 23.
32 Mikhail Bakhtin, 'Forms of Time and Chronotope in the Novel', in The Dialogic Imagination: Four Essays, ed. Michael Holquist, trans. Caryl Emerson and Michael Holquist (Austin: University of Texas Press, 1982), p. 84.
33 Bowen, Collected Impressions, p. 48.
34 In an unpublished account of literary culture and experience in wartime written in 1941, 'Writing in Wartime', Roberts's similarly alludes to wartime experience as a kind of territory: 'Living conditions are too hard or violent to affect a mature and balanced writing. The suffering . . . our own . . . is unexploded territory in the literary world'. See Lynette Roberts, 'Writing in Wartime' (1941), Harry Ransom Center, University of Texas at Austin, Lynette Roberts Collection, 3.5, p. 1.
35 Margaret R. Higonnet and Patrice L-R Higonnet, 'The Double Helix', in Behind the Lines: Gender and the Two World Wars, ed. Margaret Randolph Higonnet el al. (New Haven and London: Yale University Press, 1987), pp. 31–48 (p. 46).
36 Gill Plain, Women's Fiction of the Second World War: Gender, Power and Resistance (Edinburgh: Edinburgh University Press, 1996), p. 20.
37 Lynette Roberts, Gods with Stainless Ears, I, in Lynette Roberts: Collected Poems, ed. Patrick McGuinness (Manchester: Carcanet, 2005), p. 44. Hereafter the Collected Poems will be cited as CP.
38 Robichaud, Making the Past Present, p. 3.
39 Oxford English Dictionary, v. silt (1b): www.oed.com (last accessed 4 February 2018).
40 Peter Nicholls, 'Pound's Places', in Locations of Literary Modernism: Region and Nation in British and American Modernist Poetry, ed. Alex Davis and Lee M. Jenkins (Cambridge: Cambridge University Press, 2000), pp. 159–77 (pp. 162–70).
41 Nigel Wheale, 'Beyond the Trauma Stratus: Lynette Roberts' Gods with Stainless Ears and the Post-war Cultural Landscape', Welsh Writing in English: A Year of Critical Essays, 3 (1997), 98–117 (103); William May offers an insightful analysis of Roberts's 'optic poetics' in 'Verbal and Visual Art in Twentieth-Century British Women's Poetry', in The Cambridge Companion to Twentieth-Century British and Irish Women's Poetry, ed. Jane Dowson (Cambridge: Cambridge University Press, 2011), pp. 42–61 (p. 55).
42 John Craxton, 'Welsh Estuary Foreshore' (1943), oil on burlap, 112.30×180.30 cm, National Galleries of Scotland, Edinburgh. Quotation from: https://www.nationalgalleries.org/art-and-artists/448/welsh-estuary-foreshore (last accessed 4 February 2018).

43 Patrick McGuinness, 'Notes' to *Collected Poems*, p. 143.
44 *The Blue Bird* inspired a series of film adaptations throughout the twentieth century. Roberts may have been inspired by the technicolour film *The Blue Bird* (1940), directed by Walter Lang and starring Shirley Temple. It was Twentieth Century Fox's alternative to *The Wizard of Oz*, which had been released by MGM the previous year. A film reviewer noted in 1940 that 'One young lady . . . came back delighted from an interrupted session of The Blue Bird [by an air raid siren]. 'Let there be light!' said the Fairy on the screen – and there was lights [*sic*] – house lights, and the manager making his announcement.' See C. A. Lejeune, 'Are All Films War Films?', the *Observer*, 1940, quoted in Mark Glancy, *Hollywood and the Americanization of Britain: From the 1920s to the Present* (London and New York: I. B. Tauris and Co., 2014), p. 143.
45 There is a darker side, too: Roberts would have been aware of the solidarity shown in Wales toward Belgium, another small country, during the First World War, as encouraged by David Lloyd George's famous speech of 19 September 1914, in which he underlined the threat to the 'little five-foot-five' nations of Belgium and Serbia. In this same speech he envisaged 'a Welsh Army in the field' by invoking the military heritage of medieval Wales, presenting the Welsh as freedom fighters against the Normans and Henry IV of England. See David Lloyd George, *The Great War: Speech Delivered by the Rt. Hon. David Lloyd George at the Queen's Hall, London on September 19, 1914* (London: Hodder and Stoughton, 1914), pp. 10, 15. Linking the fates of Belgium and Wales in the current war, Roberts's reference points forward to the ruination of the enchanted self-containment of Cwmcelyn bay with the insurgence of the modern war machine.
46 John Pikoulis, 'The Poetry of the Second World War', in *British Poetry, 1900–50: Aspects of Tradition*, ed. Gary Day and Brian Docherty (Basingstoke: Macmillan, 1995), pp. 193–207 (p. 24).
47 Charles Gross, 'The Court of Piepowder', *The Quarterly Journal of Economics*, 20/2 (1906), 231–49 (231).
48 Gross, 'The Court of Piepowder', 232. A letter from T. Gwyn Jones at the Carmarthenshire County Council Education Committee to Lynette Roberts, dated 26 April 1944, indicates that Roberts subscribed to the local history journal *Carmarthenshire Antiquary* during the wartime years and made enquiries about the history of medieval sites in the area. Harry Ransom Center, University of Texas at Austin, Lynette Roberts Collection, 3.8.
49 Robert Neuwirth suggests that organizations such as the piepowder courts represented an attempt on the part of ordinary people to build their own 'social contract': 'forming a market court means that they have taken an initial step toward collective organizing and cooperative action'. See Robert Neuwirth, *Stealth of Nations: The Global Rise of the Informal Economy* (New York: Random House, 2011), p. 224. The quotation in the body of the text is from Mark Rawlinson, 'The Second World War: British Writing', in *The Cambridge Companion to War Writing*, ed. Kate McLoughlin (Cambridge: Cambridge University Press, 2009), p. 203.
50 Lynette Roberts's introduction to the 'Book of Nesta' cites as some of her sources medieval 'Laws [and] Pipe Rolls' (accounts kept by the Royal

Exchequer under the Normans, and important documents for medieval social history). In the novel itself, Rhys ap Tewdwr, Nesta's father, celebrates his ancestor Hywel Dda – considered the founder of the medieval Welsh legal system – as a great 'reformer'. Lynette Roberts, unpublished 'Book of Nesta', Lynette Roberts Collection, Harry Ransom Center, University of Texas at Austin, MS-3561, p. 2.

[51] Virginia Woolf, *A Room of One's Own and Three Guineas*, ed. Anna Snaith (Oxford: Oxford University Press, 2008), p. 238.

[52] Saunders Lewis, 'Is there an Anglo-Welsh Literature?' (Caerdydd: Urdd Graddedigion Prifysgol Cymru, 1939), p. 3.

[53] 'Evans shop' is undoubtedly a member of this chorus, but his mercantile role as shopkeeper also sets him slightly apart from the other rural workers – conjuring, perhaps, the same connection between capitalism, war and patriarchal national narratives as does Woolf in *Three Guineas*.

[54] Helene Shugart and Catherine Egley Waggoner define camp as a 'parodic, ironic, over-the-top, and often nostalgic sensibility'. See their *Making Camp: Ethics of Transgression in U.S. Popular Culture* (Tuscaloosa: University of Alabama Press, 2008), p. 1. Susan Sontag's identification of camp with a 'love of the unnatural: of artifice and exaggeration' corresponds to some extent with the style of *Gods*; Sontag also sees it as 'something of a private code, a badge of identity even, among small urban cliques.' See Susan Sontag, 'Notes on "Camp"' (1964), in her *Against Interpretation, and Other Essays* (London: Penguin, 2009), pp. 3–14 (p. 273).

[55] Jodie Medd, 'Encountering the Past in Recent Gay and Lesbian Fiction', in *The Cambridge Companion to Gay and Lesbian Writing*, ed. Hugh Stephens (Cambridge: Cambridge University Press, 2011), pp. 167–84 (p. 178).

[56] For a wide-ranging account of neo-Romanticism in British visual culture, see David Mellor (ed.), *A Paradise Lost: The Neo-Romantic Imagination in Britain 1935–55* (London: Lund Humphries, 1987); Clare Morgan also offers a summary of the interwar neo-Romantic 'zeitgeist' in 'Vanishing Horizons: Virginia Woolf and the Neo-Romantic Imagination in *Between the Acts* and "Anon"', *Worldviews*, 5 (2001), 35–57.

[57] Alexandra Harris, *Romantic Moderns: English Writers, Artists and the Imagination from Virginia Woolf to John Piper* (London: Thames and Hudson, 2010), pp. 29–30. Together with his partner Myfanwy Evans (editor of the experimental art magazine *Axis*), John Piper conducted a photographic study of medieval font sculpture in local English parish churches, which he used as the basis of his essay 'England's Early Sculptors', *Architectural Review*, 80 (1936), 157–60.

[58] Geoffrey Grigson and John Piper, 'England's Climate', *Axis*, 7 (1936), 5–9 (9).

[59] Morgan, 'Vanishing Horizons', 39.

[60] Carolyn Dinshaw, *How Soon Is Now? Medieval Texts, Amateur Readers, and the Queerness of Time* (London and Durham: Duke University Press, 2012), p. 6.

[61] Geoffrey Grigson, 'Comment on England', *Axis*, 1 (1935), 8–10 (10).

[62] Well-known artists and writers collaborated on the production of these guides: see, for example, Paul Nash's *Dorset* (1936), John Betjeman's *Devon* (1936)

and *Cornwall* (1934), and John Piper's *Oxfordshire* (1938). Eclectic texts, the *Shell Guides* combined maps and illustrations with articles on local geology, fauna and flora, dialect, and food.

63 Harris, *Romantic Moderns*, p. 10.
64 Harris, *Romantic Moderns*, p. 14.
65 Edward Blunden, 'On Pilgrimage in England: Voyages of Discovery', *Times Literary Supplement* (28 March 1942), 156–61 (156). Roberts mentions Blunden several times (and with approval) in her series of radio talks on contemporary British poetry for the British Council broadcast in May 1945, 'English Poetry Today'. See Lynette Roberts Collection, Harry Ransom Center, University of Texas at Austin, 2.3.
66 John Pikoulis, 'Lynette Roberts and Alun Lewis', *Poetry Wales* (special issue on Lynette Roberts), 19/2 (1983), 9–29 (13).
67 Patrick McGuinness, 'Introduction', in *Collected Poems*, p. xi.
68 McGuinness, 'Introduction', in *Collected Poems*, p. xii.
69 Anthony Conran, 'Lynette Roberts: The Lyric Pieces', *Poetry Wales* (special issue on Lynette Roberts), 19/2 (1983), 125–33 (132–3).
70 Victor Turner and Edith L. B. Turner, *Image and Pilgrimage in Christian Culture* (New York: Columbia University Press, 1978), pp. 13, 250–5.
71 Turner and Turner, *Image and Pilgrimage*, p. 176.
72 Cadw, 'Celtic Saints, Spiritual Places and Pilgrimage' (2001), p. 2. See *http://cadw.gov.wales/docs/cadw/publications/InterpplanCelticSaints_EN.pdfp* (last accessed 1 February 2018).
73 Turner and Turner, *Image and Pilgrimage*, p. 192.
74 Lynette Roberts, letter to Robert Graves, dated 13 December 1943, in *Diaries, Letters and Recollections*, p. 169.
75 Alex Davis and Lee M. Jenkins, 'Locating Modernisms: An Overview', in *Locations of Literary Modernism*, ed. Alex Davis and Lee M. Jenkins (Cambridge: Cambridge University Press, 2000), pp. 3–30 (p. 9).
76 Turner and Turner, *Image and Pilgrimage*, p. 7.
77 James Clifford, 'Traveling Cultures', in *Cultural Studies*, ed. Lawrence Grossberg, Cary Nelson and Paula A. Treichler (New York and London: Routledge, 1992), pp. 96–116 (pp. 97, 101).
78 Clifford, 'Traveling Cultures', p. 97.
79 Clifford, 'Traveling Cultures', pp. 100–1.
80 The title of David Jones's epic First World War poem, *In Parenthesis*, similarly implies that modern war involves a fluid form of temporality – an interlude, interval or hiatus bracketed off from the mundane temporality of peacetime.
81 Mae Henderson, 'Borders, Boundaries and Frame(works)', in *Borders, Boundaries and Frames*, ed. Mae Henderson (New York and London: Routledge, 1995), pp. 1–30 (p. 5).
82 See Angela Ingram, 'Introduction: On the Contrary, Outside of It', in *Women's Writing in Exile*, ed. Mary Lynn Broe and Angela Ingram (Chapel Hill and London: University of North Carolina Press, 1989), pp. 1–15 (p. 7), and Judith Kegan Gardiner, 'The Exhilaration of Exile: Rhys, Stead, and Lessing', in *Women's Writing in Exile*, ed. Mary Lynn Broe and Angela Ingram (Chapel Hill and London: University of North Carolina Press, 1989), pp. 133–50 (p. 134).

83 Alexandra Peat, 'Modern Pilgrimage and the Authority of Space in Forster's *A Room with a View* and Woolf's *The Voyage Out*', *Mosaic: A Journal for the Interdisciplinary Study of Literature*, 36 (2003), 139–53 (143).
84 Robichaud, *Making the Past Present*, p. 23.
85 John Wilkinson, *The Lyric Touch: Essays on the Poetry of Excess* (Cambridge: Salt, 2007), p. 179.
86 Jeremy Hooker, *The Poetry of Place* (Manchester: Carcanet, 1982), p. 35.
87 Juliette Wood, 'Perceptions of the Past in Welsh Folklore', *Folklore*, 108 (1997), 93–102 (96).
88 See Roberts's notes to *Gods with Stainless Ears* in *Collected Poems*, pp. 71–3.
89 Paul Peppis notes that many modernist artists and writers 'endeavoured to cross the "great divide" between art and life and remake both'. See his 'Schools, Movements, Manifestoes', in *The Cambridge Companion to Modernist Poetry*, ed. Alex Davis and Lee M. Jenkins (Cambridge: Cambridge University Press, 2007), pp. 28–50 (p. 28).
90 Lynette Roberts, 'A Carmarthenshire Diary', in *Diaries, Letters and Recollections*, p. 105.
91 As Charles Mundye has noted, the text of 'Câd Goddeu' ('Battle of the Trees'), from the *Book of Taliesin*, was 'reassembled' by Robert Graves and published in the twenty-first birthday issue of Keidrych Rhys's *Wales* magazine (*Wales*, 5/8–9 (1945)), and was later to inform *The White Goddess*. Alongside was a separate, related poem by Graves, 'The Blodeuwedd of Gwion ap Gwreang', dedicated to Angharad Rhys (Rhys and Roberts's daughter), which ends: 'Long and white are my fingers / As the ninth wave of the sea'. See Charles Mundye, 'Lynette Roberts and Dylan Thomas: Background to a Friendship', *PN Review*, 220, 41/2 (2014), 20–3 (23).
92 Lynette Roberts, letter to Robert Graves, dated 10 February 1944, in *Diaries, Letters and Recollections*, p. 173.
93 Lynette Roberts, letter to Robert Graves, dated 14 January 1944, in *Diaries, Letters and Recollections*, p. 170.
94 Iorwerth C. Peate, *Cymru a'i Phobl* (Caerdydd: Gwasg Prifysgol Caerdydd, 1948), p. 2.
95 Harris, *Romantic Moderns*, p. 169.
96 As part of her training at the Central School, she designed and made printed textiles, completed a wood sculpture, 'made a traditional table of my own design', and learnt gesso work and gold-leaf application. See Lynette Roberts, 'Notes for an Autobiography', in *Diaries, Letters and Recollections*, p. 197.
97 A wider discussion of the relevance of Morris's medievalist aesthetics, design principles and political thought to Roberts's poetic practice and political beliefs are beyond the scope of this essay. For a fuller treatment of these issues, see McAvoy, 'Medieval Encounters in the Writing of Lynette Roberts and Virginia Woolf', especially 184–222.
98 Jennifer Harris, 'William Morris and the Middle Ages', in *William Morris and the Middle Ages*, ed. Joanna Banham and Jennifer Harris (Manchester and Dover: Manchester University Press, 1984), pp. 1–17 (p. 3). Like John Ruskin, he felt that art was a visible record of the society that produced it, and he presented medieval craft as symptomatic of a way of life that was collective and beautiful. His medievalist craft aesthetic was popularized by

the furniture and interior decoration produced by his company, Morris & Co, during the late nineteenth and early twentieth centuries, which remained in operation until 1940.

99 Anthony Conran identifies Roberts with what he terms the 'primitive' style of John Clare and Emily Dickinson, in his *Frontiers in Anglo-Welsh Poetry*, p. 165. McGuinness argues she should more rightly be seen as 'naïve in the specific sense of the naïve painters, the tradition of Henri "Douanier" Rousseau' (see McGuinness, 'Introduction', in *Collected Poems*, p. xxxiv).

100 Daniel Williams, *Black Skin, Blue Books* (Cardiff: Cardiff University Press, 2012), p. 127.

101 As Gill Plain asserts, beneath a veneer of national togetherness, woman was seen as 'the archetypal foreign body – necessary and yet reviled' during the Second World War, often aligned with the abject figure of the spy. See Gill Plain, *Women's Fiction of the Second World War: Gender, Power and Resistance* (Edinburgh: Edinburgh University Press, 1996), pp. 23–4.

102 Esty, *A Shrinking Island*, p. 17.

103 Lynette Roberts, 'A Carmarthenshire Diary', in *Diaries, Letters and Recollections*, p. 32.

104 Conran, 'The Lyric Pieces', 129.

105 Glyn Jones, *The Dragon Has Two Tongues: Essays on Anglo-Welsh Writers and Writing*, ed. Tony Brown (Cardiff: University of Wales Press, rev. edn 2001), p. 121.

106 Conran, *Frontiers in Anglo-Welsh Poetry*, p. 176.

107 Conran, *Frontiers in Anglo-Welsh Poetry*, p. 165.

108 Plain, *Women's Fiction of the Second World War*, p. 37.

109 Roberts, 'A Carmarthenshire Diary', in *Diaries, Letters and Recollections*, p. 47.

110 Elizabeth Anderson, 'H.D.'s Tapestry: Embroidery, William Morris and *The Sword Went Out to Sea*', *Modernist Cultures*, 12/2 (2017), 226–48 (235).

111 Plain, *Women's Fiction of the Second World War*, p. 7.

112 Marea Mitchell, '"The Details of Life and the Pulsings of Affect": Virginia Woolf's Medieval Texts', *The Chaucer Review*, 51/1 (2016), 107–129 (108).

113 Anderson, 'H.D.'s Tapestry', 243.

114 Lynette Roberts, 'Lorenzo da Monaco', *Life and Letters Today*, 25/34 (1940), 300–11 (304).

115 Nigel Wheale, 'Lynette Roberts: Legend and Form in the 1940s', *Critical Quarterly*, 36/3 (1994), 4–19 (12).

116 Here, Roberts can also be seen to draw on the miniaturist tradition associated with poet and artist William Blake – a popular figure among the neo-Romantics – in order to convey the new scale of Total War, where individual men are as insignificant as insects.

117 Roberts, 'Lorenzo da Monaco', 307.

118 Roberts, 'Book of Nesta', p. 2.

119 Ben Highmore, *Ordinary Lives: Studies in the Everyday* (Abingdon, Oxon: Routledge, 2011), p. xii.

120 Roberts, 'Book of Nesta', pp. 10, 12, 16.

121 Leena Kore-Schröder, 'Who's Afraid of Rosamund Merridew?: Reading Medieval History in "The Journal of Mistress Joan Martyn"', *Journal of*

the *Short Story in English* [online], 50 (2008), 1–11 (3). See *http://jsse.revues.org/719* (last accessed 1 October 2017).
122. Eileen Power, *Medieval People* (London: Methuen, 1963 [1924]), p. 19.
123. Margiad Evans, 'Review of *Welsh Border Country* and *Old English Household Life*', *Wales*, 10 (1939), 285–6 (286).
124. Evans, 'Review', 286.
125. Lynette Roberts, letter to Alun Lewis, quoted in Pikoulis, 'Lynette Roberts and Alun Lewis', 17.
126. Angeliki Spiropoulou, *Virginia Woolf, Modernity and History: Constellations with Walter Benjamin* (Basingstoke and New York: Palgrave Macmillan, 2010), p. 27.
127. Rhys, 'Editorial' (July 1943), 4.
128. Alice Entwistle, *Poetry, Geography, Gender: Women Rewriting Contemporary Wales* (Cardiff: University of Wales Press, 2013), p. 14.
129. I refer here to Morris's much-quoted remark: 'As for romance, what does romance mean? I have heard people miscalled for being romantic, but what romance means is the capacity for a true conception of history, a power of making the past part of the present.' See William Morris, 'Address at the Twelfth Annual Meeting of the SPAB' (1889), in *William Morris: Artist, Writer, Socialist*, ed. May Morris, 2 vols (Oxford: Blackwell, 1936), I, pp. 146–7.
130. Williams, *Black Skin, Blue Books*, p. 120.
131. Walter Benjamin, *Theses on the Philosophy of History*, in *Illuminations*, ed. Hannah Arendt, trans. Harry Zohn (New York: Schocken Books, 1968), p. 255.

7

BURNT PAIN AND BLASTED SEASHELLS: LYNETTE ROBERTS'S ESTUARINE WAR WRITING

Leo Mellor

> On this vitreous monochrome of a plain
> A striped rhizome cat fled across the estuary.[1]

This juxtaposition of a glassy surface with an energized feline, crossing a space that is neither land nor sea, is seemingly only a small aside in Lynette Roberts's extraordinary long poem *Gods with Stainless Ears*. Yet Roberts's wartime work is fundamentally shaped by the particularities of the estuarine, a space that is both a boundary and always itself in cyclical flux. The personal and autobiographical nature of *Gods* means 'the estuary' she writes of (it being important enough to merit that definite article) was that of the Afon Taf below Llanybri in west Wales, the village where she spent the Second World War. This estuary, along with the wider bay beyond, shapes each of the five sections of *Gods*. Roberts described it as a 'Heroic Poem', each section beginning with a demi-Miltonic 'Argument' in prose. Each outlines and sometimes explains the action that follows, and in the very first she situates the poem in both a time and a place:

> The poem opens with a bay wild with birds and somewhat secluded from man. And it is in front, or within sight of this bay that the whole action takes place: merging from its natural state into a supernatural tension within the first six stanzas. War changes its contour. (*CP*, 44)

With its combination of coastline and active avian life, this poem is part of a complex, part-pastoral tradition of literary geography – yet the passage cited utilizes these qualities as scene setting, for an overt foregrounding of war. Conflict brings a transformative uncertainty, taking the work far from a realist mode. Such uncertainty is registered in how the very 'contour', the apparently fixed physicality of place, changes under conditions of war; yet this apparently seismic process is prefigured in how the tidal cycle alters the spatiality of the estuaries every day.

The rediscovery of Roberts's *Gods* over the past decade by readers and critics, especially since its republication in her *Collected Poems* (2005), has decisively changed several literary-critical narratives: about Welsh modernism; about gender and poetic subjectivity; and about the complexities of a 1940s culture of poetic experimentation.[2] Part of this scholarship has been to understand Roberts within her multiple contexts and cultural interstices, as Patrick McGuinness notes: 'Roberts's mind is shaped as much by ICI catalogues and newsreels, by Le Corbusier and Walter Gropius, as by the Mabinogion and *The Golden Bough*'.[3] This chapter is informed by much of the contemporary critical work on Roberts, but I want to stay close to – or at least not stray too far from – the specific intersection of time and space in a Welsh estuary that opens *Gods*. For this filmic setting of 'a bay wild with birds' is an actual physical place (sandy, muddy, marshy, treacherous in the tides) and not merely an aesthetic device. As well as being shaped by wider cultural forces, Roberts responded to the locality surrounding where she lived through the Second World War; the bioregion that comprises the sweep of the two tidal estuaries of both the Afon Tywi (River Towy) and the Afon Taf (River Taf) as they flow into bae Caerfyrddin (Carmarthen bay). The analysis that follows in this chapter is written in the belief that these estuaries, this specific bay, and the flora and fauna within it, matters both for the inspiration it brings for Roberts's Second World War works in poetry and prose – and for her precise way of apprehending the terrifying uncontainability of modern warfare.[4] By concentrating on Roberts's attentiveness to physical sensations (taken from a landscape and from those creatures that inhabit it) this mode of analysis offers a way of showing *how* she went about noting beauty, tracing violence in echoes and correspondences, and shaping grief through metaphor or analogy. Moreover, by reading Roberts's war writings in relation to the particulars of this locality, connections can also be elucidated between her precise and focused lyric poems and what McGuinness rightly sees in his introduction to *Gods* as the 'high modernist barrage of linguistic special effects, exotic preferentiality and futuristic drama' (*CP*, xii). The chapter will begin by locating her time in Llanybri biographically, and also by setting her works within a wider context of how other contemporaneous writers, in both poetry and prose, likewise found qualities of the tideline, the estuary and the island appropriate for the literature of conflict.

Throughout the 1930s, Roberts lived and worked in an astonishing variety of places: from Fitzrovia in London through to the island of Madeira, as well as taking extensive trips to Hungary and Germany.[5] But on 4 October 1939 she married Keidrych Rhys in Llansteffan (spelt Llanstephan at that time), a small village on the Tywi estuary in west Wales, and they subsequently rented a cottage a few miles away in the village of Llanybri.[6] She stayed there throughout the Second World War, apart from visits to London and to other towns where Rhys had been posted for military service. These are facts of biography and geography, but they matter for understanding the structure – and the energy – of Roberts's writings in both prose and poetry throughout the period 1939–45. Her poetry from Llanybri is shaped partly by the hostility of some villagers towards her (such as when they suspect she is a spy, an experience recounted in 'Raw Salt on Eye') and yet also by their care and friendship. Indeed *An Introduction to Village Dialect With Seven Stories* (1944), Roberts's quasi-anthropological set of seven short stories, was occasioned by the rhythm of village life – and by the tension it was held in with the world beyond. The affinities of her project with other cultural forces dedicated to reportage, especially the Mass Observation movement, have been elucidated (*DLR*, xv); but places and their wildlife – especially their birdlife – are as significant as humans and their linguistic traces when her oeuvre is considered in totality. The birds Roberts writes of – recording in her diary as she attempts to depict them and find a language for them – are largely those of the coast and marshes, such as the curlew she commented on to Robert Graves and which features in a later poem (*DLR*, 181). Yet Roberts's work is not the articulation of an essentialist place and unbroken bonds; rather in its continual linguistic energy and its unsettling vision, one at once both dirtily materialist and translucently sublime, it is closer to cultural geographer Hayden Lorimer's observation that, if poems can 'keep the map on a tilt', then 'place can buckle poetry, too. Not so much through sheer heft, but by the same forces which render place insistently elusive.'[7]

While this roughly triangular area of west Wales around Llanybri where Roberts spent the Second World War was not an island, it was bounded on two of its three sides by estuaries – and its inhabitants (human and non-human) were defined by their various relationships to the intertidal and the aquatic. The island was a potent trope in 1930s writing, from Louis MacNeice to Agatha Christie, as explored in recent scholarship.[8] An example of how lucrative (as well as ubiquitous) the trope was might be shown by the Welsh ornithologist R. M. Lockley's experience of running an observatory on the Welsh island of Skokholm in the early 1930s, which led to his series of books that mixed natural history and the lure of islands – winning him a mass readership. His titles included: *Dream Island* (1930); *The Island Dwellers* (1932); *Island Days* (1934); *The Sea's a Thief* (1936); *I Know an Island* (1938); *Early Morning Island* (1939); *The Way to an Island* (1941); *Shearwaters* (1942); *Dream Island Days* (1943); *Islands Round Britain* (1945). But both the abstracted cultural ideal of the island, and its populist recounting, also became one of the master narratives of British Second World War official culture. The island was not just a military fact – the reason for the lack of a Nazi invasion – but also a form of cultural reassurance. Its expression ranged from Low's famous 1940 cartoon after the defeat of France, depicting a British soldier on a sea-girt rock, crying out 'very well, alone', through to the quotation of Shakespeare's John of Gaunt's speech from *Richard II* – lauding 'this scepter'd isle' – which in voiceover opened Humphrey Jennings's poetic soundscape of a film, *Listen to Britain* (1942).[9]

Thinking about islands within the culture, and propaganda, of the time allows a context to Roberts's detailed geographical positioning – especially in relation to the intertidal aspects of her work and how they are so very different from such overtly island-deifying models of writing. This is, partly, a matter of practical attentiveness to biographical history: Roberts walked along the beaches and the eel-grass-thick alluvial mudflats of both the Tywi and the Taf throughout her time at Llanybri, and these walks furnished her poems with locales (both named and implied), lexical and dialect-specific terms, and significant species (especially the wading and marsh birds). These walks exposed Roberts to the ever-present tidal cycles of the estuary; forces beyond the immediacy of human history or agency.

The ordinary tidal range at the ferry point at Llansteffan, the site where Gerald of Wales crossed the Tywi in 1188, is over six metres in height, increasing to eight metres for spring tides; and therefore the estuary oscillates every day between immense sand or mudbanks and expanses of turbid water. Structures of life and work – such as the action of fishermen Roberts frequently wrote of – depended upon these rhythms. Roberts's diary entry for 17 August 1942 depicts the scene that this vast vertical tidal range created when it was at its lowest ebb:

> Today the sea went out further than usual due to the harvest tides, the sand could be seen rising in banks, lightening under the sun, dry except for a narrow channel which carried fishing boats out towards Pembrey. Here, at this brackish edge, almost 500 yards from the mark of high-tide, round, hollow, spiral holes have been left in the sand. These were dry; but it was obvious that as soon as the tide came in, the water would seep under the holes and filter high up through the sand, filling these holes with water like sinister pools, treacherously and imperceptibly. (*DLR*, 59–60)

Such awareness of tidal forces, with all their resonances in Greek and Celtic mythology, places Roberts's wartime work in a tradition of modernism's *longue durée* of interest in cycles, gyres and circles – primal forces that have physical and physiological effects on those who encounter them. Such a category of writers might include Conrad, Lawrence and Yeats – and also Robert Graves, with whom Roberts corresponded extensively. In such works, tides are often significant on a realist and descriptive level, for instance in Erskine Childers's novel *The Riddle of the Sands* (1903), but also offer a way of accessing varieties of the ineffable – such as in the works of Victor Hugo.[10] Brenda Chamberlain's *Tide-Race* (1962) offers a different perspective; an artists' memoir of Bardsey/Ynys Enlli, it charts how island life was utterly tide-dependent in the postwar years.

Indeed for all the potent symbolism accrued through modernist traditions, Roberts's tides are those of a particular place and at a very specific historical time.[11] Roberts's work in the period is instructive for suggesting how a war literature does not have to feature the violence of destruction; it can rather be a response made possible by such acts – or a retreat, with varying degrees of success, from them as the direct subject. Yet this leads towards another aspect of why the locale where Roberts spent the war years matters so much to her aesthetic. In walking these beaches and mudflats she was part of a wider transformation in British culture, one which, predating the war, had begun in the late 1930s. A renewed interest in the British landscape for a wide variety of writers and visual artists changed an overtly urban method of composition – the use of the fragment, the significant shard, the telling piece of debris – into a response to nature itself. The British surrealist went out of town. Such a transformation was especially prevalent in neo-Romantic art and it helps to open up the significance of works such as Paul Nash's *Monster Field* (1938), as a fallen tree becomes a nightmare creature, or the twisted hedges looming in the works of Graham Sutherland, or the tendrils and 'bomb-flowers' in the pictures of Ceri Richards.[12] In the view of Peter Nicholls:

> just as many of the painters of the Surrealist Group became fascinated with bio-morphic forms, so the English 'neo-Surrealist' writers tended to find their materials in 'nature' rather than in the modern, urban scene.[13]

With regard to the specific flotsam of the tideline, Roberts was not alone in being shaped by the complex contingency of what might (or might not) get washed up, but the spectrum of writers who were affected reaches far beyond the diffusion of surrealism.

Before he became a celebrated naturalist, Gavin Maxwell spent his Second World War as a soldier – firstly in London (commanding an anti-paratroop flying column in the Blitz) and then as an instructor training commandos in western Scotland, mixing proximity to death with the aesthetic possibilities offered to him by unrestricted warfare. Postwar he readjusted to civilian life by trying to set up a whaling station on the island of Soay in the Hebrides, part of an ill-begotten plan to slaughter basking sharks (*Cetorhinus maximus*) for their oil-rich livers. There is a hidden history of shell shock here; for even the authorized, and thus highly selective, biography of Maxwell makes clear that the shark fishing was pursued as a mode of (unconscious) self-medication. Maxwell's army medical notes from 1944 are direct: Dr James McDougal, the special operations executive medical officer at Arisaig, categorized him as a 'creative psychopath'.[14] Hunting sharks was a disaster personally and financially – but while doing so he had a telling experience on the shoreline in 1946, recounted in his exculpatory *Harpoon at a Venture* (1952). For his attempts to forage among the debris of the tideline became a way of seeing the chaos of war spread out and invitingly arrayed:

> after five years of sea war some of the lonelier bays had begun to look like Canadian logging rivers. [. . .] We picked our way through that fantastic litter on the tide-line as one might explore the rubble of some recently ruined city. There were ship's rafts, tanks of high-octane fuel, bales of raw rubber, great hunks of tallow, R.A.F. rubber dinghies, lifebelts – and timber, timber everywhere, like a fallen forest.[15]

To walk among such 'fantastic litter' is akin to entering a 'recently ruined city' – such as the Blitzed London he had escaped from – but this tide-line gives Maxwell materials to make his jetty and a factory, while it simultaneously tells a disordered story of unseen Atlantic battles. Such a mix of disjointed history and brutally contingent salvage value required Maxwell to concentrate hard, and quickly tow the recovered wood he wanted to Soay for his putative shark-oil factory. Yet the entire shark fishing is, as he admits retrospectively, a continuation of the war by other means (and so the quotidian reality of peacetime after demobilization does not have to be faced). However the act of attempting salvage on the tide-line shows that the shape of this continuing (inescapable) war, visible in the entropic randomness of the flotsam and debris, might not be something under your own control.

Louis MacNeice takes a rather different tone – this is his bleakly accurate observation, at the close of his poem 'Neutrality' (1942):

> But then look eastward from your heart, there bulks
> A continent, close, dark, as archetypal sin,
> While to the west off your own shores the mackerel
> Are fat – on the flesh of your kin.[16]

This is a commentary on the wartime political positioning of 'that neutral island' – Ireland – but also on the salient fact that the western coasts of the counties of Kerry, Mayo, Galway and Donegal were littered with drowned bodies throughout, and well after, the war.[17] Perhaps the most poignant part of William Golding's novel *Pincher Martin* (1956) is the initially infuriating plot twist in its final pages. After more than 100 pages of delusional visions that a shipwrecked survivor – Martin – has had on a Rockall-like rocky islet we get a denunciation, one which brutally undercuts most of the accumulated narrative – and with it all ideas of conventional temporality. A Royal Navy captain has the grim task of recovering bodies from somewhere on the west coast of Ireland:

'If you're worried about Martin – whether he suffered or not – '
They paused for a while. Beyond the drifter the sun sank like a burning ship, went down, left nothing for a reminder but clouds like smoke.
Mr Campbell sighed.
'Aye,' he said, 'I meant just that.'
'Then don't worry about him. You saw the body. He didn't even have time to kick off his seaboots.'[18]

Roberts never recovered, as far the journals tell us, anything quite so horrific from the estuaries of the Tywi and the Taf. The corporeal remains of war that she did encounter, notably the dead pilot who fell in his crumpled aircraft (*DLR*, 46), came from the air, and much of the critical work on Roberts as a war writer has, so far, been mainly based upon her responses to Blitzed cities – notably London and Swansea.

Yet Roberts's poetic response to the bombing of London – and of what she found in the aftermath of the raids – was recollected not in tranquility but in another, also war-marked, terrain: the landscape and coastline around Llanybri. In her diary for 12 June 1942, while in Llanybri, Roberts attempts to marshal her memories of the different encounters she had had over the past two years of the war, and to acknowledge the fragmentary nature of such remembrance: 'At unexpected moments, when I was working in the cottage, washing, or out in the garden, I would remember odd experiences of a closer war that I had encountered' (*DLR*, 45). Her key list of incidents includes visits to where Rhys was stationed on the east coast of England, the duration of raids, and memories of recovering bodies after an air crash. Yet her writing of poems about London is fundamentally shaped by the very distance back to Llanybri, geographically and temporally, and how such distancing both frames and intensifies experience. In Roberts's poem 'The Temple Road', written two years after a trip through bombed London, the action of memory is reawakened by the mundanity of the paint-stripping of a door. The smell of paint melting under the blowtorch then transports her from the village back into London. Sense memory unlocks a causal chain:

> There was a carpenter at my door,
> And the smell and the sound of the paint blew into
> My nostrils and ears, and gathered
> My thoughts, as I looked out of the window

> With my hands warm among the washing socks
> To the wet earth sodden with too much water
> And the green plants persisting
> Among the cavernous ruins.
> And this I remembered.
> [. . .]
> A week's devastation melted half the
> Block with the fury of rising flame-throwers.
> Then to Pimlico where I took the bus . . .
> I found warm flesh charred . . . (*CP*, 98)

It shows a scale-disregarding aesthetic that is also to be found in her prose fragment 'Swansea Raid', but one which here acts to unlock, through one specific recollection, other memories that had been repressed. Other poems, such as 'Crossed and Uncrossed', a response to visiting London in 1942 with Celia Buckmaster after a bombing raid (*CP*, 20–1), also shows a moment where sensory experience becomes frighteningly rapacious – and can lead back from London to a village where the tactile and olfactory signals of war were apparently more quotidian and unthreatening. Yet 'Crossed and Uncrossed' is also an attempt to find a point of organicist and pensive stasis, through simplicity of observation, that can act as a vantage point. This becomes clear in her telling post-raid memory of this trip, as recorded in her diary after the fires had been extinguished. It is especially fixated upon the sight of '[t]he Round Church wet and empty like a grotesque seashell' (*DLR*, 46). Amid rubble and burning libraries, debris and apparitions, the 'shell' of the church both invites attention, and offers a way of hearing something that is no longer there. Similarly, the apocalyptic poet and theorist J. F. Hendry's contemporaneous poem 'London before Invasion, 1940' opens with sculptural ruins in the aftermath of attack:

> Walls and buildings stand here still, like shells,
> Hold them to your ear. There are no echoes even
> Of the seas that once were. That tide is out
> Beyond the valleys and hills.[19]

Here, amid the morose persistence of the destroyed city, is a scale-disregarding injunction for attention – 'Hold them to your ear' – as shells of habitations are rendered into sea shells. Yet it is fruitless; the poet can no more know history, or connect with other wraiths in the city from before the bombing, than he can glimpse the Mesozoic sea that once covered the site of London; 'that tide' of war has left them stranded. For both Hendry and Roberts the 'shell' is both absence and possible aural potential, a starting place for an art of transformative imagining.

Roberts's best known piece of directly reportage-based wartime writing is the single page prose account 'Swansea Raid' (*DLR*, 103). This depicts the Luftwaffe attacks on Swansea that continued, as *Gods* notes, over the nights of 19–21 February 1941. At less than 200 words long, it is a virtuoso piece of poetic prose, first published in 1941, and then revised for inclusion in *An Introduction to Village Dialect With Seven Stories* (1944). The wreckage of the Swansea raid is not the flotsam-like debris, recollected from a distance, which shaped Roberts's poems from and about London. Rather, the vision of Swansea aflame after the attack is predicated on the viewer's distance and state of non-threatened (though empathetic) observation; very much like that at the start of *Gods* (quoted in the opening of this chapter): the scene is spread out below and before Roberts's vantage point for contemplation. And it is moreover a scene of the (wider) shoreline, the exact feature that the bombers needed to navigate by, as she expressly notes: 'from our high village overlooking the Towy we can see straight down the South Wales Coast.' (*DLR*, 103) Thus, as the bombs fall it matters that she chooses a specific verb, these '[h]igh explosives splash up blue, white, and green.' (*DLR*, 103) It opens as the heroine, self-alienating through her wartime identity number, stands watching the bombs fall on the distant city:

> Every searchlight goes up. A glade of magnesium waning to a distant hill that we know to be Swansea.
> Swansea's sure to be bad. Look at those flares like a swarm of orange bees.
> They fade and others return. A collyrium sky, chemically washed $Cu.DH_2$. A blasting flash impels Swansea to riot! (*DLR*, 103)

This is not the understanding of hollowed-out debris through carapaces of potentiality, as with the shells. Rather, this is the use of Llanybri as a vantage point for a terrifying vision, one that cannot be contained or mediated through a talismanic object such as a shell, or the combination of distance plus time. Thus, the estuary gave Roberts an aquatic connection to infinite otherness; leading to an Atlantic that stretched all the way back to her childhood home in Argentina, an ocean encompassing naval battles with its sea lanes allowing the continued survival of Britain.

Yet at the same time, against such geopolitical conflict on the vastest scale, the local and particular immediacy of the estuary – and especially its rich bird-life – made itself present in her work. Roberts studied the birds of the estuary at close hand during the war, as both living and dead subjects, as her diary entry for 15 July 1941 records:

> Today's moorhen. There was an agreement between us that if every [time] Arthur Davies shot any out-of-the-way birds by mistake, he would first bring it to me, so that I might make a study of the bird's plumage and characteristics at close quarters. This has been invaluable to me, for not only have I been able to study the change of plumage at different times of the year, but equally important to me, to know the taste of its flesh. I daresay some naturalists would squirm at this, but I believe them to be wrong in their judgment. (*DLR*, 37)

The following pages of Roberts's journal recount in detail her responses to the textures and colours of the feathers and entrails of that moorhen, but also of oystercatchers and curlews, water rails and seagulls. In this mode of visceral and detailed description, Roberts can be compared to other modern poets who took ornithology, and a reflexivity about the act of observation, as a starting point for literary creation. Roberts's approach is an antecedent to later writers such as the poet-naturalist Colin Simms, whose lifetime tracking of birds of prey in the field and in poetry resulted in *Hen Harrier Poems* (2015), a volume that followed on from his other species or genus-focused collections. Or, in a more specifically Welsh context, Roberts's interest in the birds of the estuary and marsh can be counterpointed to that in the mid to late works of the poet R. S. Thomas, works partly stimulated through Thomas's enduring friendship with the naturalist William Condry – with whom he undertook various ornithological expeditions.[20]

The lyric poems composed by Roberts during the war returned repeatedly to multiple species of (mainly wading) birds, and their habitat in the estuary. In her brief lyric 'Curlew' (*CP*, 15), a modified villanelle, the 'haunting' of the curlew is both a result of its actual imprisonment for study in her house – but also its mythic role as harbinger of death, a role that poets, especially Irish poets from Yeats to Seamus Heaney, have long explored. Roberts opens her poem:

> A curlew hovers and haunts the room
> On bare boards creak its filleted feet:
> For freedom intones four notes of doom,
>
> *Crept, slept, wept, kept*, under aerial gloom:
> With Europe restless in his wing beat,
> A curlew hovers and haunts the room. (*CP*, 15)

This is a bird that, while imprisoned, brings its 'notes of doom' – which are listened to, and interpreted, as past participles of quotidian action – and even italicized for stress. But from such notes an empathy – or communion – of sorts follows; from the particular sounds of a frightened and muddy bird to the totality of 'Europe restless in his wing beat'. No wonder that, in a later stanza, the bird is 'seeking mudsilt retreat' – the internal rhyme both stopping the continual flow of interpretation and placing the bird as other – wanting (needing?) to flee. Indeed the 'desolate phantom', as it becomes finally, is allowed to escape from the window. But the last stanza gives the lasting effect of its visitation – a ghostly presence of a curlew still 'hovers and haunts the room'. Roberts's then-husband, Keidrych Rhys, was also responding in the 1940s to the specific mystique and cultural resonances that this bird brought in its wake. But his poem 'The Curlew', a rough translation of R. Williams Parry's Welsh original, resolves away from the estuary to 'clouds, winds [and . . .] / level summer pastures of heaven'.[21] There is no such teleology possible with Roberts: the curlew is here as a warning – analogous to its own actions along the 'mudsilt' of estuary in time with the tides – of recurrence and inescapability, principles of a world beyond the apparently totalizing human conflict. In Roberts's 'Poem' – a work later reused as part of *Gods with Stainless Ears* – the mode of listing from the diary migrates into the artwork, with the vocative urgency of a persona hitting against industrial modernity and the stasis of domesticity in wartime; but beyond such aspects the 'whimbrels, redshanks, sandpipers ripple' (*CP*, 13), connecting the estuary to the world.

Connections triggered by observations can move inward into the mind as well as outward into the littoral estuary. Despite its title, 'Low Tide' (*CP*, 5–6) is not a poem that derives its potency from descriptive exactitude about tidal states; rather the tide becomes a way of knowing emotion – of absence. In this work the birds *as* birds are absent; but rather what matters is the inability of human actions to make sense of an estuarine landscape in their absence. It opens with the landscape standing in as a protagonist, selfhood diffused, and then moves to position experience spatially:

> Every waiting moment is a fold of sorrow
> Pierced within the heart.
> Pieces of mind get torn off emotionally,
> In large wisps
> Like a waif I lie, stillbound to action:
> Each waiting hour I stare and see not,
> Hum and hear not, nor, care I how long
> The lode mood lasts. (*CP*, 5–6)

This is a setting of uncertain selfhood, initially lifting away from human form, as flotsam itself; with the low tide therefore being that which both strands and reveals, allowing vulnerability to predominate. Despite a reversion to the corporeal, with a containable self by the close, the separation of the protagonist from her lover 'by the salt bar' (being both tears and the sea) is still better than the climactic claustrophobia of 'hearts . . . in clocktight rooms, / Ill found. Unused' (*CP*, 6). Such doubt over knowing and not knowing within a landscape also animates the short dialogue poem 'The Circle of C'. Here the setting is one of potentiality and gnostic menace, with a touch of Gothic (sub-Eliotic nightmare), as the persona walks amid 'cinder bats' to Cwmcelyn to ask for some kind of Delphic answer. The reply, riddle-strewn with organic menace and chemical compounds, does not satisfy: 'But what of my love I cried / As a curlew stabbed the sand' (*CP*, 7).

It is through such observational particularities that another link can be made between Roberts and the Mass Observation movement, for as has been noted she knew several of the key figures involved.[22] Mass Observation, founded in 1937 by the anthropologist Tom Harrisson, poet Charles Madge and filmmaker Humphrey Jennings, aimed through surveys and diaries to turn anthropological methods upon British culture. But its aims were never merely quantitative, and over recent years critics have come to see it as central to the changing development of a late modernist aesthetic in British culture across genres. Roberts's work lies askew to how MO has generally been seen to have impacted, for her writing is not, in the main, an uncovering of the strangeness of the collective unconscious; rather the connection comes directly in her sharp-eyed, autoethnographic, view of her surroundings – from her poems to the short stories in *Village Dialect*. For it is her method that is akin to the one encouraged by MO, a mode that Julian Huxley himself associated with 'bird-watching and natural history observation'.[23] In 'A Letter to the Dead', a recently rediscovered poem written following the death of Dylan Thomas, Roberts depicts herself as others – including Thomas – potentially saw her:

> Was I the 'Bird woman' then? 'What bird is that?' you would say,
> 'And that? And that?' impetuously as they trilled and winged away
> Sound and feather out of sight. It was on a cliff overlooking
> Your Boathouse remember? Whimbrel, sandpiper and curlew I replied
> And marveled that you did not know. *'I want to know about birds?'*
> Was your repeated reply. Then rising out of that flowing Bay
> Seven years later, the birds *yours*, were lifted on to the page,
> Recreated, made new, with us for ever.[24]

This poem offers self-narration, exploring how others might see her – even to the point where, as 'the "Bird woman"' she occupies a role as demi-human, becoming her own object of avian study. Moreover, the text is overtly placed as well as dated on the typescript – '12 February 1954; Laugharne and Llanybri, Taf Carmarthen Bay'.[25] It is thus of, as well as about, this particular tidal zone, the 'heron Priested shore' in Thomas's words, reclaiming it from the better-known poet who had put his imprimatur on the cultural cartography of this specific part of Wales.[26]

Gods not only opens with the bay as a landform – but with the active life (especially the avian life) of the bay. These are the first two stanzas of Part I of the poem, and they situate the work as depicting cyclical continuance – with everything encompassed by 'the same tide', while simultaneously showing change, novelty and rupture, glimpsed especially sharply in the verbs:

> Today the same tide leans back, blue rinsing bay,
> With new beaks scissoring the air, a care-away
> Cadence of sight and sound, poets and men
> Rediscovering them. Saline mud
> Siltering, wet with marshpinks, fresh as lime stud
>
> Whitening fields, gulls and stones attending them;
> Curlews disputing coverts pipe back: stem

> Plaintive legs deep in the ironing edge, that
> Outshines the shale, a railway line washed flat,
> Or tin splintered from a crab-green cave. (*CP*, 44)

Nigel Wheale reads this virtuosic depiction of sensations and juxtapositions as a form of 'ekphrasis – verbal painting – of the locality'.[27] This passage is indeed filled with colour and fine detail, as well as shifting points of perspective. But it is important to counterpoint this insight with Roberts's resolute interest in the tactile materiality of that which is encountered – especially in the blunt facts of matter. For instance, it is significant that the mud is 'siltering' (a rare active verb form of the silting process); the curlew is positioned vertically in the mudbanks; and against all this in the foreground the railway line across the estuary (which borders the Afon Tywi from Ferryside upstream to Carmarthen) appears initially washed flat by perspective. Together such a plethora of textured layers gives a scene that changes in depth depending on the viewer's focus – but which also, in a practical and cartographic sense, depicts a locale remade twice a day by the rising and falling of the tides. Indeed, later in *Gods* the natural world's generative ability to make art, or at least artful potential in material chaos, is glimpsed through analogy – and it is an analogy concerning depth *perception*. For the lines 'In such radium / Activity – white starlings – suspended / On string like Calder "stills"' (*CP*, 66) show how the isolation of the material object, in this case in Alexander Calder's contemporary mobiles – and not the painterly eye – might be the model for arranging the scene. Roberts here is offering an estrangement where the non-human, the object itself, might become central to organizing the appreciation of a landscape/seascape.

Such visionary (aquatic or estuarine) possibilities expressed in 'cadence of sight and sound' are counterpointed with the landlocked, human-scale routines of wartime domesticity and poverty later in Part I of the poem: 'When daily the water trudge with battering can, / Striding out of snail from sprockets of kale' (*CP*, 47). Even the recuperative visionary ending of the section cannot overturn the dichotomy, and the sea as a connective agent to 'groves of foreign / Glitter' is met with a riposte, acknowledging that the trapped nature of island life in wartime Britain can be seen in the light of both a translucent 'water mosaic of running tides' but also the 'mawkish / Litter' of wartime culture (*CP*, 51).

The possibility of art from such debris or 'litter' is a ghost somewhere in the poem behind the overt poetic narrative of the gunner and his girl in wartime. For even if the litter thrown up here by the 'running tides' is ultimately merely 'mawkish', it is coming from a 'mosaic' of experience and material matter where the juxtapositions are the revelatory acts; indeed, use of such fragmented resources might be *the* condition for an authentic art in wartime, as bomb blast actuality caught up with the preceding decade's surrealist visions of fragmentation. Such a position was common within British wartime culture, from the photographs of Lee Miller to Inez Holden's knowing aside in her novel, *It Was Different at the Time* (1943):

> One morning I walked back through the park, and saw the highest branches of a tree draped with marabout, with some sort of silk, with two or three odd stockings [and] . . . balanced on a twig was a brand new bowler hat. They had all been blown across the street from the bombed hotel opposite. A Surrealist painter who I knew slightly was staring at this, too. He said: 'Of course we were painting this kind of thing years ago, but it has taken some time to get here.'[28]

In Roberts's work, other aspects of fragmentation and partiality have also taken 'some time' to be washed up in west Wales, notably that most talismanic sound source from 'The Waste Land': the gramophone. For the 'Argument' for Part II of *Gods* opens with all natural sound – even the sound of the estuary – being juxtaposed with that most modernist piece of sonic apparatus: 'By the tidal lapping of the water a gramophone remains as the only symbol of a lost airman' (*CP*, 52). This piece of technical machinery, which allows the playing of repeatable records, is set against the continuing and unique contingency of what the bay might (or might not) reveal through sound. Such a dichotomy is intensified in the body of Part II. The vocative cry 'We must upprise O my people' (*CP*, 53) is met with a stanza giving the current situation, and opening with another command:

> Bring plimsole plover to the tensile sand
> And with cuprite crest and petulant feet
> Distil our notes into febrile weeds
> Crisply starched at the water-rail of tides:
> On gault and green stone a gramophone stands. (*CP*, 53)

This stanza has the water birds present – the plover and the water rail – but it also is a reimagining of the birds, the dark blue and black of the plover becoming shoe-like, and the water rail being the species of bird itself (*Rallus aquaticus*); and yet it is also, through the positional proposition 'at', the delineation of the boundary the marshy tideline – which forms the habitat of this bird in the debatable estuarine zone. Whatever 'notes' that can be summoned and distilled will not only be stretched but also delivered to this barrier or line of the tides.

Yet apparently emanating from the totemically placed gramophone (on its rock pedestal) are the dread tones of industrial modernity – 'saxophone towns brass out the dead' (*CP*, 53). Then against such noise the sounds continue, rather plaintively, across the bay of the birds and others. There are 'the water-cats' and the 'square slate notes'; and then the continued hymn to the avian (previously seen in 'Poem') as the counter-melody to war that stretches across two stanzas:

> wind sound
> Singular into cool and simple corners
> Round pale bittern grass and all unseen
> Unknown places of sheltered rubble
>
> Where whimbrels, redshanks, sandpipers ripple
> For the wing of living. (*CP*, 53)

Amid hints of the inescapable bombsites in the 'rubble' this passage features sound being controlled and shaped (and becoming malleable itself by such actions). This might also be the sound of the wind itself blowing, but Roberts's formulation does not settle for either aspect. Indeed, the potentiality of change comes in movements that rely upon raising or bringing as many questions as answers, whether following that 'striped rhizome cat' (*CP*, 57) or, later, the 'Marine butterflies' (*CP*, 63).

Part III of the poem offers abstraction and the freezing of time (and tide) into something beautifully petrified: '[t]he bay crystallised' (*CP*, 56); and then Part V lifts the central, semi-autobiographical, couple – the soldier and the woman – out of the bay entirely. By Part V the bay is remade into a glassy, filmic screen for the projection of an interstellar voyage, the ascension up through the 'trauma stratus' (*CP*, 65) as the science-fiction side of the poem's aeriality comes to dominate. What Roberts sees is 'the bay transformed' and then, as the couple descend from their orbital if elliptical voyage, they encounter it again:

> Salt spring from frosted sea filters palea light
> Raising tangerine and hard line of rind on the
> Astringent sky. Catoptric on waterice he of deep love
> Frees dragon from the glacier glade
> Sights death fading into chilblain ears. (*CP*, 69)

Such is the ending of the poem; it is replete with the by now familiar mixture of complex grammatical forms, mythological resonances, intense emotional gestures but shadowy individuals, and a sensual and unusual lexical set (such as 'palea': the botanical and technical term for chaff; 'catoptric': relating to mirrors and reflections).[29] But it is also the moment where the poem comes back down to earth – or rather to water. The frosted sea and the icy sheen should not disguise that at the end of such exploring we will arrive where we started and yet we might know the place for the first time. For the bay, now in this 'astringent' light of postwar modernity, has been transformed; but it has also played its part in transforming the protagonist and what her version of art – and life – might be now '*today which is tomorrow*' (*CP*, 69).

Part of the transformation has come with this acknowledgement of the passage of time – but part, a significant part, has come because this is a work shaped by two – conflicting – ways of understanding the specific geographical position of the bay – and the forces within it. For this is a poem that is interested in both tidal inevitability and the contingency of the debris of the tideline. The tide itself is the force that both drags out, and pulls in, all that debris and assorted traces, and some of this flotsam, partly linguistically and partly sonically, carries the marks of war and modernity. The tides therefore themselves hold entropy and cyclical certainty in perpetual tension: further it places human agency in discovery and arrangement of fragments in tension with forces beyond human control. For the tides are generated far beyond the earth – by the moon that is visited by the central couple in Part V of the poem. Thus Roberts's estuarine war writing, when taken in totality, can be located at such a confluence of both a tidal-based and a flotsam-filled way of thinking (and writing), differing models but both requiring attentiveness to texture and a willingness to countenance non-linearity in composition. Yet such a confluence of these models is itself a fundamentally unstable position, with individual words 'adrift' beyond any protagonist's apprehension and structure appearing overtly as imposed artifice.

So, behind (or beneath) these two differing aspects – of alluring flotsam and tidal forces – that shape Roberts's estuarine war writing there is still something else. The fears that grow through *Gods* are still fears of the writeable, and the narratable; Roberts has a trust that communicative language, even if needing an esoteric vocabulary and a disorientating grammar, can still work to capture sensations and fears. Yet what water also brings – over a geological time frame – is the potentiality for extinction, a *longue durée* where language, and the coastline, might become utterly different. Such awareness is potent, and Roberts's knowledge that these processes had happened before seems to suggest implicitly that it might occur again. Indeed, her diary from August 1942 shows this being rendered into physicality – with the example of a shell, not now as comparator of blitzed buildings on bomb sites but rather as a missive and a fragile testimony. The diary shows her finding an explanation for the abundance of the aquatic periwinkle, 'transparent pale pink snail shells lying among the hedges', around Llanybri:

> [t]he frequency with which these pink shells can be found among the Spring violets and primroses can mean but one thing; that at one time the sea must have covered this particular part of the valley and had since withdrawn. (*DLR*, 60)

The decisive calmness of this observation needs perhaps to be set against the apocalyptic vision in Roberts's poem 'Fifth of the Strata'. For the aquatic here in Roberts also brings the potential for a total remaking of the land itself, a reordering of that which is certain – whether politically or geographically.[30] In this poem the vision seems proleptically, terrifyingly, modern – a way of seeing how the trauma of the Second World War might allow other, even more totalizing traumas (of climate change in our contemporary readings) to be imagined upon knowable topography:

> And the sea will insist
> Persuade a path to follow,
> Longs eagerly to cover

> The green valley pastures:
> To flow forward along
> The sunken ribbed coomb
> And dry river-bed . . . endlessly.
> And it will succeed
> Tomorrow follow
> All gravel roads
> And rise slowly around
> The Dragon's scaled Fort;
> To leave nothing of Wales
> But white island shining
> The crest of Snowdon
> Glittering with dark wintry-ice. (*CP*, 17)

The politics of helplessness before inundation, and the inundation of politics by rising tides seem to make this an uncomfortably prescient poem for the contemporary reader. Such an apparently proleptic vision is made possible by the stimulus of the specific locale and ecosystem. If Roberts is to be studied and enjoyed by readers now, and understood as central to Welsh modernism, it is important to acknowledge such cartographic precision: the sweep of the two tidal estuaries of the Tywi and the Taf as they flow into bae Caerfyrddin (Carmarthen bay). This specific place, from which her war writing emerged, is by its nature not a simple or static landscape, but *because* of this complexity it allowed for a way of thinking about nature-through-war (and war-through-nature), one unmatched in any other comparable poet, in an oeuvre of works that remain uniquely beautiful and terrifying.

Notes

[1] Lynette Roberts, *Collected Poems*, ed. Patrick McGuiness (Manchester: Carcanet, 2005), p. 57. All further references to this volume will be given in the text as *CP*.
[2] See, for example, in terms of modernism, John Goodby and Chris Wigginton, 'Welsh Modernist Poetry: Dylan Thomas, David Jones, and Lynette Roberts', in *Regional Modernisms*, ed. Neal Alexander and James Moran (Edinburgh: Edinburgh University Press, 2013), pp. 160–83. To help understand the aesthetic possibilities inherent in Roberts's work as historically contingent see Charles Mundye, 'Outside the Imaginary Museum: Mythology and Representation in the Poetry of Lynette Roberts and Keidrych Rhys', *PN Review*, 40/2 (2013), 23–8; and to appreciate her prosody and complexity see

John Wilkinson's essays on Roberts collected as two chapters, 'Frostwork and The Mud Vision' and 'The Water-Rail of Tides', in his *The Lyric Touch: Essays on the Poetry of Excess* (Cambridge: Salt, 2007).

3 Patrick McGuinness, 'Introduction' to Lynette Roberts, *Diaries, Letters and Recollections* (Manchester: Carcanet, 2008), p. xv. All further references to this volume will be given in the text as *DLR*.

4 The complexity of Roberts's position as a war poet has been acknowledged in some work, notably my own *Reading the Ruins: Modernism, Bombsites and British Culture* (Cambridge: Cambridge University Press, 2011), pp. 109–15. See also Anthony Conran, 'Lynette Roberts: War Poet', *Anglo-Welsh Review*, 65 (1979), 50–62, also published in *The Cost of Strangeness: Essays on the English Poets of Wales* (Llandysul: Gomer, 1982), and Nigel Wheale, 'Lynette Roberts: Legend and Form in the 1940s', *Critical Quarterly*, 36/3 (1994), 4–19.

5 For biographical details see McGuinness's 'Introduction' to the *Collected Poems*, p. xiii.

6 This chapter can be usefully read in conjunction with the Ordnance Survey map of the area at 1:25,000 scale, number 177 (Explorer series).

7 Hayden Lorimer, 'Poetry and Place: the Shape of Words', *Geography*, 93/3 (2008), 181, cited in 'Introduction: Poetry & Geography', in *Poetry and Geography: Space and Place in Postwar Poetry*, ed. Neal Alexander and David Cooper (Liverpool: Liverpool University Press, 2013), pp. 4–5.

8 See, for example, John Kerrigan, 'Louis MacNeice among the Islands', in *Modern Irish and Scottish Poetry*, ed. Fran Brearton, Edna Longley and Peter Mackay (Cambridge: Cambridge University Press, 2010), pp. 58–86.

9 For a vast but nuanced overview of islands in (mainly Western) culture see Marc Shell, *Islandology: Geography, Rhetoric, Politics* (London: Stanford University Press, 2014).

10 See Hugh Aldersey-Williams, *Tide: The Science and Lore of the Greatest Force on Earth* (London: Viking, 2016), pp. 201–5.

11 The date of the diary entry quoted – 17 August 1942 – happens to have been a significant turning point in the war, for in the mid-afternoon the first raid by US aircraft was made on a European target. Eighteen B-17 Flying Fortress bombers, based at RAF Polebrook, attacked the marshalling yards at Rouen-Sotteville, France.

12 See David Mellor (ed.), *A Paradise Lost: The Neo-Romantic Imagination in Britain, 1935–55* (London: Lund Humphries, 1987).

13 Peter Nicholls, 'Surrealism in England', in *The Cambridge History of Twentieth-Century English Literature*, ed. Laura Marcus and Peter Nicholls (Cambridge: Cambridge University Press, 2005), pp. 396–416 (p. 414).

14 Douglas Botting, *Gavin Maxwell: A Life* (London: Harper Collins, 1991), p. 57.

15 Gavin Maxwell, *Harpoon at a Venture* (London: Rupert Hart-Davies, 1952), pp. 50–1.

16 Louis MacNeice, *Collected Poems*, ed. E. R. Dodds (Oxford: Oxford University Press, 1967), p. 202.

17 See Claire Wills, *That Neutral Island: A Cultural History of Ireland during World War II* (London: Faber, 2008), pp. 128–9.

18 William Golding, *Pincher Martin* (London: Faber, 1956), pp. 223–4.

[19] Collected in *The White Horseman*, ed. J. F. Hendry and Henry Treece (London: Routledge, 1941), p. 60.
[20] Letters between Thomas and Condry are part of the Condry collection, National Library of Wales, GB 0210 WMCOND.
[21] Keidrych Rhys, *The Van Pool: Collected Poems*, ed. Charles Mundye (Bridgend: Seren, 2012), p. 158.
[22] See McGuinness, 'Introduction', in *Diaries, Letters and Recollections*, p. xv.
[23] Julian Huxley, 'Forward', *Mass Observation* (London: Fredrick Muller, 1937), p. 7.
[24] Lynette Roberts, 'A Letter to the Dead', *PN Review*, 220, 41/2 (2014), 18.
[25] See Charles Mundye, 'Lynette Roberts and Dylan Thomas: Background to a Friendship', *PN Review* 220, 41/2 (2014), 20–3.
[26] Dylan Thomas, 'Poem in October', in the *Dylan Thomas Omnibus: Under Milk Wood, Poems, Stories and Broadcasts* (London: Weidenfeld & Nicolson, 1995), p. 73.
[27] Nigel Wheale, 'Beyond the Trauma Stratus: Lynette Roberts' *Gods with Stainless Ears* and the Post-war Cultural Landscape', *Welsh Writing in English: A Yearbook of Critical Essays*, 3 (1997), 98–117 (103).
[28] Cited in Mellor, *Reading the Ruins*, p. 86.
[29] See McGuinness's 'Notes', *Collected Poems*, p. 146.
[30] John Brannigan uses this poem as part of his wider history of how writers have reimagined the topography of the British Isles, through visions of rising seas, for aesthetic or ideological ends. See his *Archipelagic Modernism* (Edinburgh: Edinburgh University Press, 2015), p. 3.

8

LISTENING AND LOCATION
IN THE POETRY OF LYNETTE ROBERTS

Zoë Skoulding

The poems of Lynette Roberts demand concentrated listening as much as they describe her listening to environmental sound, particularly of war, of birds and the bilingual everyday speech of Llanybri, the small village in west Wales where she lived as an outsider with a limited knowledge of Welsh. Roberts's work encodes a lived context in which a new malleability of sound derived from film and radio occasioned a reflexive awareness of the listener's role as well as sharpened attention to the sounded quality of landscape. Roberts is equally interested in the poetic and musical traditions that surround her in Welsh culture, though she hears them as new and unfamiliar: hers is, as Patrick McGuinness writes, 'the modernism of anticipation, not nostalgia'.[1] The renewal of perception associated with modernist practice may be considered from an ecological perspective since, as Eric F. Clarke comments, '[i]n ecological theory, perception and meaning are closely related. When people perceive what is happening around them, they are trying to understand, and adapt to, what is going on'.[2] Meaning in an ecological sense is actively constructed in that adapting to 'what is going on' is part of a dynamic relationship with the exterior world. The premise of this chapter is that paying attention to Roberts's listening can reveal the processes of adaptation that take place in and through her work, and can inform us about the environment to which she is adapting. It is an environment contoured by non-human, cultural and political factors, all of which are manifested through sound and in turn influence the sound of Roberts's own poems.

Rather than using deliberate techniques of estrangement, Roberts's work may instead be viewed as an effort to adapt to relatively unfamiliar conditions, the senses brought into play to explore changing environments, whether non-human, cultural or political, or all of those things simultaneously. By focusing often on sound, Roberts brings listening to the fore in the sense described by Jean-Luc Nancy, for whom '[t]o be listening is always to be on the edge of meaning', as attention strains towards what is not, or not yet, fully understood.[3] Because it takes place over time, listening has a relationship with the future, operating in the area of the unknown rather than the already assimilated, the futures to which Roberts attends including the postwar technological age as well as the future nation of Wales, particularly in Part V of her major modernist poem *Gods with Stainless Ears*.[4] It is this emphasis on deciphering the present and future that distinguishes Roberts's work from a dominant strain of Welsh writing in English that has tended to highlight the rural past, particularly under the influence of R. S. Thomas, in a tradition that has obscured her reputation.

In highlighting the ecological and acoustic dimensions of Roberts's poetry, I am not suggesting that it gives us any kind of privileged access to the 'voice' of the natural world; Jonathan Bate, for example, has argued that the role of the poet is 'to determine whether the earth will sing or be silent'.[5] However, like Matthew Jarvis, I see

> manifest problems . . . with the sense that poetry should be tied to a particular programme . . . and the rhetorical attempt to align a linguistic art form with non-human sounds by calling the latter 'earth's own poetry' in an apparent effort to claim poetry as the primary cultural mode in which the earth can be remembered.[6]

A further problem arises in a bilingual context such as Wales where the earth might be expected to sing in one language or another, thereby underpinning nationhood as in some sense 'natural'. Turning away from critical schema of these kinds, this chapter is concerned with the ways in which language and perception are situated in Roberts's work, and how they in turn situate the reader as attention is constantly drawn to sounds in the landscape and to the unfamiliar sounds at the borders of cohabiting sounds and languages. Sometimes perception of the physical environment seems to be very directly represented, for example in onomatopoeic references to bird calls, but the dense surfaces of Roberts's poems, where her English is often inflected by Welsh, scientific vocabulary and unexpectedly futuristic or archaic usages, mean that attention is also drawn to the intricacy of language as a signifying system. It is impossible to separate perceived sound from signification since the two shape each other; in what follows I will be locating Roberts's work, and her view of her environment, through this tension.

Roberts's perception of her environment is neither passive nor static, but an active means of participation in a strengthened awareness of Welsh identity that was emerging during the Second World War. This was articulated by, among others, her husband Keidrych Rhys, whose editorship of *Wales* asserted the distinctiveness of Welsh culture and its independence from England. His project was described in the following terms by Denys Val Baker, quoted by Rhys in his editorial in 1945:

> The revived *Wales*, heralding a Welsh renaissance, re-emphasizes the fact that the war has made the Welsh realise that they are a nation with a country, a people, a culture and a tradition *different* from England's to fight for. There is a new wave of national feeling in our people. While hoping eventually for self-government, Wales is particularly anxious to bring together the divided 'progressive elements' and differing national viewpoints of Wales.[7]

Inhabiting Welsh culture also means inhabiting Wales as a physical space. Baker discusses the impossibility of returning to a pre-war Wales in which national symbols were celebrated but the 'real people' were 'exported like cattle, in their thousands, to England.'[8] He goes on to observe that *Wales* under Rhys's editorship, by contrast, calls for writers and artists to 'tramp up and down their countryside', taking ownership of the physical as well as the symbolic landscape.[9] Inhabiting a place is always of primary importance to Roberts, who writes on the first page of 'A Camarthenshire Diary' that 'Keidrych says I have some funny ideas about poets. I have. I think good real living is more important than spreading yourself on paper', and she goes on to state her wish to be 'just a normal person who can take my full share of responsibility.'[10] For Roberts, this includes a commitment to the practicalities of impoverished village life. It also means living with a language that is not her own, but which defines the diverse culture of a future autonomous Wales by marking its separation from Englishness; listening to the confluence of languages is part of Roberts's 'share of responsibility'.

Roberts brings a sharp and purposeful attention to her quotidian life in rural Wales: in her writing, to inhabit the land in an everyday sense is to construct its potential for political independence. However, in listening to spaces that are culturally and ecologically complex, Roberts creates a basis for imagining a national identity founded not on sameness but on sonic complexity. Sound brings distant events into collision with immediate surroundings: the impact of a world war on local rural life is accentuated in the way her poetry juxtaposes the sound of enemy aircraft with the sounds of birds marking out their own territories independently of human activity, such as 'Curlews disputing coverts' who 'pipe back' on the first page of *Gods with Stainless Ears*.[11] The Welsh-language epigraphs of the same poem likewise make room for difference: the sound of Welsh, whether as a language that Roberts understands imperfectly, or in the way it inflects English, is another recognition of competing territorial claims. By foregrounding the sounds of Welsh and birdsong, Roberts attends to claims on space that might be seen as conflicting with her own predominantly anglophone and human point of view. Listening, then, is a form of attention to otherness that undermines the emphasis on unity and control enforced through military aggression.

The question of territory is addressed in both human and ornithological terms in Roberts's work under a sky resounding with planes, sirens and the calls of birds. These different perspectives produce different forms of listening and subjectivity, as in the following stanzas:

> O the cut of it, woe sharp on the day
> Scaled in blood, the ten-toed woodpecker,
> A dragon of wings 1 6 2 0 B 6
> 4 punctuates machine-gun from the quarry pits:
> Soldiers, tanks, lorry make siege on the bay.
>
> Freedom to boot. CONCLAMATION. COMPUNCTION.
> Kom–pungk'–shun: discomforts of the mind deride
> Their mood. Birds on the stirrups of the waterbride
> Flush up, and out of time a tintinnabulation
> Of voice and feather fall in and out of the ocean sky. (*CP*, 45).

The staccato listing of numbers echoes the machine-gun fire, drawing attention to a situation that is equally threatening to human and non-human inhabitants of the landscape. In his description of this kind of perception, Roland Barthes usefully highlights the shared experience of humans and animals:

> Based on hearing, listening (from an anthropological viewpoint) is the very sense of space and of time, by the perception of degrees of remoteness and of regular returns of phonic stimulus. For the mammal, its territory is marked out by odors and sounds; for the human being – and this is a phenomenon often underestimated – the appropriation of space is also a matter of sound.[12]

For Barthes, territory is the space of potentially threatened safety. The primary form of listening, shared by humans and animals, is alert, focused on interpreting danger and responding to it.[13] It is accompanied in humans by two other forms of listening, the deciphering of signs, and with particular relevance to music, the '*shimmering* of signifiers', in which the listener keeps interpretation in suspension.[14] All three forms of listening are brought into play by the reader, who, like the startled birds, must stay on the alert, since for listening to be activated, sound cannot be fully assimilated to meaning. The deciphering of signs in these stanzas has been discussed by several critics, including John Wilkinson, who remarks how punning, a sonic technique reliant on a shift in signification, 'produces the deeply sardonic "freedom to boot," associating "freedom" with conscription and violence'.[15] Andrew Webb, writing elsewhere in this volume, suggests that 'COMPUNCTION. / Kom–pungk'-shun' is a quotation from Winston Churchill's 1941 speech in County Hall.[16] Its phonetic transcription therefore jolts it out of the logic of signification and into nuances of sound as mediated by film or radio. Midway, the stanza switches to focus on the alarm of birds as they 'Flush up', placing 'discomforts of the mind' between media reportage and disturbance in the natural world (*CP*, 45). Each element, however, is separately sounded and co-existing in the landscape. In the intriguing phrase 'stirrups of the waterbride', sense is led by sound through the pattern of rhyme, which holds attention just long enough for the elements of the image to come together (*CP*, 45). It is possible to read 'waterbride' in association with the legends of Welsh water fairies as documented by Sir John Rhŷs, and 'stirrups' with the white horses of the sea, or foam splashed up by the birds, but because of the emphasis on a sonic pattern ('deride'/'birds'/'bride'), the signifier 'shimmers' in and out of focus rather than delivering an unambiguous sign, leaving a cluster of interpretative possibilities.[17] These instabilities trace Roberts's own activity of perception, through which rural Wales is experienced as militarized and media saturated as well as mythological and ecologically diverse. Her poetry is informed by cultural information like the structure of filmic narrative, as here in its cutting between scenes, but it also mimics birdsong, for example in the relentlessness of 'mind'/'deride'/'bride'/'time'/'sky', in much the same way that birds appear to mimic the sounds of human activity.

In its openness to the multiple external factors that shape our experience of an environment, Roberts's work demonstrates an ecological sensibility in which human and non-human lifeworlds are audibly connected. Drawing on the writings of James Gibson, Eric F. Clarke explains that:

> Rather than considering perception to be a constructive process, in which the perceiver builds structure into an internal model of the world, the ecological approach emphasizes the structure of the environment itself and regards perception as the pick-up of that already structured perceptual information.[18]

This statement has implications for Roberts, who in this view may be seen neither as an autonomous creator nor as the Barthesian scriptor in a purely intertextual landscape, but as an active listener open to a complex world. According to Clarke, 'Perceptual information' includes language because 'for human beings *every* circumstance and experience is cultural'.[19] Adaptation and learning are central to a dynamic process in which 'perceivers pick up information from all parts of the environment – cultural and natural'; perception is never passive, as understanding and perception shape each other.[20] The structural use of sound in the poem creates equivalencies between moments of disjunction and heightened attention that link different aspects of the environment, for example where the movement of the birds as they 'Flush up' is paralleled in that of aircraft:

> Into euclidian cubes grid air is planed.
> Propellers scudding up grit and kerosene, braid
> Hulls waled 5 mile hollow, spidering each man stark

> On steelweb, hammering in rivets ambuscade
> Interrupted by sirens screaming tirade. (*CP*, 47)

Here, the birds are replaced by the mechanical propellers, the alarm of the birds by the alert of sirens. Punning makes the aircraft cut into the 'planed' air. Rhyme, instead of resolving sound, wrenches language into unexpected combinations like the slightly archaic 'ambuscade' and the use of 'tirade', with no article, to turn the siren into an abrupt form of speech as well as giving an echo of its sound. In this abrasive military context, human activity is defamiliarized, fused with metallic surfaces, but remains part of a continuum with the natural world, as in the phrase 'spidering each man stark / On steelweb'.

Roberts was aware, as her prose writings reveal, of the importance of listening in her daily life. The connections that most interest her are the links between movement, music, song and speech, the ways in which these are formed in the context of rural work in a particular environment, and their refraction through literary contexts. In her essay 'An Introduction to Village Dialect', Roberts suggests that the patterns of everyday speech around her are connected with long histories of dance and song, particularly the repetitive structure of the carol or rondel.[21] As McGuinness remarks: 'the article's interest lies less in its factual and scholarly accuracy than in the insights it gives us into Roberts's ideas about spoken and literary language, between ancient forms and current dialect, and about the relationship between past and present.'[22] Another way of putting this would be to say that her observations suggest a highly perceptive and situated response to her lived environment, material and aural, rather than abstracted linguistic knowledge. Her poetry, as a dynamic process, knows more than can be articulated in her poetics, yet her comments on her own work still offer valuable insights into listening. Observing the etymology of *carol* in Old French, where it meant 'to dance in a ring', Roberts links it with a passage by Giraldus from his 1188 *Itinerarium Cambriae* (*The Journey Through Wales*):

> You may see men or girls, now in the church, now in the churchyard, now in the dance, which is led around the churchyard with a song, on a sudden falling on the ground as in a trance, then jumping up in a frenzy, and representing with their hands and feet, whatever work they have unlawfully done on feast days; you may see one man put his hand to the plough, and another, as it were, goad on the oxen, mitigating their sense of labour, by the usual rude song.[23]

As well as mentioning the way in which these rhythms are continued in contemporary work songs, Roberts goes on to note a connection between the circular pattern of the rondel and the repetitions in the speaking patterns around her, such as, for example, these phrases heard in Llanybri: '*Did you hear the* thunder, it was very cold last night. The *thunder* it was terrible. Did you hear the *thunder*, Mrs Davies?'[24] Although she suggests that such idioms may be found across Europe, she compares the speech of Llanybri with specific examples from Gerard Manley Hopkins, Pierre Loti's depiction of Breton, James Joyce and J. M. Synge.[25] While her inclination is to ascribe these similarities to the rhythms of working on the land, a more obvious explanation for the patterns she hears might be the juxtaposition of English with another language, and the influence of Welsh syntax on English, which would have parallels in Breton and Irish contexts.

Although Roberts claims in *Village Dialect* to 'have arrived at the essence of all languages of the soil', this suggests an unproblematic link between language and locale that her poetry interestingly contradicts.[26] Listening, as Eric F. Clarke suggests following Barthes, may present us with language that seems to have 'a fixed character in practice', even though it has evolved as a sign system in arbitrary ways.[27] Roberts's comment on language and soil suggests an essential and non-arbitrary link between language and landscape that does not exist, but might sound as though it does because of language's naturalization in a particular context over time. At the same time, because she is listening simultaneously to Welsh and English as well as to non-human sounds, her own language responds to plurality rather than the singularity of 'essence'. More recent and contrasting articulations of place in Welsh poetry can be illuminating in this respect. Alice Entwistle draws attention to the following passage by Gillian Clarke as typifying the entanglement of place and identity:

> From where I write I see a landscape open like a book, a landscape of valleys and hills typical of the view from the . . . writing desk of many a Welsh writer from any of the seven counties of Wales . . . I can name the fields on my side of the valley, and a few on the other side. Valleys, and a land that is tilted to face its neighbour, make for tight communities and open lives.[28]

Like Roberts, Clarke writes with a close, sensual interest in the landscape she inhabits, and there is a suggestion here that the sloping formation of the land itself contributes to its neighbourliness. This is not a hypothesis that is easily transferable to other contexts (one might consider the hills surrounding Sarajevo, for example), but a wish to locate an intrinsic quality of Welshness in a static understanding of landscape. Entwistle usefully observes that in this passage, Clarke, who was born in Cardiff, is 'a (belated) product of the landscape she constructs from her desk', and that her remarks are 'haunted' by what Jasmine Donahaye identifies as 'uncomfortable questions about essentialism, about "authentic" or legitimate culture, about rights, about ethnicity, language and experience embedded in landscape' stemming from a construction of place 'as a fixture'.[29]

There is a very different process at work in Roberts's poetry, one that emerges when the ear rather than the eye is foregrounded. She may well survey landscape and name the fields of her locality, but she does not read it like the open book that presents itself to Clarke. In the opening of *Gods with Stainless Ears*, she describes 'All this Saint Cadoc's / Estuary: and that bell tolling, Abbey paddock', in a filmic sweep that incorporates sound and movement through its repetitive echo of the bell (*CP*, 44). The sensory richness of the landscape cannot be captured in purely visual language; it demands an auditory and tactile exploration that stretches language's capacity to name, for example 'Saline mud / Siltering, wet with marshpinks', where onomatopoeia makes contextual sense of 'siltering', with its suggestion of silt, filtering and slithering (*CP*, 44). The poem does not assume the comprehensibility of the landscape but approaches it as an unfamiliar space to be explored through language. This lack of familiarity extends to those among whom Roberts lives, and a much edgier form of belonging is signalled, for example, in 'Raw Salt on Eye', which records the wartime villagers' accusations of 'spycraft' against the incomer in their midst.[30]

Locality, for Roberts, is intensified by the co-existence of human and non-human activity as acute attention is given to the confluences of sound and language at a given moment. In 'Curlew', for example, the drama of a bird caught indoors is intensified by the language and sound of war.[31] The remoteness of war is brought close through the exploration of the birdcall and its relation to the 'notes of doom' signalled by aircraft (*CP*, 15). Immediate sense perception of the bird's cry comes simultaneously with the thought of the sky as a zone of international conflict; the two are inseparable, mutually exclusive and oscillating as they are explored through language that is itself part of the sounded environment. With 'Europe restless in his wingbeat', the bird 'Captured, explodes a chill sky croon / *Wail-ing . . . pal-ing*' as its cry blurs into the noise of planes or sirens (*CP*, 15). In ecological terms, the poem links perception and the search for meaning by using the sound of the birdcall as a device to 'translate' and estrange English in the italicized sections such as '*Crept, slept, wept, kept*'. Roberts explains her technique to Robert Graves: 'I tried to use the exact [qualities] of a curlew's call which so often breaks with those 4 shrill notes.' She admits, however, that 'Shagreen bleat is *bad* as you point out. I had in mind the shagreen quality of its legs, the greezing gooseflesh of its voice.'[32] This willingness to accept judgement on her own work points to the dominant aesthetic of the time, a taste for clarity that precluded such a blending of image (the texture of the curlew's legs) and affect (the feeling produced by its cry). What is 'bad' in these terms might also apply to the lines ' . . . *purring burbling trilling soft sweet / Syllables of sinuous sound to a liquid moon*', which echo the typical bubbling sound of a curlew's song to a point that strains 'natural' English expression by making the language seem overloaded (*CP*, 15). The poem may be heard simultaneously in the context of human structures of language, which are foregrounded because they are estranged and thus no longer seem 'natural', and an effort to mediate those structures via the non-human or 'natural' world.

Such observations and comments in Roberts's diaries and letters reveal her writing as part of an intense, continuous and self-conscious activity of perception. Her work might also be considered in the light of Alva Noë's proposition that perception is not passive reception, but that 'we enact the perceptual world by skilful exploration'.[33] Enacting the perceptual world changes our relationship with place, and the actions that are significant here are those that bind Roberts into her locale, and the everyday rural life on which her Welsh identity is founded. In 'Bird Notes' in her diary of 15 July 1941, she records the agreement that

> if ever Arthur Davies shot any out-of-the-way birds by mistake, he would first bring it to me, so that I might make a study of the bird's plumage and characteristics at close quarters. This has been invaluable to me, for not only have I been able to study the change of plumage at different times of the year, but equally important to me, to know the taste of its flesh.[34]

While 'Curlew' places the bird within the sounds of the living environment, the acquisition and consumption of its body as described above places the author within the seasonal patterns and relationships of the rural locale, forming a tight connection between observation, listening, writing and the kind of 'good real living' to which Roberts aspires. The poem is part of a wider exploration of relationships between humans, animals, land and language in which social interaction is part of the sensory knowledge gained.

'Curlew' is structured as a villanelle, a form itself derived from the country dances that intrigue Roberts in her introduction to *Village Dialect*. It is to the villanelle that she also returns in Part I of *Gods with Stainless Ears*, quoted above, in which the lines 'Interrupted by sirens screaming tirade' and 'Into euclidian cubes grid air is planed' are subtly mutated through several repetitions in an echo of this form (*CP*, 47). Her intention, she writes, is to suggest 'Factory hands and repetitive lines' in a pattern adapted from the villanelle to reflect the 'muddled and intense thought' of the first years of the war, before 'clear, cold, and austere sight is regained' (*CP*, 43). The use of the villanelle for 'Curlew' creates the same oppressive intensity, before culminating in the bird's release at the end of the poem:

> Till window, wide, frees thin mails of plume,
> Fluting voice and shade through cloud's moist sleet:
> A curlew hovers and haunts the room. (*CP*, 15)

The final line places the bird back inside the room as a ghost of itself but also as a sonic reverberation: the effect of repetition in the poem is that it continues to repeat in the reader's memory after the poem has ended. It might be considered in the light of Nancy's remark that 'All sonorous presence is . . . made of a complex of returns [*renvois*] whose binding is the resonance or "sonance" of sound', since unlike presence perceived through sight or touch, which is instant and motionless, 'sonorous presence is . . . essentially mobile'. It vibrates 'from the come-and-go between the source and the ear, through open space.'[35] The contours of this space are both physical and cultural, because culture can only be known in its physical manifestations, and indeed culture in Roberts's work is shown to be intimately tied to its physical surroundings. The curlew's cry haunts the same landscape as enemy aircraft and the languages in which both of these things might be described. Roberts's ability to place human activity within the context of a non-human world without erasing either is unusual for its time and increasingly relevant to our contemporary ecological crisis.

Although Roberts was not satisfied with the poem, her response to Robert Graves is particularly illuminating where she defends it, stating: 'I *did* want to get the feeling of frustration in relation to the bird's imprisonment & lack of wholesome environment *in relation* to all peoples living in the world today.'[36] The sense of formal entrapment is therefore a response to a worldwide problem; the to and fro of the bird's 'sonorous presence' is one that locates the poem in a global context. The curlew's crisis is not replaced or anthropomorphized in relation to war, but is placed in a resonant relationship with it. The relation between the 'notes of doom' and 'freedom' is sound-led, but the doomed freedom is both the bird's and Europe's, which is what makes our attention oscillate between birdsong, human conflict and its potential outcome (*CP*, 15). Whereas in 'Moorhen', another of Roberts ornithological poems, the bird under observation is 'without interference / Or compound political tags', suggesting immunity from the human world of war, our perception of the curlew is inseparable from its backdrop of war and the daily struggle for survival on the home front.[37] As readers of the poem we bring an attention that is shaped by Roberts's own listening to the conditions in which she found herself.

By paying attention to the global dimensions of a local, domestic incident, Roberts reveals the ambitious scope of her work, which is to recast her locality in heroic terms, by showing that the here and now of the poem, as experienced through listening, is always connected with elsewhere. There is a precedent for this in the landscape of Nonconformist Wales in which a biblical topography is mapped on to rural everyday life through placenames, and in *Gods with Stainless Ears* the epigraph to Part IV is typical of the saturation of locality with mythical dimensions. Lines from Dyfnallt's 'Cri Madonna' weave together wartime Llanybri and Nazareth:

> Un eich amynedd yn ddi-feth
> Un yn eich croes a'ch cri,
> Mair, mam Iesu o Nasareth
> A' Mari o Llanybri.
>
> The same your patience unfailing,
> The same your cross and your cry,

Mary mother of Nazareth
And Mary of Llanybri. (*CP*, 60)

Roberts's interest in this poem is not the kind of transcendent spiritual endurance that is reflected for example in R. S. Thomas's later poem on a similar theme, 'Pietà'.[38] What seems more relevant to Roberts is the coincidence of the naming of her own village and the extension of contemporary suffering into a mythological past, but her rationale for its inclusion is the experience of listening to the Welsh language. Providing the translation above in the notes, she comments:

> I have intentionally used Welsh quotations as this helps to give the conscious compact and culture of another nation. The village of Llanybri, around which the poem is set, is Welsh speaking. Most of the people, *with the exception of the older generation*, can also speak English; either better than we can, or with a strange imagery and intonation found in common with all peasants of the soil. (*CP*, 76)

Leaving aside its inadvertently condescending ethnographic perspective, this statement reveals the presence of Welsh in the poem as relating particularly to a lived context. Quotations used as epigraphs often signal a specific literary hinterland, and those by Dafydd ap Gwilym in Part II might be seen in this light, but the others seem to serve a different purpose, which is to assert the relationship of language with the landscape in which it is performed. Most of the epigraphs are from the Bible, which is in some ways surprising given that Roberts at this time viewed religion as 'a supplanted dogma and out of date'.[39] The fact of their being quoted in Welsh adds little in terms of semantic meaning, but because the language of the Bible is a resonating presence in the mid-twentieth century Welsh rural community, embedded in the inner ear from its recitation in churches and chapels, there is a symbolic and performative meaning in the sound of biblical Welsh: it is part of the soundscape. It is clear from Roberts's note about 'compact and culture' that she sees a close continuity between the written Welsh of the quotations and the spoken Welsh of everyday situations, despite differences in register, for both are part of the lived environment. Through the iteration of Welsh texts in her poem, Roberts acts on what she hears, adapting to the presence of Welsh by using the most substantial work in translation that she has to hand – the Bible.

There is a paradox in that this cultural meaning derived from the sound of Welsh is one that is more audible to Roberts than to the Welsh speakers among whom she lives. Eric F. Clarke describes the particularly sharp awareness of sound that accompanies the experience of listening to an unknown language:

> when a person hears what a sound means (i.e. understands the sound in relation to its source), it becomes more difficult to detect the sound's distinctive features. Speech perception provides a striking case of this: it is a common experience when listening to the sounds of an unfamiliar foreign language to notice the huge variety and specific qualities of the sounds that make up the language – to be quite acutely aware, in other words, of continuously variable acoustical features but to understand nothing. To a native speaker/listener, however, these are paradoxically far more difficult to detect even though they are the critical features that enable the language to function as a communicative medium at all.[40]

The use of biblical texts in Welsh allows the predominantly English-speaking reader, and to some extent Roberts herself, to hear the sound of the language dislodged from its signification. In her notes, Roberts remarks on the slipperiness of the English translation from Acts: 'These men are full of new wine', commenting: 'Here the English translation is incorrect as the original Greek word implies sweet wine. John Kitto, DD, FSA, has pointed this out. The Welsh rendering is *Gwin* (the G a mutation), *win* meaning wine, *melus*: sweet' (*CP*, 70). This explanation signals that the Welsh texts are destined for a reader who will not speak Welsh, but Roberts reminds her readers that the King James version is itself no less a translation, emphasizing that English exists alongside other languages. The point is a minor one (since new, unfermented wine may also be sweet), but it is significant in displacing the power structures in which the two languages traditionally exist as minority and metropolitan languages. For the intended anglophone reader, the Welsh epigraphs are an interference with the signals of communication, and are thus perceived as noise or silence, but Roberts is making the point that the Bible's translation into English cannot be assumed to be transparent, or to have greater authority.

Discords and silences in listening are a means of juxtaposing English with other kinds of sound organization. In Part IV, pain at losing a child is suggested by what Roberts, appropriating musical terminology to her own rather different purposes, describes as 'discordant fifths', perhaps relating to the five-line stanzas and irregular rhyme schemes (*CP*, 60). The speaker's sense of loss eats away at the five-line stanza structure at one point, causing whole lines to disappear:

> O LOVE was there no barddoniaeth?
> No billing birds to be – coinheritor?
>
> The night sky is braille in a rock of frost. (*CP*, 61)

Despite the Welsh epigraphs, the many inventive lexical choices, and overall linguistic adventurousness that define *Gods*, this is one of the few occasions where Roberts uses Welsh in the body of the poem, and it is notable that it is the Welsh word for poetry. The impossibility of conveying either the Welsh language or birdsong in English suggests that the silence of the empty lines is the point at which language breaks its limits, but at the same time it is an opening to alternative perspectives on absence, conveyed in musical harmony (or disharmony), *barddoniaeth* and birdsong. This is paralleled in the shutdown of vision in the image of the sky as 'braille' (*CP*, 61) – meaning is present, but beyond the limits of the linguistic perspective of the poem.

Roberts had experimented with the Welsh-language form of the *englyn* in her poem 'Broken Voices', noting the influence of R. Williams Parry as well as Graves, whom she believes to be the only other poet to have attempted this complex form (which involves a syllable count and a set pattern of internal rhyme) in English (*CP*, 38). An emphasis on a collective voicing is suggested in the second stanza:

> Now one mouth twisting twelve tongues – of the flock
>   Unlocked the padlocked lungs:
>   Slung a trail of steaming dung
>   Blocking path of two not sung.[41]

If the effect of the form here is to produce a degree of awkwardness, it introduces an aesthetic that has a striking influence on Roberts's subsequent work, as again in Part IV of *Gods*, where the dense sonic patterning is recalled, if not exactly reproduced, in the alliteration, assonance and internal rhyme of a stanza such as this one:

> So double hurt was hard to console. Heart hatched
> Shrived nerves each day in valley clove. Stretched

> Mind tight into scarlet umbrella. Slatched
> Nowhere the deflated ropes of blood. Wrenched
> Harbouring heartbreak that is a crack grailed. (*CP*, 61)

The bodily estrangement of miscarriage is articulated through a poetics that resists naturalization, with caesuras isolating rhymed words and therefore drawing attention to rhyme as a violent disturbance to expectation rather than a soothing repetition. The element of formal constraint in *cynghanedd*, the Welsh practice of 'singing in chains' in Mererid Hopwood's term, can produce this effect.[42] The apparently effortless transcendence of such a form is an impressive mastery, but anti-mastery may also be deliberately deployed, for example in the contemporary Welsh-language poet Twm Morys's 'My First Love was a Plover', a 'cywydd for Canadians' that includes the lines 'We ate leeks at a lakeside / I caressed her crest, and cried'.[43] His poem reverses the familiar pattern of a dominant language encroaching on a less powerful one through a minoritizing or deterritorializing strategy that hears English through the prism of Welsh rather than vice versa. In Morys's example the effect is irony and comic bathos, whereas for Roberts the estranging of English is also an estranging of the body and its perceptions, a radical vulnerability. Her work reminds us that perception is rooted not only in the lived experience of place but also in the body as a gendered, cultured space.

By attending to the listening that takes place in Roberts's work, we also focus on a poetic process that responds to a highly complex literary, political and physical environment, and one that cannot be fully explained through reference to the techniques of high modernism. Tony Conran describes Roberts as a 'primitive' in the sense that '"primitive" and modernist can often be regarded as two sides of the same [coin]', while McGuinness relates her poetry to naive painting, suggesting that it has 'an enabling – and in the best sense unsophisticated – belief in language's sufficiency'.[44] Although his explanation of her difference from the modernism of Pound and Eliot is helpful, her work need not necessarily be seen within a binary of modernist literary sophistication versus an idiosyncratic 'home-made' aesthetic, a contrast that places her poetry too easily within the gendered expectations of the period in which she wrote. It is true that Roberts's description of her process can reveal a particular kind of playful innocence, for example in relation to 'Rainshiver', in which 'Rain freezes our senses. Our gills fill with a drill motion: / Chills the air and stills the billing birds'.⁴⁵ In her diary of 23 June 1940, Roberts describes the constraint of using as many 'long thin letters' as possible to look like rain, which results in a linguistic excessiveness to match the excessive weather.⁴⁶ Although this seems naive, when the technique is echoed and some of the same text reworked in *Gods with Stainless Ears*, it takes on an altogether different character, no longer a whimsical experiment but part of a sustained process of subjecting English to a range of contextual pressures:

> Grisaille freezes the sense; crines
> The gills into a drill motion; stills-shrills
> The singing birds to kill; Drips rills
> From envelopes, pustule eyes and hat, (*CP*, 62)

In the light of what Roberts says about her experiment in 'Rainshiver', the effect produced here may be seen in terms of the visual effects of rain, but the proliferation of the doubled 'l' has the accidental effect of making the text look like Welsh, and when read aloud the intense repetition of sound estranges English, making its sounds as noticeable as they would be a 'foreign' language, which is what English effectively is in the locale in which Roberts is writing.

Understanding the potential of English to be heard as foreignness or noise is part of Roberts's vision of a Wales that encompasses 'differing national viewpoints'.⁴⁷ As explained in *Wales* these must cohere as a foundation to hopes of independence.⁴⁸ To turn one's attention to noise is to acknowledge the fullness of one's immediate surroundings, whether environmental, political, cultural, or all three. Roberts notices how 'OK saltates the cymric hearth and / BBC blares from Bermondsey tongue', 'saltates' being an intriguing word choice, denoting loose particles of earth or sand swept along by wind or water and deposited on a different surface (*CP*, 48). The image, as Webb and Daniel Hughes observe in their chapters in this volume, contrasts the looseness and mobility of the English language with the burial or suffocation of Welsh, as 'Old women die folded in skirts, their culture / Entombed' (*CP*, 48). However, both languages are, in *Gods with Stainless Ears*, positioned within a wider multilingual context. In the line 'Embrowns himmel hokushai' at the beginning of Part III, the syntactically odd placing of 'embrowns' launches us into German and Japanese references: the German heavens inflected by a Hokusai woodcut (*CP*, 56). In the opening of Part IV, the same sound is echoed in a different sky: 'I, rimmeled, awake before the dressing sun', where 'rimmel' is both a brand of make-up and the Spanish word for mascara, *el rimel* (*CP*, 60). In the pun on eye/I, there is a swivelling between cultural perspectives on a hinge of echoed sound, a challenge to the confrontational binaries of war. Rather than rooting the perceiving subject in a fixed and familiar territory, Roberts's poems develop through the activity of perception; place is a process of discovery that respects the existence of other, unknown perspectives. Her listening is simultaneously an imaginative projection of a future Wales in all its cultural and ecological diversity, and a means of locating herself in her daily environment, where multiple languages and lives intersect.

Notes

1. Patrick McGuinness, 'Introduction', in Lynette Roberts, *Collected Poems*, ed. Patrick McGuinness (Manchester: Carcanet, 2005), p. xxx. All further references to this volume will be given in the text as *CP*.
2. Eric F. Clarke, *Ways of Listening: An Ecological Approach to the Perception of Musical Meaning* (Oxford: Oxford University Press, 2005), p. 6.
3. Jean-Luc Nancy, *Listening*, trans. Charlotte Mandell (New York: Fordham University Press, 2007), p. 7.
4. For a fuller discussion of examples see Zoë Skoulding, 'Film, Gramophones and the Noise of Landscape in Dylan Thomas and Lynette Roberts', in *Reading Dylan Thomas*, ed. Edward Allen (Edinburgh: Edinburgh University Press, 2017), pp. 138–54.
5. Jonathan Bate, *Song of the Earth* (London: Pan Macmillan, 2011), p. 282.
6. Matthew Jarvis, *Welsh Environments in Contemporary Poetry* (Cardiff: University of Wales Press, 2008), pp. 7–8.
7. Keidrych Rhys, 'Editorial', *Wales*, 4/6 (1945), 4.
8. Rhys, 'Editorial' (1945), 4.
9. Rhys, 'Editorial' (1945), 4.
10. Lynette Roberts, 'A Carmarthenshire Diary', entry for 3 November 1939, in *Diaries, Letters and Recollections*, ed. Patrick McGuinness (Manchester: Carcanet, 2008), p. 3.
11. Lynette Roberts, *Gods with Stainless Ears*, in *Collected Poems*, p. 44. All further references are to this edition and are given in the body of the text.
12. Roland Barthes, 'Listening', in *The Responsibility of Forms: Critical Essays on Music, Art and Representation*, trans. Richard Howard (Oxford: Basil Blackwell, 1985), pp. 245–60 (p. 246).
13. Jean-Luc Nancy, cited above, describes this experience not as listening but as hearing, because 'to hear a siren, a bird, or a drum is already each time to understand the rough outline of a situation, a context if not a text'. See his *Listening*, p. 6. There are differences of definition between his analysis

and that of Barthes, but I have drawn more on Barthes's perspective here because of his stronger emphasis on the continuity between human and animal listening.
14. Barthes, 'Listening', p. 259.
15. John Wilkinson, *The Lyric Touch* (Cambridge: Salt, 2007), p. 193.
16. Andrew Webb, '"What changes break before us": Semi-peripheral Modernity in Lynette Roberts's Poetry and Prose', pp. 90–1 above.
17. Sir John Rhŷs, *Celtic Folklore: Welsh and Manx* (Oxford: The Clarendon Press, 1901), pp. 11–18.
18. Clarke, *Ways of Listening*, p. 17.
19. Clarke, *Ways of Listening*, p. 40.
20. Clarke, *Ways of Listening*, p. 40.
21. Lynette Roberts, 'An Introduction to Village Dialect', in *Diaries, Letters and Recollections*, pp. 107–24 (pp. 120–2).
22. McGuinness, *Diaries, Letters and Recollections*, p. 224.
23. Roberts, 'An Introduction to Village Dialect', pp. 119–20.
24. Roberts, 'An Introduction to Village Dialect', p. 123, italics in original.
25. Roberts, 'An Introduction to Village Dialect', p. 123.
26. Roberts, 'An Introduction to Village Dialect', p. 119.
27. Clarke, *Ways of Listening*, p. 40.
28. Gillian Clarke, quoted in Alice Entwistle, *Poetry, Geography, Gender: Women Rewriting Contemporary Wales* (Cardiff: University of Wales Press, 2013), p. 4.
29. Jasmine Donahaye, quoted in Entwistle, *Poetry, Geography, Gender*, pp. 4–5.
30. Lynette Roberts, 'Raw Salt on Eye', in *Collected Poems*, p. 6.
31. Lynette Roberts, 'Curlew', in *Collected Poems*, p. 15. All further references are to this edition and are given in the body of the text.
32. Lynette Roberts, 'Letter to Robert Graves', dated 18 December 1944, in *Diaries, Letters and Recollections*, p. 180.
33. Alva Noë, *Varieties of Presence* (Cambridge: Harvard University Press, 2012), p. 59.
34. Roberts, 'A Carmarthenshire Diary', entry for 15 July 1941, in *Diaries, Letters and Recollections*, p. 37.
35. Nancy, *Listening*, p. 16.
36. Lynette Roberts, 'Letter to Robert Graves', dated 18 December 1944, in *Diaries, Letters and Recollections*, p. 181.
37. Lynette Roberts, 'Moorhen', in *Collected Poems*, p. 16.
38. R. S. Thomas, *Pietà* (London: Rupert Hart-Davis, 1966).
39. Roberts, 'A Carmarthenshire Diary', entry for 17 June 1940, in *Diaries, Letters and Recollections*, p. 18.
40. Clarke, *Ways of Listening*, p. 34.
41. Lynette Roberts, 'Broken Voices', in *Collected Poems*, p. 9.
42. Mererid Hopwood, *Singing in Chains: Listening to Welsh Verse* (Llandysul: Gomer, 2004).
43. Twm Morys, *www.brunel.ac.uk/__data/assets/pdf_file/0014/111155/Twm-Morys-Cerdd-Dafod-A-Poet-Introduces-a-Welsh-Metrical-Tradition.pdf* (last accessed 15 January 2016).
44. Anthony Conran, *Frontiers in Anglo-Welsh Poetry* (Cardiff: University of Wales Press, 1997), p. 166; McGuinness, *Collected Poems*, p. xxxvi.

[45] Lynette Roberts, 'Rainshiver', in *Collected Poems*, p. 26.
[46] Roberts, 'A Carmarthenshire Diary', entry for 23 June 1940, in *Diaries, Letters and Recollections*, p. 21.
[47] Rhys, 'Editorial' (1945), 4.
[48] Rhys, 'Editorial' (1945), 4.

9

LYNETTE ROBERTS'S *THE ENDEAVOUR*: A GENERIC ADVENTURE

Charles Mundye

In late December 1953 T. S. Eliot wrote Lynette Roberts a characteristically gloomy and cautious Christmas letter. Eliot had published both Roberts's *Poems* (1944) and *Gods with Stainless Ears* (1951) with Faber, but now he was urging her towards a change of direction:

> Certainly I will be one of your references for a Scholarship . . . I hope that you succeed; but at the same time it strikes me that to try to live on one grant after another is a very precarious way of life, and that you will have to try to find a regular job in the end. It would be a good thing to learn short-hand and typing. But a job of some kind you must have, eventually.[1]

After this closing injunction his best wishes for 1954 must have had a slightly hollow ring. Roberts was also corresponding with Robert Graves, to whom she outlined the proposed subject for her Leverhulme scholarship application in more detail:

> I put in for poetry research with an emphasis on rhythm in relation to social and national environment . . . An example of what I mean is for instance the rumba and dance rhythms of today and how in studying African rhythms in order to get at the basic nucleus of these jazz rhythms, I found the true source and poetically unadulterated version of the present samba rhythms used in Brazil filtered into our own poetic metres.[2]

This energetic proposal draws attention to the ambition of Roberts's thinking: interdisciplinary and international before such requirements would become the sine qua non of the successful grant application. Eliot was right in part to highlight the precariousness of such plans; despite the eminence of the referees, the scholarship never materialized. However, neither did Roberts give in to the inevitable 'regular job', and Eliot may or may not have known at the time that her third and final published book *The Endeavour: Captain Cook's First Voyage to Australia* was already with the printers. By comparison with the first two it was destined to be a minor commercial success. That Eliot should recommend regular paid employment reflects his own doubting approach to the role of the professional writer, and recalls the distrust in which he held Ezra Pound's well-meaning Bel Esprit scheme to free Eliot from his employment in a bank thirty years earlier.[3] That he should suggest Roberts use her typewriter not for creative writing but for what was then such functionally gendered employment might also remind us of the very particular challenges and obstacles facing the woman writer trying to make a living from writing in the 1950s.

Lynette Roberts's *The Endeavour* has so far eluded the renewed critical interest in her writing, which has otherwise firmly located her as an important figure for Welsh writing in English and for poetic modernism. It has also fallen through the various nets that have recently trawled through mid-twentieth century writing looking to recover such devalued genres as historical and middlebrow fiction, genres often inhabited by women writers. I will situate Roberts's text in terms of such renewed interests, and will further examine how the text relates to, and modifies, current critical attempts to reconsider both the stretch and constitution of modernism itself. In doing so I will reflect more generally on such critical categories as late modernism and intermodernism. That none of these important engagements with often-ignored writing should have picked up on Roberts's *The Endeavour* is testament to what an unusual book in many respects it is, and how difficult it is to classify Roberts in any of the usual ways. However, Eliot's desire to consign her to a typing pool in his 1953 Christmas letter is perhaps proleptic of the subsequent critical neglect of the mid-century woman writer more generally, and also draws our attention to various aesthetic and commercial questions facing a late modernist woman writer at a point when modernism was losing whatever currency and dominance it once had. Renewed attention to Roberts's *The Endeavour* and its contexts provides a unique opportunity to re-evaluate the contested and evolving understanding of mid-century literary thinking and practice, especially as it relates to modernism and its aftermaths.

In pursuing this critical recovery, I will draw on Roberts's largely unpublished correspondence with two other writers who are often difficult to classify, and who each in very different ways disrupt the usual narratives of twentieth-century literary modernism. For a period of over ten years Edith Sitwell was an encouraging mentor and friend to Roberts. As with Roberts, Sitwell's work as a poet and novelist has been neglected and marginalized for too long. The reputation of Robert Graves, the third major correspondent in focus here, has fared better, but from the 1920s onwards he became a self-styled literary outsider, with traditional narratives of twentieth-century writing often defined by his exception to them.[4] The professional relationship between Graves and Roberts was deeply important to both, and its nature and extent has not yet been properly explored. This chapter goes some way to explaining it further.

In 1953 Eliot's Christmas letter was sent to Roberts's address at the caravan, Bell's Wood, Bayford, Hertfordshire. Her ten-year-long marriage to editor and poet Keidrych Rhys broke up in 1949, and her itinerant address was enabled by the purchase of a caravan that was initially sited at the graveyard in Laugharne, where she lived for a short period from summer 1949 in the immediate aftermath of her separation from Rhys.[5] One principal advantage of the caravan was that it gave Roberts a degree of physical freedom: she could relatively easily and affordably move the location of her home according to pragmatic need, opportunity and existential desire. The caravan was also a physical manifestation of a more metaphorical sense of freedom, expressed in an earlier letter to Robert Graves: 'I had to catch an early bus into Carmarthen and felt like a migrating bird who practises a smooth, clear, powerful flight over a large section of the sky before dispatching on his holiday trip abroad. I felt *really happy*'.[6] The immediate context for this heady sense of freedom was her marital separation and subsequent plans to move to Mallorca, in part to be near Robert Graves and his partner Beryl. Yet a general sense of existential restlessness, deracination and a complex idea of home is perhaps more deeply located beneath this gently mock-epic account of a daily bus trip. These preoccupations find expression in the idea that was to become *The Endeavour*, and they are there in her earlier writing too. In the early stages of the Second World War her diary compares bird migration with her own desire to move away from Llanybri, registering similar sentiments to those expressed in her later letter to Graves:

> I find it [the wind] refreshing to my general mood of disturbance which occurs just before the birds' first migratory flight. But the question arises, where shall I go and when? For instinct cannot altogether guide those who are caught in the chains of culture and a barbaric civilisation . . . But we are at war so there remains only 'chance' or fate to guide our footsteps.[7]

We can see the same sense of affinity with migratory birds in her poem 'The Orange Charger', a poem about the robin, who:

> loves to migrate
> And not to migrate,
> Or sits with wistful isolation
> In the perennial springs of the Azores.[8]

Here Roberts combines an attentiveness to detailed natural history with a deep sense of the way in which the bird in question is a metaphorical idealization of the lyric-poetic voice itself.

Robert Graves and Lynette Roberts were regular correspondents when she first tried writing historical fiction in the 1940s, and Graves became something of a role model for Roberts at this time. Roberts sent him the manuscript of the 'Book of Nesta', her unpublished story of a medieval Welsh princess, and Graves gently upbraided her for introducing an anachronistic potato into her landscape of medieval Wales.[9] Roberts had tried 'Nesta' on Eliot at Faber, but it was unlikely ever to be their kind of book, regardless of the wartime paper rationing that Eliot used as partial excuse.[10] 'Nesta' never did find a publisher, and the manuscript was considered lost until very recently rediscovered in the archives of the Harry Ransom Center, Texas. But with her second full-length prose work *The Endeavour*, Roberts secured a contract from a publisher, signed 1 September 1953, and she was able to write excitedly to Beryl and Robert Graves:

> I have just sent my complete MSS of Capt James Cook's first voyage taken from all the ship's journals. This is the first time this has been done. Always before authors have been greedy to concentrate on his *whole* life. My book only covers a concentration of 3 years . . . The publishers are *Peter Owen Ltd* a young and honest firm.[11]

The contract provided reasonably good terms: her royalty statement for 1 July 1954, after only a few months of sales, indicates 1,502 copies sold at full price and 296 on special export terms, bringing in a total for the author of £132.[12] In declining Roberts's new book of poems in May 1953, T. S. Eliot had remarked *en passant* that *Gods with Stainless Ears* had not sold well; the change in genre, then, meant a minor change in fortune at the very least.[13] Retailing at 16s., and published in cloth with a powder-blue dust jacket illustrated by a close-up scene from Thomas Luny's *c*.1790 painting of 'The Bark, *Earl of Pembroke*, later *Endeavour*, leaving Whitby Harbour in 1768', the book was destined for a broader reading public than her previous volumes of poems. The advertisements on the dust jacket are illustrative of a truly independent and quirky publisher who nevertheless sought commercial success: Roberts's *The Endeavour* was keeping company with biographies of Colette and Emily Brontë, and two volumes relating to the Marquis de Sade. Next to these is an advert for a reprint of 'Dr Sitwell's only novel', *I Live under a Black Sun*, first published in 1937, and reprinted by Peter Owen in 1953. The publisher's catalogue was to develop with books of popular travel and geography, including C. C. Vyvyan's *Down the Rhone on Foot* (1955), and *Temples and Flowers: A Journey to Greece* (1955), and A. R. de Carteret's *The Story of Sark* (1956). Francis Cunynghame's *Reminiscences of an Epicure* (1955) rubbed shoulders with texts by Cesare Pavese, Herman Hesse, Ezra Pound and Jean Cocteau. It is an interesting question as to which company Roberts was keeping on this extraordinarily varied and internationalist list, in part because her book is so very generically ambiguous.

The Endeavour tells the story of Captain James Cook (1728–1779), perhaps the most famous of eighteenth-century adventurers, and his first great three-year voyage, which started from Plymouth in August 1768, stopping in Madeira and Rio de Janeiro, before rounding Cape Horn to Tahiti to observe the transit of Venus across the sun on 3 June 1769. From there the expedition moved onwards, firstly to a circumnavigation of New Zealand, and then to the east coast of Australia, which Cook carefully charted and explored for the first time. Here Cook and his crew had variously problematic encounters with the indigenous peoples, shot, ate and skinned a kangaroo, and were nearly shipwrecked on the Great Barrier Reef near the place they named Cape Tribulation. They put in for repairs in Batavia (now Jakarta), where many of the crew and gentlemen were lost to malaria and related illness, and then faced the long voyage home round the Cape of Good Hope, reaching the English port of Deal in July 1771. It was ostensibly a voyage of scientific discovery, and in this Cook was accompanied by the wealthy scientist Joseph Banks, who employed on board a small army of assistants, including the artist Sydney Parkinson, to record their discoveries. It was also very much a voyage of imperial ambition; the charting and claiming of hitherto unknown lands in the name of King George was a principal aim, especially after Cook opened the secret second set of orders in Tahiti that instructed him to push on further south to search for the mythical Great Southern continent. The journey has been subsequently endowed with talismanic power, and generated significant controversy, ever since. But what attracted Roberts to the subject in the late 1940s and early 1950s? In her introduction to *The Endeavour* she gives us a small clue through a single point of biographical identification: 'With regard to dramatization: I have been shipwrecked on the rocks when the ship contained monkeys, snakes and animals collected from an expedition returning from the Amazon, and no dramatic account could express the full individual impact of such a mishap.'[14] Roberts directs us to the significance of her own first-hand experience of shipwreck, and ensuing evacuation, as a passenger on board the British cruise liner *Hilary*, which accidentally ran aground in reduced visibility at Carmel Head, Anglesey, in April 1939. The ship had started its voyage in Manaós, northern Brazil, travelled hundreds of miles along the Amazon river, and then stopped at various points in the Atlantic, picking up holiday makers en route to Liverpool, including Lynette Roberts and her friend and fellow writer Celia Buckmaster, who had been on a working holiday on the island of Madeira. The ensuing *Daily Mail* report of the incident made particular mention of the two independent and artistic women writers:

> Two London girls were the heroines of the long wait while the rescue ship arrived – 28-years-old Miss Lynette Roberts and her 24-years-old companion, Miss Celia Buckmaster, poet and authoress, of King's Bench Walk . . . who were returning from a holiday in Madeira.
> Miss Buckmaster sat at the piano in the third-class lounge, idly picked out a tune. Miss Roberts, who lives in Newman Street, W., took it up, began to sing.
> Soon, all the passengers in the lounge had joined in.
> 'We treated it as a joke', Miss Roberts said to me, 'but I was very nervous. We could just see the rocks ahead. It was so quiet in the fog'.

Miss Buckmaster was anxious over the manuscript of a novel she was writing, pictures she had painted, her canary in a cage. All were saved.[15]

A similar concern for the safety of the scientific and artistic records of their voyage would have been passing through the minds of Joseph Banks and Sydney Parkinson when in June 1770 Cook's *Endeavour* was caught fast on the jagged edge of what became known as Endeavour Reef, with the significant difference that they were in a completely unknown part of the world, with no-one to save them but themselves. Nevertheless, the incident off Holyhead allowed at least one point of connection between the great captain, his assembled crew, and Lynette Roberts herself. Also, it was by no means Lynette Roberts's first stop in Madeira, for as she later noted in a radio talk: 'for the British born in the Argentine there are many sea voyages'.[16]

In recounting a seemingly remote eighteenth-century narrative of global exploration and discovery, Roberts was telling a tale much closer to home than might at first be apparent, for Cook's voyage connects a number of geographies of deep personal significance to Roberts's sense of origin and identity. Telling the story of Cook's now legendary restlessness allows her to voice her own experience of travel, and to consider how such geographical movements map on to other kinds of international, mythopoeic, linguistic and cultural crossings, as I will demonstrate. Roberts's father Cecil Roberts was a very senior engineer whose career took him to Argentina, where he had a significant role in building the railways. It was here that Roberts subsequently spent much of her childhood, as documented in her 'Radio Talk on South American Poems'. Travelling frequently between her South American childhood home and Britain, she had significant first-hand experience as a passenger on the same sea route of the first leg of Cook's outbound voyage. Further, Cecil Roberts was born in Australia in 1880, his father's family having emigrated wholesale to Adelaide from Wales in 1843 aboard the ship *Madras*. Roberts's maternal family were also Welsh émigrés to the Australia that Cook's initial voyage had opened up to colonial settlement. In recounting Cook's voyage of discovery, Roberts is exploring questions of family identity, shadowing her own experience and that of her immediate ancestors in the telling. It is important to note in this respect that her father died in late November 1949, in the midst of the difficulties of her divorce. She told Graves the news in an intensely moving letter: 'Robert, He's *dead*. My beloved father. And it is wretchedly so, since

I had looked forward to seeing him after the divorce was through. I remember so well his tears when he had kissed me goodbye fifteen years ago and they surprised me'.[17] There's a sense of double exile and double loss in this passage, but the letter vacillates between near-mindless grief and a way back towards life, as does an uncollected poem, 'Out of the Paw of Night', written around the same time, which parallels the letter:

> Out of the paw of night
> And out of my sodden self
> A cry like the whining of the wind:
> A filter of salt covers my eyes
> Banks of sand rise in my throat
> On hearing the foul news of his death.
> Death so finite; so unacceptable.[18]

The metaphorization of coast and sea in the poem resonates distantly in the sea narrative she was about to begin, which took her back to her father via Captain Cook's navigation of South America and Australia.

Roberts's particular narrative choice also enables her to explore a variety of very familiar natural histories. Much of the Atlantic and South American flora and fauna encountered and even discovered for European eyes by the *Endeavour* expedition would have been familiar to Roberts from first-hand experience, and the narrative provides many opportunities for her to extend her repertoire of writing on natural history subjects. The narrative of Cook's journey also allowed Roberts to engage with the scientific and artistic representation of exotic fauna and flora. We should also remember one further biographical detail: when she came to London as a young woman she trained with domestic scientist and author Constance Spry, and subsequently became a self-employed professional florist, setting up a company under the name of Bruska from her Newman Street address and supplying exotic flowers at 100 per cent mark-up to high-class clients.[19]

The gentleman botanist Joseph Banks accompanying Cook was in his exotic element when he arrived on Brazilian soil for the first time in 1768. In his journal he describes some of the plant and animal life that he encountered:

These were chiefly the parasitic plants, especially *Renealmiæ* (for I was not fortunate enough to see one *Epidendrum*) and the different species of *Bromelia*, many not before described. *Karratas* I saw here growing on the decayed trunk of a tree sixty feet high at least, which it had so entirely covered that the whole seemed to be a tree of *Karratas* ... Add to these that the whole country was covered with the beautiful blossoms of *Malpighiæ, Bannisteriæ, Passifloræ,* not forgetting *Poinciana* and *Mimosa sensitiva*, and a beautiful species of *Clusia*, of which I saw great plenty; in short the wildest spots here were varied with a greater quantity of flowers, as well as more beautiful ones, than our best-devised gardens; a sight infinitely pleasing for a short time, though no doubt the eye would soon tire with a continuance of it.

The birds of many species, especially the smaller ones, sat in great abundance on the boughs, many of them covered with most elegant plumage. I shot *Loxia brasiliensis*, and saw several specimens of it. Insects also were here in great quantity, many species very fine, but much more nimble than our European ones, especially the butterflies, almost all which flew near the tops of the trees, and were very difficult to come at, except when the sea breeze blew fresh, which kept them low down among the trees where they might be taken. Humming birds I also saw of one species, but could not shoot them.[20]

The artist Sydney Parkinson was employed to create images of their discoveries first-hand, and his journal records the same occasion, rather more briefly: 'I soon discovered a hedge in which there were many very curious plants in bloom, and all of them quite new to me. There were so many, that I even loaded myself with them'.[21] These various journals kept by the voyagers of *Endeavour* provide Roberts with much of her source material. Parkinson, a man of few words here, let his brush do the talking; indeed, as part of her intensely detailed research for the book, Roberts visited the library of the Natural History Museum and worked through the originals of Sydney Parkinson's many drawings and watercolour paintings made on the voyage.[22]

The following excerpt from Roberts's chapter 'Botanical Pursuits', which describes the same Brazilian landing by Banks and Parkinson, demonstrates a complex combination of Roberts's professional skills as a writer and natural historian. She writes in what might be termed a visual poetic style, combining first-hand observations with complex passages of ekphrasis based on Parkinson's work to give an astonishingly detailed variation on Banks's own experiential account:

> The powdery atmosphere that stood around the soft falls of mimosa, yellow and sweet. The grey feathery leaf-tips stirring, as a heavier perfume

from thick waxy bells guided them to climbing branches that stretched high and grew as they stood to watch. Drifting down from the tall and gnarled branches of the trees hung bunches of orchids, as profuse and as large as a flowering bush: and varied aerial plants of *Bromelia* and the parasite *Renealimæ* with stems like wires and flowers like insects. They felt the strangeness around them, and they must have appeared odd to the flowers, as they rolled and tumbled, still used to the continual movement of the ship and unable to account for the motionless land.

Banks stood again before another delight. A decayed tree sixty feet high was completely covered with *Karratas* so that the tree could not be seen. And around it gathered many weird insects and tropical bees. Prussian blue butterflies as large as birds flew fast and high above the trees; too high for them to be caught. And humming birds, just the one variety, were continually fluttering low in front of the blossoms; sipping with their long slender beaks the nectar at the base of each flower. Every feather of their one-inch body scaled with soft iridescent feathers. Their wings moving so rapidly that they could not be seen.

'Please God he will miss,' whispered Parkinson to himself.

And Banks, who was an extremely good shot and very keen to get one of these humming birds, failed in the attempt.

Through more glades of blue-green slatted leaves. Past scarlet *Poinsettia*, whose huge spread of red leaf-pattern against the smaller starlike bushes and flamboyant climbers and blossoming *Malpighiæ* and *Bannisteriæ*, took some time before Banks and his party could disengage their eyes. And then in an open shaft of light Passion Fruit climbed up and over a dark glossy bush. The yellowing leaves and the auricle eyes of its flowers, no small wonder to behold. The stamens radiating from the centre in the form of bright blue filaments like the iris of an eye. All laid like feathers, against the lime-green of its sepals on which these stamens rest . . .

'I must live,' said Parkinson, 'if only to finish drawing these beautiful plants'.[23]

Banks in his own journal imagines his eye eventually tiring at the sight of the visual richness of the flora, which is something you could never imagine hearing from Roberts. She is the most visual of poets, and her writing is frequently vivid with detailed colour. The visual richness of her literary imagination is perhaps no surprise, given that she was also herself an artist of significant talent, whose paintings have been exhibited on at least one occasion.[24] In prose passages such as this, Roberts continues the attention to particular detail that is so characteristic of her poetry: consider this by way of comparison from *Gods with Stainless Ears*, and from a Welsh rather than Brazilian landscape:

> Corymb of coriander: each ray frosted
> Incandescent: by square stem held, hispid,
> And purple spotted. Twice pinnate with fronds
> Of chrome. Laid higher than the exulted hedge;
> By pure collated disc of daisy glittering
>
> White on a red powdered stem.[25]

But the visual poetry of *The Endeavour* has also to accommodate a dramatization of action, and in the passage above Roberts fleshes out the sensitivities of Parkinson by imagining him wish for Banks to miss his attempt at shooting the hummingbird. At times Parkinson seems to take on the perspective that is closest in spirit to the narrative voice itself: the artistic eyes through which the rest is witnessed, at least to the point of his death, which she alludes to here with ironic prolepsis.

In considering what drew Roberts to this historical project above all others, I have so far considered the narrative of *The Endeavour* to be a specific kind of displaced or relocated autobiography, offering Roberts the opportunity to explore particular aspects of natural history and its visual and descriptive representations. But such a many-faceted text is no one thing alone. It has perhaps more obvious generic affinity with the documentary narrative, with travelogue, and with popular history. In her introduction to the text Roberts avoids the terms novel and fiction, preferring to designate it as an attempt at a 'comprehensive survey' and a 'study', thus emphasizing its supposed historical authenticity and veracity.[26] The publicity blurb on the dust jacket also eschews the term novel, preferring instead to describe the text as one of 'the classics of sea literature'. But the text is clearly novelistic in form and tone, and its connections to the genre of historical fiction are difficult to ignore.

Writing on British women's historical fiction of the 1950s, Diana Wallace observes:

> Silenced by the consensus society which relegated them to the domestic sphere, women writers used the historical novel to enter the male world, and to tackle some of the most pressing questions of the post-war world, linking them to an exploration of masculinity itself.[27]

Roberts's *The Endeavour* has fallen into the same obscurity as many of the historical fictions that Wallace considers to be necessary to recasting perceptions of the political and literary conservatism of the period, and the more predominant genres and categorizations that tend to reflect it (think, in the years immediately following publication of *The Endeavour*, of the coalescing of kitchen-sink realism, the Angry Young Men, and, in poetry, the Movement). Certainly *The Endeavour* enabled Roberts to avoid the consensus-society fate embodied so succinctly in Eliot's idea of the regular typing job, at least for a short while, and in many respects it is equally disruptive of some the neater literary-historical categorizations of the mid century, a point to which I will return later. It is also significant that throughout the text Roberts inhabits the perspectives of a series of male protagonists, although the omniscient narrative voice includes and controls the various male journal narratives incorporated within it, sometimes lifting passages otherwise verbatim but converting them from first person to third person. Roberts takes sustained phrases wholesale from the various journals and accounts of the voyage, so that lines from Cook's journal will jostle side-by-side in dialogue with lines from Banks's journal and those of others. Consider, by way of example, the imbrication of the original biographical-historical narratives by Banks and Cook in the third-person narrative in this passage from the shipwreck scene:

> The beating of the ship upon the rocks continued with such vigour that scarcely anyone could keep their legs steady on deck and they were compelled to hold on as best they could.
>
> Decayed stores, guns, ballast, hoop staves, oil jars, firewood, fresh water and their casks rolled between decks and broke loose as they were mustered ready to throw overboard. The crew peered into that very stretch of sea as it swallowed up these treasures amounting to some fifty tons which up till now had been so valuable to them. The moonlight picked out the sheathing boards which kept hitting the sides of the ship like a lost child. Then at midnight her false keel came away, so that they watched the disintegration of their ship.[28]

This passage is constructed out of lines from Banks's journal: 'All this time she continued to beat very much, so that we could hardly keep our legs upon the quarter-deck';[29] then from Cook's journal: 'but threw overboard our Guns, Iron and Stone Ballast, Casks, Hoop Staves, Oil Jarrs, decay'd Stores, etc. . . . by this time we had thrown overboard 40 or 50 Tuns weight';[30] before returning to Banks's journal: 'By the light of the moon we could see her sheathing-boards, etc., floating thickly around her, and about twelve her false keel came away.'[31] Sometimes borrowed phrases are descriptive of events or observations, and at others they are converted into direct speech or dialogue, but all are incorporated seamlessly into Roberts's own narrative, with the acknowledgment that she is doing so located only in a note within the introduction.[32] This incorporation of different narrative voices by direct borrowing in order to create a narrative inclusive of, but distinctly different from, those original sources is familiar modernist practice, and here deployed in popular genre writing. The narrative strategy is often, as here, concerned with fleshing out the emotional registers excluded from but implicit in the original journal entries. In this respect Roberts's very striking exploration of the psychological interior of Sydney Parkinson's fear at the point of shipwreck in June 1770 is a telling invention. Parkinson's own journal account is very much influenced by the subgenre of perilous adventure narrative: 'we were, at this period, many thousand leagues from our native land, (which we had left upwards of two years,) and on a barbarous coast, where, if the ship had been wrecked, and we had escaped the perils of the sea, we should have fallen into the rapacious hands of savages.'[33] Roberts's more subtle descriptive gesture both sympathizes with and humanizes the masculinist adventure narrative by showing us his interior thought process and a concomitant physical response to the emotional fall-out: 'Parkinson was vomiting, searching inwardly for his mother. They rushed past him along the gangways, taking various routes up to the deck.'[34]

Wallace has elsewhere observed that '[h]istorical fiction has always been a hybrid form, mixing two elements which seem diametrically opposed – fact and fiction, reality and romance, truth and lies – and because of this it has attracted a great deal of criticism.'[35] This observation rings true for *The Endeavour*, both in its constitution from history and imagination, and indeed in terms of its reception. Perhaps the most high-profile contemporary review in high-literary mode came from the *Times Literary Supplement*, and the kinds of criticism directed at it open up once more those telling questions about the nature of the crisis of identity in thinking about mid-century writing and the reception of anything resembling modernist style. The wonderfully phlegmatic reviewer S. Barrington Gates wrote in bemusement:

some projects in literature are almost certain to fail, and Miss Roberts's study of Cook's first voyage seems to demonstrate one of them . . . Reality, however hard, brutal, tedious, jerky, dull, is what we should get; any literary effort to embellish and smooth the story lessens the approximation.

This doctrine has some admirable elements but is crippled by its neglect of the vital question of focus . . . when such material [the various first-hand accounts of the voyage] is to be combined a unity must be imposed by the chronicler, and if this necessity is denied the result is likely to be a good deal odder than the events on which it concentrates.

In this difficult book Miss Roberts bids us, in effect, to try to look in several directions at once. This strain seems to have affected her own prose, which contains an extraordinary number of verbless and disconnected sentences. Continuity, that is what we sigh for as we are jerked into Miss Roberts's next shot before we have grasped what we are looking at. Perhaps, indeed, the truth about her experiment is that the difficulties she presents to the reader would be brilliantly resolved on the screen.[36]

It is an extraordinary idea that Roberts's written style is more odd or exotic than the story of Cook's adventures themselves, and one that registers the extent of Barrington Gates's stylistic discombobulation. This is not the first time that Roberts's tendency towards dissociation had been criticized; even Graves and Eliot had been on at her about it in relation to her poetry in the previous decade.[37] Part of what Barrington Gates dislikes is the modernism inherent in such a scheme of silent collage, with Roberts kaleidoscoping the various accounts into spectacular narrative colour, presenting simultaneous narrative and dramatic perspective through reconstituting dislocations of syntax. Further, Barrington Gates's question about whether this is possibly the wrong medium for the narrative is more likely a result of his feeling uncomfortable with the book's generic pluralism. And to what extent is this discomfort a reaction to Roberts's modernism persisting into the 1950s, and to make matters worse persisting in popular genre writing, where it just should not belong?

That Edith Sitwell's only (historical) novel was republished by Peter Owen in 1953 once again brings to the fore the extent of the literary connections and friendships behind the scenes of mid-century modernism. In 1953 Peter Owen also published Max Wykes-Joyce's biographical study *Triad of Genius: Part 1: Edith and Osbert Sitwell*, and a letter from Sitwell to Roberts on 31 January 1954 refers to Roberts's having reviewed this text, as well as Sitwell's latest volume of poems *Gardeners and Astronomers*. By this point Roberts had been corresponding regularly with Sitwell for many years, and in 1951 dedicated *Gods with Stainless Ears* to her. In the same letter, written from Sunset Boulevard, Sitwell outlined to Roberts her involvement in the aftermath of their mutual friend Dylan Thomas's death in November, and meeting Peter Ustinov who had written a thinly disguised satirical play based on the Sitwells. Sitwell also observes: 'You are the only young woman who can write. I have always said so, and I continue to say so. I long for your description of Cook's first voyage – which sounds exactly the kind of book that enthrals me.'[38]

The first face-to-face meeting of the two great modernist woman poets in 1943 was a rather inauspicious occasion, and one recorded in Roberts's essay 'Tea with the Sitwells', which describes an awkward afternoon encounter with Sitwell and a polite metropolitan coterie, at which the elder poet was at her most performatively inscrutable. Among Roberts's gently humorous analysis of peculiar social mores is a particularly telling observation on a turn in conversation when Sitwell and composer Constant Lambert suggested contemporary art needed to simplify in response to the preceding decades of modernist complexity. Roberts writes:

> Simplicity. I know that the simplicity which Lambert wants is not that which Edith Sitwell means. He has made the same mistake as her reviewers. Today simplicity cannot be taken apart from its age, must be *part of it*. It is the lack of this acceptance which makes the application of the word so impossible for most people to accept. Pastoral ding dong is OUT.[39]

This meeting took place at around the time Lynette Roberts was writing her long heroic poem *Gods with Stainless Ears*, and reaching her modernist apotheosis both in terms of style and subject matter. In this poem and elsewhere, there is a particular immediacy to her poetic modernism, conveyed through her creation of a living language from the legends and landscape of the small Welsh village where she lived for much of the war. While the range of *Gods with Stainless Ears* both in terms of style and subject is radically ambitious, it is nevertheless one that begins on a domestic scale and site, focusing on the local experience of war on the home front. Pastoral ding-dong, however, it certainly is not, and its clarity is the hard and difficult clarity of a particular kind of high modernism.

In the same account of tea with the Sitwells, Roberts points out a specific paradox representative of some of the broader complex anxieties inherent in 1940s and 1950s modernism, writing: 'Here then were two distinguished persons, a poet [Sitwell] and composer [Lambert], demanding a return to simplicity, and perhaps we can say of both that they are the most complicated examples of that art that we have ever had.'[40] The point is well made, for only six years before this meeting Sitwell published *I Live under a Black Sun* for the first time. This is a generically complex historical fiction that reimagines the eighteenth-century quasi-biographical life of Jonathan Swift into the period of World War I. This is also partly autobiography: both in the central narrative of repeatedly failed love, and in the minor narrative of love triumphing in successful postwar reconciliation, Sitwell is encoding aspects of her own experience as writer, lover and literary champion, and she herself flagged up some of the generic ambiguities of her text: 'It is an allegory, in a sense . . . The reason I put Swift into modern clothes is because the spirit of the modern world is power gone mad. And Swift was power gone mad'.[41] As Jean Radford observes: 'Sitwell's novel . . . is a collage of quotations taken from Swift (some modernized, some not), poetic descriptions of nature and imagery drawn from Owen, Eliot, Lawrence, and other contemporaries. The result is a generic mix, a montage of pastoral, letters, romance, war, fiction, jeremiad, satire and social protest.'[42]

The collage of quotations from eighteenth-century sources, the poetic description of the natural world and the generic conflation are all common to Roberts's text as well. Radford also indicates that Sitwell's biographer, Victoria Glendinning, someone we may reasonably expect to be on side, does not like its 'confusion of intent and execution'.[43] As Patrick McGuinness has observed: 'It seemed inevitable that Roberts's poetry would be charged with "obscurity", a charge often levelled against women poets of a modernist bent – Mina Loy, Marianne Moore, Laura Riding, to mention just three (it is always the men who are "learnèd" and the women who are "obscure").'[44] Perhaps it is no surprise to see similar accusations levelled against the prose of both Sitwell and Roberts.

In addition to the focus on women's historical fiction there has been much recent and important work in reclaiming other forgotten or undervalued writing of the early and mid century. In respect of women's middlebrow fiction Nicola Humble has been instrumental in reclaiming 'both the term and body of literature to which it was generally applied in the four decades from the 1920s to the 1950s', arguing that 'convenient literary fictions like "Modernism", "the Auden generation", "the angry young men" leave little space for writers like Rosamond Lehmann, Rose Macaulay, Elizabeth Bowen, and Elizabeth Taylor'.[45] Kristin Bluemel and others have posited the new term of intermodernism in an attempt to classify and reclaim the significance of those writers excluded from traditional versions of the modernist canon owing to their characteristic tendency to locate 'their responsibilities, as writers, primarily to "the people" '.[46] Much of the spirit of this work in terms of the political and national consciousness of mid-century writing has shared ground with those critics proposing late modernism as a literary-historical category, most notably Jed Esty, Marina Mackay and Tyrus Miller. Miller writes: 'The "unseasonable forms" spun out by late modernist writers, however, signify more than just patchwork in the otherwise unbroken facade of literary history. Untimely phenomena like late modernist fiction represent breaking points, points of nonsynchronism, in the broad narrative of twentieth-century cultural history.'[47] It is implicit here that such broad narratives are of course problematic and provisional. As Miller further observes:

> 'Late modernism,' like 'modernism,' refers to a significant set of family resemblances between writers during a certain period of time. It is a construction of the work of analysis, which allows these resemblances to be disclosed and judged. As a historical category, it stands and falls on the persuasiveness with which it helps bring these resemblances to light.[48]

But Sitwell and Roberts do not fit easily into any of these re-evaluated narratives either, and their very different versions of late modernism do not obviously map onto any of these recent attempts at categorization. Roberts's own recent recovery from obscurity is part of a reinvigorated interested in Welsh writing in English. Her modernism is a very significant part of the story of Welsh modernism as its own potentially distinct category, and certainly her texts represent potential breaking points in, for instance, Jed Esty's arguments in *A Shrinking Island: Modernism and National Culture in England*, which focuses on a largely London-centric late modernism. Apart from the dedicated interest of a small number of professional and amateur enthusiasts, Sitwell's writing remains thoroughly in the shadows.

In their 1943 discussion of simplicity, Roberts, Sitwell and friends were reflecting on how variously an artist might value or understand and interpret that need. Such an impetus was to become central to the predominant narratives about British literary tendencies of the 1950s, from the Angry Young Men to writers of the Movement. In one respect, at least, and in part through its presentation as seemingly popular genre writing, Roberts's *The Endeavour* marks a significant stage in the simplification of her writing voice in comparison to her earlier poetry. However, her narrative is constructed on the founding principles and subjects that underlie her modernist poetics, and any concentration on the process of simplification per se would be to miss those ways in which her prose style is visually poetic, deploys simultaneous multiple narrative perspective through silent collage, and concentrates on those same questions of existential restlessness and border crossings that make her such an engagingly complex writer. While the generally accepted periodizations of modernism are stretched ever further forward, and while the stylistic and conceptual determinants become ever broader, there is still much work to be done to restore those writers of the 1940s and 1950s who remain unquantifiable by or elusive to current categorizations, and in so doing to modify those categorizations to do the work we need them to do.

As further demonstration of Roberts's generic restlessness, in her private papers there is a nine-page manuscript of a version of *The Endeavour* for children. On Banks and Parkinson's illicit expedition onto Brazilian soil she writes with characteristic sensitivity to generic register:

> As they drew near the gay flowers glittered in their faces. Sparkling with dew, they were as large and fragile as candy floss. There were flowers which grew down from the branches of the trees, out of the trunks of the trees and flowers which grew with no roots at all. And it was a strange and wonderful sight. They saw humming birds as small as a thimble with tiny feathered wings.[49]

And in the mid 1960s Roberts was planning a further generic translation of *The Endeavour* into a television serialization: a letter from Peter Owen to Roberts on 16 July 1966 revealed the book was out of stock, but nevertheless the publisher recommended an agent to try to take the television idea forward.[50] An eight-part sketch for the proposed serialization also survives in her papers, putting the emphasis on drama and spectacle: 'Part V: They sail North Island find cannibals, warriors who seek opportunities to show off their courage, huge birds seen *yards* long? A boy on *Endeavour* is stolen by cannibals.'[51] Roberts was a great believer in the potential of film as a medium for the creation and dissemination of poetry, declaring for example at her wartime tea with the Sitwells her desire that poetry readings should in future be shown through the medium.[52] The idea, which came to nothing, might at least have pleased Barrington Gates.

Roberts's daughter Angharad Rhys remembers that early copies of *The Endeavour* came with an advertising band around the dust jacket claiming that the book was 'more exciting than the Kon-Tiki', drawing comparison with the very popular book and film based on the Norwegian adventurer Thor Heyerdahl's 1947 voyage from Peru to the Polynesian islands in a balsa-wood raft.[53] Roberts's own adventurous plans to move to Mallorca in the early 1950s did not materialize, but in writing the story of Cook's first voyage Roberts achieved a version of migratory freedom through a generic adventure that reconnected with aspects of a personal past through imaginative historical prose. The rediscovery of such a text, and the exploration of the networks that helped enable it, provides us with a very different way to think about the nature and status of mid-century writing, and also indicates the distance still to go in understanding those often misrepresented decades and their authors, forced to the edge of discussion by the tyrannies of prevailing literary-historical narratives.

Notes

[1] T. S. Eliot, unpublished letter to Lynette Roberts, 28 December 1953. A copy of the letter is among Lynette Roberts's family papers. The original is held in the Harry Ransom Center, University of Texas at Austin. Reproduced by permission of Faber and Faber on behalf of the Estate of T. S. Eliot.

[2] Lynette Roberts, unpublished letter to Robert Graves, 21 January 1954. This, and subsequent quotations from the unpublished correspondence, are reproduced by permission of the President and Fellows of St John's College, Oxford, and the Estate of Lynette Roberts.

[3] The scheme was designed in 1922 with a plan to provide Eliot with enough money to give up conventional work in order to devote himself to literature. For an account of the scheme and Eliot's reaction to it, see A. D. Moody, *Ezra Pound: The Epic Years, 1921–1939* (Oxford: Oxford University Press, 2014), pp. 35–8.

[4] For an account exploring the idea of Graves's self-imposed exile see Patrick McGuinness, 'Donald Davie and Robert Graves: Some Notes and a Letter', *Gravesiana*, 1/4 (1997), 333–45.

5 Roberts returned to the same graveyard in November 1953, a month before Eliot's Christmas letter arrived, to attend the funeral of her friend Dylan Thomas.
6 Roberts, unpublished letter to Robert Graves, 16 September 1949.
7 Lynette Roberts, 'A Carmarthenshire Diary', in *Diaries, Letters and Recollections*, ed. Patrick McGuinness (Manchester: Carcanet, 2008), p. 25.
8 Lynette Roberts, 'The Orange Charger', *Life and Letters*, 60/139 (1949), 232–3. Reprinted in 'Three Uncollected Poems', ed. Charles Mundye, *PN Review*, 40/2 (2013), 28–9.
9 Graves, letter to Roberts, 13 February 1944, in *Poetry Wales* (special issue on Lynette Roberts), 19/2 (1983), 51–124 (67). A proportion of the Roberts and Graves correspondence is here published as 'The Correspondence between Lynette Roberts and Robert Graves', and I quote from this published source where possible.
10 Eliot, unpublished letter to Roberts, 11 April 1945.
11 Roberts, unpublished letter to Beryl and Robert Graves, 12 September 1953.
12 The statement is in the Roberts family papers.
13 Eliot, unpublished letter to Roberts, 27 May 1953.
14 Lynette Roberts, *The Endeavour: Captain Cook's First Voyage to Australia* (London: Peter Owen, 1954), p. 11.
15 Anon., 'Girls Stage Cabaret as Ship Grounds', *Daily Mail* (10 April 1939), 9.
16 Lynette Roberts, 'Radio Talk on South American Poems', in *Collected Poems*, ed. Patrick McGuinness (Manchester: Carcanet, 2005), p. 111.
17 Roberts, letter to Graves, 4 November 1949. The letter is partially published in the *Poetry Wales* correspondence, but with mistranscriptions.
18 Lynette Roberts, 'Out of the Paw of Night', *Poetry London*, 5/21 (1951), 13–14.
19 Roberts, *Diaries, Letters and Recollections*, pp. 203–4.
20 Joseph Banks, *Journal of the Right Hon. Sir Joseph Banks*, ed. Joseph D. Hooker (London: Macmillan, 1896), p. 29.
21 Sydney Parkinson, *A Journal of a Voyage to the South Seas* (London: Printed for Stanfield Parkinson, the Editor: and sold by Messrs Richardson and Urqhuart; and others, 1773), p. 4.
22 In a two-page manuscript summary of the project she writes: 'There are also the sensitive watercolour drawings by Sydney Parkinson, a draughtsman who died on this voyage. These are bound in weighty holly-green volumes which take almost two men, or one stumbling and bent under the weight, to lift off the shelves.' Roberts family papers.
23 Roberts, *The Endeavour*, pp. 48–50.
24 'A crowded and enthusiastic company presented themselves at the opening of the Exhibition of Paintings by Welsh Artists at the Mansard Gallery on Thursday, the 15th January . . . Lynette Roberts shows the originals of her Llanybri landscapes already well-known in reproduction, the colouring which we see for the first time has a likeness to tender ceramics and pervades and intangible feminine charm. Kyffin Williams seems remarkably at home with a palette knife'. Ixion, 'Review: Art Exhibition', in *Wales*, 7/28 (1948), 482–3 (482).
25 Roberts, *Collected Poems*, p. 53.
26 Roberts, *The Endeavour*, p. 9.

27 Diana Wallace, *The Woman's Historical Novel: British Women Writers, 1900–2000* (Basingstoke: Palgrave Macmillan, 2005), p. 104.
28 Roberts, *The Endeavour*, p. 199.
29 Banks, *Journal*, p. 275.
30 James Cook, *Captain Cook's Journal during his First Voyage Round the World*, ed. W. J. L. Wharton (London: Elliot Stock, 1893), p. 275.
31 Banks, *Journal*, p. 275.
32 'Analysing these [journal entries] from day to day, and when possible quoting the authentic writings from each person as they speak, for instance when there is a conflict between Banks and Cook, or Cook and his officers, I have deliberately used their own way of relating these thoughts, so that each personality grows out of his own statements.' See Roberts, *The Endeavour*, p. 9.
33 Parkinson, *A Journal*, p. 142.
34 Roberts, *The Endeavour*, pp. 197–8.
35 Diana Wallace, 'Difficulties, discontinuities and differences: Reading women's historical fiction', in *The Female Figure in Contemporary Historical Fiction*, ed. Katherine Cooper and Emma Short (Basingstoke: Palgrave Macmillan, 2012), p. 208.
36 S. Barrington Gates, 'Cook's Voyage', *Times Literary Supplement* (30 April 1954), 283.
37 For a discussion of Eliot's and Graves's criticisms see Charles Mundye, 'Outside the Imaginary Museum: Mythology and Representation in the Poetry of Lynette Roberts and Keidrych Rhys', *PN Review*, 40/2 (2013), 23–8.
38 Edith Sitwell, unpublished letter to Roberts, 31 January 1954. A copy of the letter is among the Roberts family papers. The original is held in the Harry Ransom Center, University of Texas at Austin. Reproduced by permission of Peters Fraser & Dunlop on behalf of the Estate of Edith Sitwell.
39 Lynette Roberts, 'Tea with the Sitwells', in *Diaries, Letters and Recollections*, pp. 145–8 (p. 148).
40 Roberts, 'Tea with the Sitwells', p. 147.
41 Quoted in Jean Radford, 'Modernist Melancholy: Edith Sitwell's Black Sun', in *At Home and Abroad in the Empire: British Women Write the 1930s*, ed. Robin Hackett, Freda Hauser and Gay Wachman (Newark: University of Delaware Press, 2009), p. 213.
42 Radford, 'Modernist Melancholy', p. 208.
43 Radford, 'Modernist Melancholy', p. 208.
44 Roberts, *Collected Poems*, p. xxxiii.
45 Nicola Humble, *The Feminine Middlebrow Novel, 1920s to 1950s: Class, Domesticity, and Bohemianism* (Oxford: Oxford University Press, 2001), pp. 1–2.
46 Kristin Bluemel (ed.), *Intermodernism: Literary Culture in Mid-Twentieth-Century Britain* (Edinburgh: Edinburgh University Press, 2009), p. 1.
47 Tyrus Miller, *Late Modernism: Politics, Fiction, and the Arts between the World Wars* (Berkeley and London: University of California Press, 1999), p. 12.
48 Miller, *Late Modernism*, p. 22.
49 Roberts, unpublished manuscript. Roberts family papers.
50 The letter is among the Roberts family papers.

[51] Roberts, unpublished manuscript. Roberts family papers.
[52] Roberts, 'Tea with the Sitwells', pp. 146–7.
[53] Personal communication.

Select Bibliography

Primary Sources

Beale, Anne, *The Vale of the Towey* (London: Longman, Brown, Green, and Longmans, 1844).
—, *Traits and Stories of the Welsh Peasantry* (London: George Routledge and Company, 1849).
Bowen, Elizabeth, *Collected Impressions* (London: Longmans, 1950).
Burton, P. H., unpublished letter to Roberts, 17 November 1948. Lynette Roberts Collection, Harry Ransom Center, University of Texas at Austin.
Cook, James, *Captain Cook's Journal during his First Voyage Round the World*, ed. W. J. L. Wharton (London: Elliot Stock, 1893).
Davies, Sioned (ed. and trans.), *The Mabinogion* (Oxford: Oxford University Press, 2007).
Eliot, T. S., 'The Waste Land', in *The Waste Land and Other Poems* (London: Faber, 1990).
—, unpublished letter to Roberts, 11 April 1945. Lynette Roberts Collection, Harry Ransom Center, University of Texas at Austin.
—, unpublished letter to Lynette Roberts, 27 May 1953. Harry Ransom Center, University of Texas at Austin.
—, unpublished letter to Lynette Roberts, 28 December 1953, Lynette Roberts Collection, Harry Ransom Center, University of Texas at Austin.
Golding, William, *Pincher Martin* (London: Faber, 1956).
Graves, Robert, letter to Roberts, 13 February 1944, in *Poetry Wales* (special issue on Lynette Roberts), 19/2 (1983), 51–124 (67).
Hemans, Felicia, *'The Domestic Affections' and Other Poems* (London: T. Cadell and W. Davies, 1812).

—, *A Selection of Welsh Melodies* (London: J. Power, 1822).
—, 'The Homes of England', *Blackwood's*, 21 (1827), 392.
Hendry, J. F., and Henry Treece (eds), *The White Horseman* (London: Routledge, 1941).
Jones, David, *In Parenthesis* (London: Faber and Faber, 1961).
Lewis, Alun, *Selected Poems of Alun Lewis*, ed. Jeremy Hooker and Gweno Lewis (London: Unwin, 1981).
MacNeice, Louis, *Collected Poems*, ed. E. R. Dodds (Oxford: Oxford University Press, 1967).
Mansfield, Katherine, *The Collected Letters of Katherine Mansfield*, ed. Vincent O'Sullivan and Margaret Scott (Oxford: Oxford University Press, 1996).
—, *The Collected Stories of Katherine Mansfield* (London: Penguin, 2001).
Maxwell, Gavin, *Harpoon at a Venture* (London: Rupert Hart-Davies, 1952).
Parkinson, Sydney, *A Journal of a Voyage to the South Seas* (London: Printed for Stanfield Parkinson, the Editor: and sold by Messrs Richardson and Urqhuart; and others, 1773).
Philips, Katherine, 'To my Lord Archbishop of Canterbury his Grace 1664', in *The Collected Works of Katherine Philips, the Matchless Orinda*, ed. Patrick Thomas, Germaine Greer and R. Little, 3 vols (Stump Cross: Stump Cross Books, 1990–3), I, p. 239, ll. 1–10.
Rhys, Keidrych, *The Van Pool: Collected Poems*, ed. Charles Mundye (Bridgend: Seren, 2012).
Roberts, Lynette, 'To Keidrych Rhys', *Wales*, 10 (1939), 278–9.
—, *El Dorado*, in Collected Poems, ed. Patrick McGuinness (Manchester: Carcanet, 2005), pp. 115–29.
—, 'Poem', *Wales*, 11 (1939–40), 302.
—, 'Lorenzo da Monaco', *Life and Letters Today*, 25/34 (1940), 300–11.
—, 'Letter from Lynette Rhys', National Library of Wales, David Jones Papers CT7/2 (MS: 1943).
—, 'The Orange Charger', *Life and Letters*, 60/139 (1949), 232–3.
—, 'Out of the Paw of Night', *Poetry London*, 5/21 (1951), 13–14.
—, *The Endeavour: Captain Cook's First Voyage to Australia* (London: Peter Owen, 1954).
—, *Collected Poems*, ed. Patrick McGuinness (Manchester: Carcanet, 2005).
—, 'Radio Talk on South American Poems', in *Collected Poems*, ed. Patrick McGuinness (Manchester: Carcanet, 2005), pp. 107–14.
—, *Diaries, Letters and Recollections*, ed. Patrick McGuinness (Manchester: Carcanet, 2008).
—, 'A Carmarthenshire Diary', in *Diaries, Letters and Recollections*, ed. Patrick McGuinness (Manchester: Carcanet, 2008), pp. 3–93.

—, 'Coracles of the Towy', in *Diaries, Letters and Recollections*, ed. Patrick McGuinness (Manchester: Carcanet, 2008), pp. 133–8.

—, *Gods with Stainless Ears*, in *Collected Poems*, ed. Patrick McGuinness (Manchester: Carcanet, 2005), pp. 41–78.

—, 'An Introduction to Village Dialect', in *Diaries, Letters and Recollections*, ed. Patrick McGuinness (Manchester: Carcanet, 2008), pp. 107–24. Originally published as *An Introduction to Village Dialect With Seven Stories* (Carmarthen: The Druid Press, 1944).

—, 'Notes for an Autobiography, in *Diaries, Letters and Recollections*, ed. Patrick McGuinness (Manchester: Carcanet, 2008), pp. 191–219.

—, 'Simplicity of the Welsh Village', in *Diaries, Letters and Recollections*, ed. Patrick McGuinness (Manchester: Carcanet, 2008), pp. 127–32.

—, 'Tea with the Sitwells', in *Diaries, Letters and Recollections*, ed. Patrick McGuiness (Manchester: Carcanet, 2008), pp. 145–8.

—, 'Village Dialect: Seven Stories', in *Diaries, Letters and Recollections*, ed. Patrick McGuinness (Manchester: Carcanet, 2008), pp. 94–106. Originally published as *An Introduction to Village Dialect With Seven Stories* (Carmarthen: The Druid Press, 1944).

—, 'A Letter to the Dead', *PN Review*, 220, 41/2 (2014), 18–19.

—, unpublished 'Book of Nesta', Lynette Roberts Collection, Harry Ransom Center, University of Texas at Austin, MS-3561.

—, 'Undated Correspondence', National Library of Wales, David Jones Papers CT3/6, 149–50.

—, unpublished letter to Alun Lewis (undated, *c.*1940–1), Alun Lewis Collection, National Library of Wales, Aberystwyth.

—, letter to Robert Graves, *c.*7 May 1944, in *Diaries, Letters and Recollections*, ed. Patrick McGuinness (Manchester: Carcanet, 2008), pp. 176–7.

—, unpublished letter to Beryl and Robert Graves, 12 September 1953, St John's College, Oxford.

—, unpublished letter to Robert Graves, 16 September 1949, St John's College, Oxford.

—, unpublished letter to Robert Graves, 4 November 1949, St John's College, Oxford.

—, unpublished letter to Robert Graves, 21 January 1954, St John's College, Oxford.

—, unpublished. 'Writing in Wartime' (1941) Lynette Roberts Collection, Harry Ransom Center, University of Texas at Austin, 3.5.

Sitwell, Edith, unpublished letter to Lynette Roberts, 31 January 1954, Lynette Roberts Collections, Harry Ransom Center, University of Texas at Austin, 4.3–4.

Thomas, Dylan, *The Collected Letters of Dylan Thomas*, ed. Paul Ferris (London: Dent, 1985).
—, *A Dylan Thomas Treasury: Poems, Stories and Broadcasts* (London: Phoenix, 2001).
Thomas, R. S., *Pietà* (London: Rupert Hart-Davis, 1966).
Treece, Henry, 'Two at the Table', in *I Cannot Go Hunting Tomorrow* (London: Grey Walls Press, 1946), pp. 111–21.
Woodcock, George, *Letter to the Past* (Toronto: Fitzhenry and Whiteside, 1982).
Woolf, Virginia, 'Modern Fiction', in *Collected Essays*, ed. Leonard Woolf, 3 vols (London: Hogarth, 1966 [1919]), II, pp. 106–7.
—, *Virginia Woolf, Selected Short Stories*, ed. Sandra Kemp (London: Penguin Classics, 2000 [1921]).
—, *The Waves* (Oxford: Oxford University Press, 2014 [1931]).
—, *A Room of One's Own and Three Guineas* (Oxford: Oxford University Press, 2008).

Secondary Sources

Anon., 'A New Novel by Miss Beale of Llandeilo', *The Welshman* (22 October 1869), 6.
Anon., 'Girls Stage Cabaret as Ship Grounds', *Daily Mail* (10 April 1939), 9.
Aldersey-Williams, Hugh, *Tide: The Science and Lore of the Greatest Force on Earth* (London: Viking, 2016).
Alexander, Neal, and David Cooper (eds), *Poetry and Geography: Space and Place in Postwar Poetry* (Liverpool: Liverpool University Press, 2013).
Anderson, Benedict, *Imagined Communities: Reflection on the Origin and Spread of Nationalism* (London: Verso, 1983; rev. edn, 2006).
Anderson Elizabeth, 'H.D.'s Tapestry: Embroidery, William Morris and *The Sword Went Out to Sea*', *Modernist Cultures*, 12/2 (2017), 226–48.
Bakhtin, Mikhail, 'Forms of Time and Chronotope in the Novel', in *The Dialogic Imagination: Four Essays*, ed. Michael Holquist, trans. Caryl Emerson and Michael Holquist (Austin: University of Texas Press, 1982), pp. 84–258.
Banks, Joseph, *Journal of the Right Hon. Sir Joseph Banks*, ed. Joseph D. Hooker (London: Macmillan, 1896).
Barthes, Roland, *The Responsibility of Forms: Critical Essays on Music, Art and Representation*, trans. Richard Howard (Oxford: Basil Blackwell, 1985).
Batchelor, Jennie, and Cora Kaplan (eds), *The History of British Women's Writing*, 10 vols (Basingstoke and New York: Palgrave Macmillan, 2010–18).

Bate, Jonathan, *Song of the Earth* (London: Pan Macmillan, 2011).
Beddoe, Deirdre, *Out of the Shadows: A History of Women in Twentieth-Century Wales* (Cardiff: University of Wales Press, 2000).
Benjamin, Walter, *Theses on the Philosophy of History*, in *Illuminations*, ed. Hannah Arendt and trans. Harry Zohn (New York: Schocken Books, 1968).
Bluemel, Kristin (ed.), *Intermodernism: Literary Culture in Mid-Twentieth-Century Britain* (Edinburgh: Edinburgh University Press, 2009).
Blunden, Edward, 'On Pilgrimage in England: Voyages of Discovery', *Times Literary Supplement* (28 March 1942), 156–61.
Bohata, Kirsti, *Postcolonialism Revisited* (Cardiff: University of Wales Press, 2004).
Botting, Douglas, *Gavin Maxwell: A Life* (London: Harper Collins, 1991).
Bradbury, Malcolm, 'The Cities of Modernism', in *Modernism 1890–1930*, ed. Malcolm Bradbury and James McFarlane (Harmondsworth: Penguin, 1991), pp. 94–104.
Brannigan, John, *Archipelagic Modernism* (Edinburgh: Edinburgh University Press, 2015).
Broomfield, Stuart, *Wales at War: The Experience of the Second World War in Wales* (Stroud: The History Press, 2009).
Chandler, Alice, *A Dream of Order: The Medieval Ideal in Nineteenth-Century English Literature* (London: Routledge and Kegan Paul, 1971).
Clarke, Eric F., *Ways of Listening: An Ecological Approach to the Perception of Musical Meaning* (Oxford: Oxford University Press, 2005).
Clifford, James, 'Travelling Cultures', in *Cultural Studies*, ed. Lawrence Grossberg, Cary Nelson and Paula A. Treichler (New York and London: Routledge, 1992), pp. 96–116.
Conran, Anthony, 'Lynette Roberts: War Poet', *Anglo-Welsh Review*, 65 (1979), 50–62.
—, *The Cost of Strangeness: Essays on the English Poets of Wales* (Llandysul: Gomer, 1982).
—, 'Lynette Roberts: The Lyric Pieces', *Poetry Wales* (special issue on Lynette Roberts), 19/2 (1983), 125–33.
—, *Frontiers in Anglo-Welsh Poetry* (Cardiff: University of Wales Press, 1997).
Crawford, Robert, 'Macdiarmud in Montrose', in *Locations of Literary Modernism: Region and Nation in British and American Modernist Poetry*, ed. Alex Davis and Lee M. Jenkins (Cambridge: Cambridge University Press, 2000), pp. 35–56.
Davis, Alex, and Lee M. Jenkins, 'Locating Modernisms: An Overview', in *Locations of Literary Modernism*, ed. Alex Davis and Lee M. Jenkins (Cambridge: Cambridge University Press, 2000), pp. 3–30.

Dearnley, Moira, '"I Came Hither, A Stranger": A View of Wales in the Novels of Anne Beale (1815–1900)', *The New Welsh Review*, 1/4 (1989), 27–32.

Dilworth, Thomas, *Reading David Jones* (Cardiff: University of Wales Press, 2008).

Dinshaw, Carolyn, *How Soon Is Now? Medieval Texts, Amateur Readers, and the Queerness of Time* (London and Durham: Duke University Press, 2012).

Doyle, Laura, and Laura Winkiel (eds), *Geomodernisms: Race, Modernism, Modernity* (Bloomington and Indianapolis: Indiana University Press, 2005).

Edwards, Hywel Teifi, '"Y Pentre Gwyn" and "Manteg": from Blessed Plot to Hotspot', in *Beyond the Difference: Welsh Literature in Comparative Perspectives*, ed. Alyce von Rothkirch and Daniel Williams (Cardiff: University of Wales Press, 2014), pp. 8–20.

Edwards, O. M., *Cartrefi Cymru* (Wrecsam: Hughes a'i Fab, 1896).

Entwistle, Alice, *Poetry, Geography, Gender: Women Rewriting Contemporary Wales* (Cardiff: University of Wales Press, 2013).

Esty, Jed, *A Shrinking Island: Modernism and National Culture in England* (Princeton: Princeton University Press, 2003).

Evans, Margiad, 'Review of *Welsh Border Country* and *Old English Household Life*', *Wales*, 10 (1939), 285–6.

Ferris, Paul, *Dylan Thomas: The Biography* (London: Dent, 1999).

Flay, Claire, *Dorothy Edwards* (Cardiff: University of Wales Press, 2011).

Fleure, H. J., *Wales and Her People* (Wrexham: Hughes and Son, 1926).

Friedman, Susan Stanford, *Mappings: Feminism and the Cultural Geographies of Encounter* (Princeton: Princeton University Press, 1998).

—, 'Periodizing Modernism: Postcolonial Modernities and the Space/Time Borders of Modernist Studies', *Modernism/modernity*, 13/3 (2006), 425–43.

Gardiner, Judith Kegan, 'The Exhilaration of Exile: Rhys, Stead, and Lessing', in *Women's Writing in Exile*, ed. Mary Lynn Broe and Angela Ingram (Chapel Hill and London: University of North Carolina Press, 1989), pp. 133–50.

Garrity, Jane, *Step-daughters of England: British Women Modernists and the National Imaginary* (Manchester and New York: Manchester University Press, 2003).

—, 'Modernist Women's Writing: Beyond the Threshold of Obsolescence', *Literature Compass*, 10/1 (2013), 15–29.

Gasiorek, Andrzej, *A History of Modernism* (Chichester: Wiley and Blackwell, 2015).

Gates, S. Barrington, 'Cook's Voyage', *Times Literary Supplement* (30 April 1954), 283.
Geertz, Clifford, *The Interpretation of Cultures* (New York: Basic Books, 1973).
George, David Lloyd, *The Great War: Speech Delivered by the Rt. Hon. David Lloyd George at the Queen's Hall, London on September 19, 1914* (London: Hodder and Stoughton, 1914).
Glancy, Mark, *Hollywood and the Americanization of Britain: From the 1920s to the Present* (London and New York: I. B. Tauris and Co. Ltd, 2014).
Goodby, John, 'Dylan Thomas and the Poetry of the 1940s', in *The Cambridge History of English Poetry*, ed. Michael O'Neill (Cambridge: Cambridge University Press, 2010), pp. 858–78.
—, *The Poetry of Dylan Thomas: Under the Spelling Wall* (Liverpool: Liverpool University Press, 2013).
—, and Chris Wigginton, 'Welsh Modernist Poetry: Dylan Thomas, David Jones, and Lynette Roberts', in *Regional Modernisms*, ed. Neal Alexander and James Moran (Edinburgh: Edinburgh University Press, 2013), pp. 160–83.
Gramich, Katie, *Twentieth-Century Women's Writing in Wales: Land, Gender, Belonging* (Cardiff: University of Wales Press, 2007).
Grigson, Geoffrey, 'Comment on England', *Axis*, 1 (1935), 8–10.
—, and John Piper, 'England's Climate', *Axis*, 7 (1936), 5–9.
Gross, Charles, 'The Court of Piepowder', *The Quarterly Journal of Economics*, 20/2 (1906), 231–49.
Harris, Alexandra, *Romantic Moderns: English Writers, Artists and the Imagination from Virginia Woolf to John Piper* (London: Thames and Hudson, 2010).
Harris, Jennifer, 'William Morris and the Middle Ages', in *William Morris and the Middle Ages*, ed. Joanna Banham and Jennifer Harris (Manchester and Dover: Manchester University Press, 1984), pp. 1–17.
Henderson, Mae, 'Borders, Boundaries and Frame(works)', in *Borders, Boundaries and Frames*, ed. Mae Henderson (New York and London: Routledge, 1995), pp. 1–30.
Hickman, Miranda, 'Modernist Women Poets and the Problem of Form', in *The Cambridge Companion to Modernist Women Writers*, ed. Maren Tova Linett (Cambridge: Cambridge University Press, 2010), pp. 33–46.
Highmore, Ben, *Ordinary Lives: Studies in the Everyday* (Abingdon: Routledge, 2011).
Higonnet, Margaret R., and Patrice L.-R. Higonnet, 'The Double Helix', in *Behind the Lines: Gender and the Two World Wars*, ed. Margaret

Randolph Higonnet et al. (New Haven and London: Yale University Press, 1987), pp. 31–48.

Hobsbawm, Eric, *Nations and Nationalism since 1780: Programme Myth, Reality* (Cambridge: Cambridge University Press, 1990).

—, and Terence Ranger (eds), *The Invention of Tradition* (Cambridge: Cambridge University Press, 1983).

Hooker, Jeremy, *The Poetry of Place* (Manchester: Carcanet, 1982).

Hopwood, Mererid, *Singing in Chains: Listening to Welsh Verse* (Llandysul: Gomer, 2004).

Humble, Nicola, *The Feminine Middlebrow Novel, 1920s to 1950s: Class, Domesticity, and Bohemianism* (Oxford: Oxford University Press, 2001).

Humm, Maggie, 'Women Modernists and Visual Culture', in *The Cambridge Companion to Modernist Women Writers*, ed. Maren Tova Linnet (Cambridge: Cambridge University Press, 2010), pp. 146–59.

Huxley, Julian, *Mass Observation* (London: Fredrick Muller, 1937).

Hynes, Samuel, *The Auden Generation: Literature and Politics in England in the 1930s* (London: The Bodley Head, 1976).

Ingram, Angela, 'Introduction: On the Contrary, Outside of It', in *Women's Writing in Exile*, ed. Mary Lynn Broe and Angela Ingram (Chapel Hill and London: University of North Carolina Press, 1989), pp. 1–15.

Ixion, 'Review: Art Exhibition', in *Wales*, 7/28 (1948), 482–3.

Jarvis, Matthew, *Welsh Environments in Contemporary Poetry* (Cardiff: University of Wales Press, 2008).

Johnes, Martin, *Wales Since 1939* (Manchester: Manchester University Press, 2012).

Jones, Glyn, *The Dragon Has Two Tongues: Essays on Anglo-Welsh Writers and Writing*, ed. Tony Brown (Cardiff: University of Wales Press, rev. edn, 2001).

Kerrigan, John, 'Louis MacNeice among the Islands', in *Modern Irish and Scottish Poetry*, ed. Fran Brearton, Edna Longley and Peter Mackay (Cambridge: Cambridge University Press, 2010), pp. 58–86.

Kore-Schröder, Leena, 'Who's Afraid of Rosamund Merridew?: Reading Medieval History in "The Journal of Mistress Joan Martyn" ', *Journal of the Short Story in English* [online], 50 (2008), 1–11 (3). See *http://jsse.revues.org/719*.

Kronfeld, Chana, *On the Margins of Modernism: Decentering Literary Dynamics* (Berkeley and London: University of California Press, 1996).

Lewis, Eiluned, and Peter Lewis, *The Land of Wales* (London: Batsford, 1937).

Lewis, Saunders, *Egwyddorion Cenedlaetholdeb ('Principles of Nationalism')* (Caerdydd: Cymdeithas Plaid Cymru Archive Society, 1975 [1926]), pp. 1–19.

—, 'Is there an Anglo-Welsh Literature?' (Caerdydd: Urdd Graddedigion Prifysgol Cymru, 1939).

Linett, Maren Tova, 'Modernist Women's Literature – an Introduction', in *The Cambridge Companion to Modernist Women Writers*, ed. Maren Tova Linett (Cambridge: Cambridge University Press, 2010), pp. 1–16.

Lootens, Tricia, 'Hemans and Home: Victorianism, Feminine "Internal Enemies," and the Domestication of National Identity', *PMLA*, 109/2 (1994), 238–53.

Lorimer, Hayden, 'Poetry and Place: the Shape of Words', *Geography*, 93/3 (2008), 181–2.

Macalister, R. A. S., *The Secret Languages of Ireland* (Cambridge: Cambridge University Press, 1937).

McAvoy, Siriol, 'The Presence of the Past: Medieval Encounters in the Writing of Virginia Woolf and Lynette Roberts' (unpublished PhD thesis, Cardiff University, 2016).

McGuinness, Patrick, 'Donald Davie and Robert Graves: Some Notes and a Letter', *Gravesiana*, 1/4 (1997), 333–45.

Mao, Douglas, and Rebecca L. Walkovitz, 'The New Modernist Studies', *The Modern Language Association of America*, 123/3 (2008), 737–47.

Marcus, Jane, 'Alibis and Legends: The Ethics of Elsewhereness, Gender and Estrangement', in *Women's Writing in Exile*, ed. Mary Lynn Broe and Angela Ingram (Chapel Hill and London: University of North Carolina Press, 1989), pp. 269–94.

Marcus, Sharon, 'Feminist Criticism: A Tale of Two Bodies', *PMLA*, 121/5 (2006), 1722–8.

Martineau, Harriet, 'Cheshire Cheese', *Household Words* (2 September 1854), 52–6.

Matthews, David, *Medievalism: A Critical History* (Cambridge: D. S. Brewer, 2015).

May, William, 'Verbal and Visual Art in Twentieth-Century British Women's Poetry', in *The Cambridge Companion to Twentieth-Century British and Irish Women's Poetry*, ed. Jane Dowson (Cambridge: Cambridge University Press, 2011), pp. 42–61.

Medd, Jodie, 'Encountering the Past in Recent Gay and Lesbian Fiction', in *The Cambridge Companion to Gay and Lesbian Writing*, ed. Hugh Stephens (Cambridge: Cambridge University Press, 2011), pp. 167–84.

Mellor, David, (ed.), *A Paradise Lost: The Neo-Romantic Imagination in Britain 1935–55* (London: Lund Humphries, 1987).

Mellor, Leo, *Reading the Ruins: Modernism, Bombsites and British Culture* (Cambridge: Cambridge University Press, 2011).

Miller, Tyrus, *Late Modernism: Politics, Fiction, and the Arts Between the World Wars* (Berkeley and London: University of California Press, 1999).

Mitchell, Marea, '"The Details of Life and the Pulsings of Affect": Virginia Woolf's Medieval Texts', *The Chaucer Review*, 51/1 (2016), 107–29.

Moody, A. D., *Ezra Pound: The Epic Years, 1921–1939* (Oxford: Oxford University Press, 2014).

Moretti, Franco, 'Conjectures on World Literature', *New Left Review*, 1 (2000), 54–68.

—, 'More Conjectures on World Literature', *New Left Review*, 20 (2003), 73–81.

Morgan, Clare, 'Vanishing Horizons: Virginia Woolf and the Neo-Romantic Imagination in *Between the Acts* and "Anon" ', *Worldviews*, 5 (2001), 35–57.

Morgan, Eluned, *Dringo'r Andes* (Y Fenni: Y Brodyr Owen, 1904).

Morris, William, 'Address at the Twelfth Annual Meeting of the SPAB' (1889), in *William Morris: Artist, Writer, Socialist*, ed. May Morris, 2 vols (Oxford: Blackwell, 1936), I, pp. 146–7.

Mundye, Charles, 'Outside the Imaginary Museum: Mythology and Representation in the Poetry of Lynette Roberts and Keidrych Rhys', *PN Review*, 40/2 (2013), 23–8.

—, 'Lynette Roberts and Dylan Thomas: Background to a Friendship', *PN Review*, 220, 41/2 (2014), 20–3.

Murfin, R., and S. M. Ray (eds), *The Bedford Glossary of Critical and Literary Terms* (Boston: Bedford/St Martin's, 2009).

Nancy, Jean-Luc, *Listening*, trans. Charlotte Mandell (New York: Fordham University Press, 2007).

Neuwirth, Robert, *Stealth of Nations: The Global Rise of the Informal Economy* (New York: Random House, 2011).

Nicholls, Peter, 'Pound's Places', in *Locations of Literary Modernism: Region and Nation in British and American Modernist Poetry*, ed. Alex Davis and Lee M. Jenkins (Cambridge: Cambridge University Press, 2000), pp. 159–77.

—, 'Surrealism in England', in *The Cambridge History of Twentieth Century English Literature*, ed. Laura Marcus and Peter Nicholls (Cambridge: Cambridge University Press, 2005), pp. 396–416.

Noë, Alva, *Varieties of Presence* (Cambridge: Harvard University Press, 2012).

Peat, Alexandra, 'Modern Pilgrimage and the Authority of Space in Forster's *A Room with a View* and Woolf's *The Voyage Out*', *Mosaic: A Journal for the Interdisciplinary Study of Literature*, 36 (2003), 139–53.

Peate, Iorwerth C., *The Welsh House: A Study in Folk Culture* (London: The Honourable Society of Cymmrodorion, 1940).

—, *Cymru a'i Phobl* (Caerdydd: Gwasg Prifysgol Caerdydd, 1948).
Peppis, Paul, 'Schools, Movements, Manifestoes', in *The Cambridge Companion to Modernist Poetry*, ed. Alex Davis and Lee M. Jenkins (Cambridge: Cambridge University Press, 2007), pp. 28–50.
Pikoulis, John, 'Lynette Roberts and Alun Lewis', *Poetry Wales* (special issue on Lynette Roberts), 19/2 (1983), 9–29.
—, 'The Poetry of the Second World War', in *British Poetry, 1900–50: Aspects of Tradition*, ed. Gary Day and Brian Docherty (Basingstoke: Macmillan, 1995), pp. 193–207.
Piper, John, 'England's Early Sculptors', *Architectural Review*, 80 (1936), 157–60.
Plain, Gill, *Women's Fiction of the Second World War: Gender, Power and Resistance* (Edinburgh: Edinburgh University Press, 1996).
Plate, Liedeke, *Transforming Memories in Contemporary Women's Rewriting* (Basingstoke and New York: Palgrave Macmillan, 2011).
Pollard, Charles W., *New World Modernisms: T. S. Eliot, Derek Walcott, and Kamau Brathwaite* (Charlottesville: University of Virginia Press, 2004).
Power, Eileen, *Medieval People* (London: Methuen, 1963 [1924]).
Pratt, Mary Louise, *Imperial Eyes* (London: Routledge, 1992).
Prescott, Sarah, '"That private shade, wherein my Muse was bred": Katherine Phillips (1632–1664) and the Poetic Spaces of Welsh Retirement', *Philological Quarterly*, 88/4 (2009), 345–64.
Radford, Jean, 'Modernist Melancholy: Edith Sitwell's Black Sun', in *At Home and Abroad in the Empire. British Women Write the 1930s*, ed. Robin Hackett, Freda Hauser and Gay Wachman (Newark: University of Delaware Press, 2009), pp. 203–21.
Ramazani, Jahan, *A Transnational Poetics* (Chicago: University of Chicago Press, 2009).
Rawlinson, Mark, 'The Second World War: British Writing', in *The Cambridge Companion to War Writing*, ed. Kate McLoughlin (Cambridge: Cambridge University Press, 2009), pp. 197–211.
Reed-Danahay, Deborah, 'Introduction', in *Auto/ethnography: Rewriting the Self and the Social* (Oxford: Berg, 1997), pp. 1–17.
Rees, Dylan, *Carmarthenshire: the Concise History* (Cardiff: University of Wales Press, 2006).
Rees, W. J., *The Lives of the Cambro-British Saints* (Llandovery: William Rees; London: Longman; Abergavenny: J. H. Morgan, 1853).
Renan, Ernest, 'What is a Nation?', trans. Martin Thom, in *Nation and Narration*, ed. Homi K. Bhabha (London and New York: Routledge, 1990), pp. 8–22.

Rhŷs, John, *Celtic Folklore: Welsh and Manx* (Oxford: The Clarendon Press, 1901).
Rhys, Keidrych, 'Editorial', *Wales*, 3/1 (1943), 4–6.
—, 'Editorial', *Wales*, 3/3 (1944), 4–6.
—, 'Editorial', *Wales*, 4/6 (1945), 4–6.
Roberts, Glyn, 'The Welsh School of Writers', *The Bookman*, 84 (1933), 248–9.
Roberts, Gwyneth Tyson, *The Language of the Blue Books: the Perfect Instrument of Empire* (Cardiff: University of Wales Press, 1998).
Robichaud, Paul, *Making the Past Present: David Jones, the Middle Ages, and Modernism* (Washington DC: The Catholic University of America Press, 2007).
Sala, Nicoletta, 'Fractal Geometry in the Arts: An Overview across the Different Cultures', in *Thinking in Patterns: Fractals and Related Phenomena in Nature*, ed. Miroslav M. Novak (Singapore, River Edge, New Jersey, and London: World Scientific, 2004), pp. 177–88.
Santos, Irene Ramalho, *Atlantic Poets: Fernando Pessoa's Turn in Anglo-American Modernism* (Hanover: University Press of New England, 2003).
Savage, Mike, Gaynor Bagnall and Brian Longhurst, *Globalization and Belonging* (London and Thousand Oaks: Sage, 2005).
Schensul, J. J., and M. D. Lecompte, *Designing and Conducting Ethnographic Research* (Walnut Creek: AltaMira, 1999).
Schulz, Felix Robin, *Death in East Germany, 1945–1990* (New York: Berghahn Books, 2013).
Shell, Marc, *Islandology: Geography, Rhetoric, Politics* (London: Stanford University Press, 2014).
Shugart, Helene, and Catherine Egley Waggoner, *Making Camp: Ethics of Transgression in U.S. Popular Culture* (Tuscaloosa: University of Alabama Press, 2008).
Sivaramamurti, C., *The Painter in Ancient India* (New Delhi: Abhinav Publications, 1978).
Skoulding, Zoë, 'Film, Gramophones and the Noise of Landscape in Dylan Thomas and Lynette Roberts', in *Reading Dylan Thomas*, ed. Edward Allen (Edinburgh: Edinburgh University Press, 2017), pp. 138–54.
Smith, Kieron, ' "Constructing the Map": Welsh Criticism of Caradoc Evans', *Almanac*, 16 (2012), 89–120.
Sontag, Susan, 'Notes on "Camp" ' (1964), in her *Against Interpretation, and Other Essays* (London: Penguin, 2009), pp. 3–14.

Spiropoulou, Angeliki, *Virginia Woolf, Modernity and History: Constellations with Walter Benjamin* (Basingstoke and New York: Palgrave Macmillan, 2010).

Stephens, Meic (ed.), *The New Companion to the Literature of Wales* (Cardiff: University of Wales Press, 1998).

Stephens, Thomas, *The Literature of the Kymry* (London: Longmans, Green and Co., 1876).

Stevens, Catrin, *Iorwerth C. Peate* (Cardiff: University of Wales Press, 1986).

Thomas, M. Wynn, '*My People* and the Revenge of the Novel', *New Welsh Review*, 1 (1988), 17–22.

—, *Corresponding Cultures: The Two Literatures of Wales* (Cardiff: University of Wales Press, 1999).

Tschiffely, A. F., *This Way Southward: The Account of a Journey Through Patagonia and Tierra Del Fuego* (London: William Heinemann, 1940).

Turner, Victor, and Edith L. B. Turner, *Image and Pilgrimage in Christian Culture* (New York: Columbia University Press, 1978).

Verma, Neelam, *Traditions: A Complete Book of Indian Arts and Crafts Motifs* (Mumbai: English Edition Publishers and Distributors, 2005).

Wainwright, Laura, 'New Territories in Modernism: Anglophone Welsh Writing, 1930–49' (unpublished PhD thesis, Cardiff University, 2010).

Walkovitz, Rebecca L., *Cosmopolitan Style: Modernism Beyond the Nation* (New York: Columbia University Press, 2006).

Wallace, Diana, *The Woman's Historical Novel: British Women Writers, 1900–2000* (Basingstoke: Palgrave Macmillan, 2005).

—, 'Difficulties, discontinuities and differences: Reading women's historical fiction', in *The Female Figure in Contemporary Historical Fiction*, ed. Katherine Cooper and Emma Short (Basingstoke: Palgrave Macmillan, 2012), pp. 206–21.

Warwick Research Collective [WReC], *Combined and Uneven Development: Towards a New Theory of World-Literature* (Liverpool: Liverpool University Press, 2015).

Watkins, Vernon, 'Review of *In Parenthesis*', *Wales*, 5 (1938), 184.

Wheale, Nigel, 'Lynette Roberts: Legend and Form in the 1940s', *Critical Quarterly*, 36/3 (1994), 4–19.

—, 'Beyond the Trauma Stratus: Lynette Roberts' *Gods with Stainless Ears* and the Post-war Cultural Landscape', *Welsh Writing in English: A Yearbook of Critical Essays*, 3 (1997), 98–117.

Wigginton, Chris, 'Welsh Modernist Poetry: Dylan Thomas, David Jones, and Lynette Roberts', in *Regional Modernisms*, ed. Neal Alexander and James Moran (Edinburgh: Edinburgh University Press, 2013), pp. 160–83.

Wilkinson, John, *The Lyric Touch: Essays on the Poetry of Excess* (Cambridge: Salt, 2007).
Williams, Daniel, 'Welsh Modernism', in *The Oxford Handbook of Modernisms*, ed. Peter Brooker, Andrzej Gasiorek, Deborah Longworth and Andrew Thacker (Oxford: Oxford University Press, 2010), pp. 797–816.
—, *Black Skin, Blue Books* (Cardiff: Cardiff University Press, 2012).
Williams, Glyn, *The Desert and the Dream: A Study of Welsh Colonization in Chubut, 1865–1915* (Cardiff: University of Wales Press, 1975).
—, *The Welsh in Patagonia: The State and the Ethnic Community* (Cardiff: University of Wales Press, 1991).
Williams, Raymond, *Marxism and Literature* (Oxford: Oxford University Press, 1977).
—, *Culture* (London: Fontana, 1981).
—, 'Welsh Culture', in *Who Speaks for Wales? Nation, Culture, Identity*, ed. Daniel Williams (Cardiff: University of Wales Press, 2003).
—, *The Politics of Modernism: Against the New Conformists* (London and New York: Verso, 2007 [1989]).
Wills, Claire, *That Neutral Island: A Cultural History of Ireland during World War II* (London: Faber, 2008).
Wisherman, Ulla, and Ilze Klavina Mueller, 'Feminist Theories on the Separation of the Private and the Public: Looking Back, Looking Forward', *Women in German Notebook*, 20 (2004), 184–97.
Wood, Juliette, 'Perceptions of the Past in Welsh Folklore', *Folklore*, 108 (1997), 93–102.
Zagarell, Sandra A., 'Narrative of Community: The Identification of a Genre', *Signs: Journal of Women in Culture and Society*, 13/3 (1988), 498–527.

Electronic Sources

The Blue Bird, dir. Walter Lang (MGM 1940).
Cadw, 'Celtic Saints, Spiritual Places and Pilgrimage' (2001), p. 2: *http://cadw. gov.wales/docs/cadw/publications/InterpplanCelticSaits_EN.pdfp*.
Churchill, Winston, speech at County Hall on 14 July 1941. See https://www. nationalchurchillmuseum.org/do-your-worst-well-do-our-best.html. See also *https://www.youtube.com/watch?v=cRBGfYVOELk*.
Listen to Britain, dir. Humphrey Jennings and Stewart McAllister (1942).
Morys, Twm, *www.brunel.ac.uk/__data/assets/pdf_file/0014/111155/Twm-Morys-Cerdd-Dafod-A-Poet-Introduces-a-Welsh-Metrical-Tradition.pdf*.
The Routledge Encyclopedia of Modernism (2016): *www.rem.routledge.com*.

Index

Note: works by Lynette Roberts (LR) appear directly under title; works by others under author's name

A
Aaron, Jane, 5
Aeneas of Troy, 138
Alexander, Neil, 10
Aneirin (sixth-century bard), 131
Argentina, 2, 12, 24, 27, 29–33, 37–8, 42–3, 47–8, 136, 203
'Argentine Railways' (LR; poem), 64n13
Arnold, Matthew, 51
Arts and Crafts Movement, 15, 140
autoethnography, 73
Axis (magazine), 133

B
Baker, Denys Val, 179
Baldwin, Archbishop of Canterbury, 138
Ball, John (fictional/historical figure), 108–9
Banks, Joseph, 202–5, 208, 214
Barthes, Roland, 181
Beale, Anne, 51–2, 54–5, 61–2
  Country Courtships (novel), 66n60
  The Vale of the Towey (reissued as *Traits and Stories of the Welsh Peasantry*), 53
Becket, Thomas, Archbishop of Canterbury, 122
Beddoe, Deirdre, 5, 90
Bell, Idris, 48
Bellamy, Kathleen, 127
Benjamin, Walter, 124, 145
Bible, Holy: language, 189–96
birds and bird-life, 157, 165–71, 177, 179–80, 182–3, 185, 200
Black Book of Carmarthen, The, 96, 126
Blake, William, 153n116
'Blood and Scarlet Thorns' (LR; poem), 64n13
Blue Bird, The (film), 149n44
Bluemel, Kristin, 6, 213
Blunden, Edward: 'On Pilgrimages in England' (essay), 134
'Book of Nesta, The' (LR; unpublished novel), 19n38, 102, 122, 127, 140, 144, 150n50, 200

Book of Taliesin, The, *see* Taliesin
Borges, Jorge Luis, 44n10
Bowen, Elizabeth, 127–8, 213
Bradbury, Malcolm, 20n57
Brett, Dorothy, 57
'Broken Voices' (LR; poem), 191
Brownell, Sonia (*later* Orwell), 3
Bruska (company), 204
Brutus of Troy, 118n4, 138
Buckmaster, Celia, 163, 202–3
Buenos Aires, 2, 24
Burne-Jones, Sir Edward, 143

C

Cadoc, St (Cattwg), 126
Camaldolese Gradual (choir book), 144
camp: as term, 150n54
Canterbury Tale, A (film), 125
Carmarthenshire
    changes through modernity, 87–9
    in LR's work, 86
    in wartime, 89–90, 92
    see also Llanybri
'Carmarthenshire Diary, A' (LR), 26, 39, 80, 146n6, 179
Carroll, Lewis: *The Hunting of the Snark*, 112
Carteret, A. R. de: *The Story of Sark*, 201
Catraeth (legendary battle), 91, 109, 131–2
Central School of Arts and Crafts, London, 5, 74, 140
Chamberlain, Brenda, 9, 142
    Tide-Race, 159
Chandler, Alice, 125
Chaucer, Geoffrey, 121, 125, 134
Childers, Erskine: *Riddle of the Sands*, 159
Chislehurst caves, Kent, 7, 17n13

Christie, Agatha, 158
Churchill, Winston S., 92, 181
'Circle of C, The' (LR; poem), 36, 167
Clare, John, 153n99
Clarke, Eric F., 177, 182, 184–5, 190
Clarke, Gillian, 184
Clifford, James, 137
Coleridge, Samuel Taylor: *Rime of the Ancient Mariner*, 82
Collected Poems (LR; ed. Patrick McGuinness), 8, 12, 156
Condry, William, 165
Conrad, Joseph, 159
Conran, Anthony, 8–9, 60, 95, 126, 135, 141, 192
Cook, Captain James, 14, 200–4, 208, 210
'Coracles of the Towy' (LR; essay), 52, 86–7, 97
Crawford, Robert, 7
Craxton, John: 'Welsh Estuary Foreshore' (painting), 130
'Crossed and Uncrossed' (LR; poem), 163
Cunynghame, Francis: *Reminiscences of an Epicure*, 201
'Curlew' (LR; poem), 165–6, 185–8
Cwmcelyn, 89, 167

D

Dafydd ap Gwilym, 94, 126, 189
Dante Alighieri: *Divine Comedy*, 122
Davies, Arthur, 186
Davies, Edward ('Celtic'), 46n18
Davies, Rhys, 68
Davies, Rosie, 26, 34, 53–5, 59–61, 75, 77–8, 81, 88
Davis, Alex, 136
Deininger, Michelle, 5, 11, 13
Dickens, Charles, 76
Dickinson, Emily, 143, 153n99

Dictionary of Welsh Biography, The, 51
Dilworth, Thomas, 112, 116
Donahaye, Jasmine, 185
Douglas, Keith, 130
Druid Press, Carmarthen, 56, 58
Dyfnallt (John Dyfnallt Owen), 41
Dynevor Park, Llandeilo, 37–8

E

'Earthbound' (LR; poem), 122, 141–2
Edwards, Dorothy, 67–8
   Rhapsody, 68
   Winter Sonata, 125
Edwards, Sir O. M.: *Cartrefi Cymru*, 45n11
El Dorado (LR; verse drama), 12, 34, 37
Eliot, T. S.
   advises LR to take regular job, 197–8, 208
   British identity, 50
   champions LR, 7
   correspondence with LR, 4
   invokes Middle Ages, 122
   on low sales of *Gods with Stainless Ears*, 201
   LR visits in London office, 46n19
   on LR's dissociation, 210
   modernism, 124, 192
   publishes LR, 102, 105, 197
   Little Gidding, 122
   Murder in the Cathedral, 122
   The Waste Land, 82
Endeavour (ship), 201, 204–5
Endeavour, The: Captain Cook's First Voyage to Australia (LR)
   modernism in, 14, 198–9
   narrative, 201–2, 205–10, 214
   proposed TV serialization, 214–15
   success, 198
   version for children, 214

Entwistle, Alice, 184–5
Epynt, Breconshire, 91
Esty, Jed, 124, 141, 213
   A Shrinking Island, 213
Evans, Sir Arthur, 138
Evans, Caradoc, 101, 103
   My People, 67, 101–2
Evans, John, 32
Evans, Margiad *see* Whistler, Peggy
Evans, Myfanwy, 150n57

F

Ferryside, 87
Field, The (magazine), 52
'Fifth Pillar of Song, The' (LR; collection): rejected, 7
'Fifth of the Strata' (LR; poem), 173
'Fisherman' (LR; story), 81-2
Flay, Claire, 67
floor patterns: in LR's 'Tiles', 76–7
formation: as term, 102
'Fox' (LR; story), 57, 59, 69, 73–5
Freeman, Kathleen, *The Intruder and Other Stories*, 68
Friedman, Susan Stanford, 9, 11–12

G

Garbutt, Ruby (LR's mother)
   death, 2
   sings Spanish lullabies to LR as child, 17n7, 34
Gardiner, Judith Kegan, 137
Garrity, Jane, 5, 9
Gates, S. Barrington, 209–10
Geertz, Clifford, 72
Geoffrey of Monmouth, 138
Gerald of Wales (Giraldus Cambrensis), 121, 140, 159
   Itinerium Kambriae (*Itinerary through Wales*), 36, 138, 183

Gibson, James, 182
Giraldus Cambrensis *see* Gerald of Wales
Glendinning, Victoria, 212
Glissant, Edouard, 16
Gododdin, Y (medieval poem), 92, 109, 113, 125, 131–2
Gods with Stainless Ears (LR)
  anti-Establishment sentiments, 114–15
  anticipates postwar benefits, 97
  apocalyptic tone, 114
  challenges concept of Allied victory, 96
  cites *Lives of Cambro-British Saints*, 102
  dedicated to Edith Sitwell, 4, 211
  early sources, 138
  on experience and effect of war, 53, 89–95, 98, 105–11, 114, 128, 131, 164
  invokes Dante's *Divine Comedy*, 122
  on Llanybri, 36
  on lost origins, 138
  low sales, 201
  LR's notes to, 137
  medieval references, 126–7, 131–3, 145
  on miscarriage, 49, 94–5, 111
  modernism in, 85, 105–7, 156, 170, 211
  on need for myth, 39
  place in, 129–30, 137, 155, 168, 171–2, 188, 194
  and poetic form, 13, 131, 187, 191, 193
  as requiem for war dead, 40
  small detail in, 143, 207
  sound and listening in, 180, 185
  structure, 105, 114–16, 128–9
  supernatural/magic section, 95–6
  and Welsh culture and identity, 104–5, 107–12, 116–17
  Welsh myth in, 96–7
  Welsh quotations in, 41–2
Golding, William: *Pincher Martin*, 160
Goodby, John, 8, 10
Gowland, David, 44n4
Gramich, Katie, 3, 5, 11, 132
Graves, Robert
  correspondence and relations with LR, 4, 14, 70, 102, 121–2
  interest in cyclic movements, 159
  and LR's application for scholarship, 197
  and LR's argument for myth, 39
  and LR's 'Book of Nesta', 140
  and LR's disbelief in collective gatherings for poets, 136
  on LR's dissociation, 210
  and LR's longing to write *penillion* (ballad form), 33
  and LR's migrations, 199–200
  and LR's poem on the curlew, 157, 188, 1186
  and LR's puzzlement over Taliesin phrase, 37
  and LR's reaction to father's death, 203
  and LR's use of words in *Gods with Stainless Ears*, 40
  and LR's Welsh identity, 48–9
  in Mallorca, 199
  mythography, 35–6
  published in *Wales*, 119n13
  reputation, 199
  style, 9
  translates 'Câd Goddeu' ('Battle of the Trees'), 139
  uses Welsh-language poetic form, 191
  The White Goddess, 35, 48

INDEX

'Graveyard' (LR; story), 70, 78–9
Grigson, Geoffrey, 133
Gruffydd, W. J., 41
Guest, Lady Charlotte, 146n3

H

Harris, Alexandra, 133–4, 140
Harrisson, Tom, 167
Hawthorne, Nathaniel: *The Scarlet Letter*, 25
H.D. (Hilda Doolittle), 142
Heaney, Seamus, 165
Hemans, Felicia, 55
Henderson, Mae, 13
Hendry, J. F.: 'London before Invasion, 1940' (poem), 163–4
Hernández, José: *Martín Fierro*, 31, 33
Heseltine, Nigel, 119n
Higgonet, Margaret and Patrice, 128
Highmore, Ben, 144
Hilary (cruise liner), 202
Holden, Inez: *It Was Different at the Time*, 170
Homer, 138, 140
Hooker, Jeremy, 468
Hopkins, Gerard Manley, 29, 184
Hopwood, Mererid, 192
Horizon (magazine), 7
Household Words (magazine), 76
Hudson, W. H., 32, 44n10
Hughes, Cadvan, 33
Hughes, Daniel, 4, 11, 13, 193
Hugo, Victor, 159
Humble, Nicola, 212
Humm, Maggie, 5
Huxley, Julian, 168

I

impressionism, 61–2
Ingram, Angela, 6, 137

Introduction to Village Dialect With Seven Stories, An (LR), 13, 45n11, 54, 56–7, 59–61, 69–83, 87, 157, 164, 168, 183–4
islands: in LR's writings, 158

J

Jameson, Storm, 68, 122
Jantzen, Operation (Second World War), 91
Jarvis, Matthew, 178
Jenkins, Lee, 136
Jennings, Humphrey, 46n20, 158, 167
Jews: persecuted by Nazis, 127
Jones, David
  belief in future Welsh resurgence, 117–18
  biblical allusions in, 113–14, 116
  correspondence and relations with LR, 4, 102–4, 117
  illustrations and engravings, 103
  influenced by war and Wales, 20n63, 110, 116–17
  invokes Middle Ages, 122, 125
  and modernism, 101–2, 106, 108, 113–14
  paintings, 39
  published by T. S. Eliot, 102
  Welsh identity, 104–5
  In Parenthesis, 11, 13, 104–6, 108–13, 116–17, 125, 151n80
Jones, Glyn, 45n15, 68, 101–2
Joyce, James
  as exile, 50
  speech, 184
  Finnegans Wake, 36
Julian of Norwich, 122

K

Kafka, Franz, 119n13
Kingdom Come (journal), 70

Kitto, John, 190
Kronfeld, Chana, 11

L
Lady of the Lake (legend), 25
'Lady of Llyn y Fan Fach' (folk tale), 61
Lambert, Constant, 211–12
'Lamentation' (LR; poem), 4–5, 64n21, 90
language: LR's views on, 183–4
Lawrence, D. H., 50, 159
Lehmann, Rosamond, 213
Lessing, Doris, 6
'Letter to the Dead, A' (LR; poem), 168
Lewis, Alun, 3, 5–6, 55, 134–5
   'All Day it has Rained' (poem), 60
Lewis, Eiluned, 68
Lewis, Saunders, 126, 132
   Egwyddorion Cenedlaetholdeb (*Principles of Nationalism*), 126
Lewis, Wyndham: friendship and correspondence with LR, 3
Life and Letters Today (magazine), 7, 81, 122, 143
Listen to Britain (documentary film), 46n20, 158
Llansteffan peninsula, 85–6, 89, 91, 97
Llanybri
   and English-language broadcasts, 92
   George Woodcock on, 87
   language, 184
   LR's life in, 1, 3, 6–7, 14, 27–30, 32, 36, 38–43, 48–9, 63, 80, 90, 119n12, 128, 132, 135–7, 157, 180, 188–9
   in wartime, 164
Lloyd George, David, 149n45

Llyn y Fan Fach ('lake of the small peak'), 25–6
Llywarch Hen, 125, 133
Lockley, R. M., 158
Lorenzo da Monaco, 122, 143–4
Lorimer, Hayden, 157
Loti, Pierre, 184
Low, David, 158
'Low Tide' (LR; poem), 166–7
Loy, Mina, 9, 212
Luny, Thomas: 'The Bark, *Earl of Pembroke*, later *Endeavour*, Leaving Whitby Harbour in 1768' (painting), 201

M
Mabinogion, 38, 114, 121, 125
McAllister, Stewart, 46n20
Macaulay, Rose, 213
McAvoy, Siriol, 56
MacDiarmid, Hugh, 119n13
McDouglas, Dr James, 160
McGuinness, Patrick
   on accusations of obscurity against LR, 212
   compares LR's poetry to naive painting, 192
   edits LR's *Collected Poems*, 8
   on influences on LR, 156
   on LR as outsider, 3
   on LR's interest in recording life, 72
   on LR's *Introduction to Village Dialect*, 70
   on LR's 'Maeterlinck blue' reference, 130
   on LR's modernism, 157, 177
   on LR's 'Poem from Llanybri', 134
   on LR's view of language, 183
   on LR's work in Llanybri, 62

Mackay, Marina, 213
MacNeice, Louis, 158
   'Neutrality' (poem), 160
Madge, Charles, 167
Maeterlinck, Maurice: *The Blue Bird*, 130
Mansfield, Katherine, 12, 57, 62
   'At the Bay' (story), 58
Mao, Douglas, 10
Marcus, Sharon, 9
Martin, Clara I.
   Bearing Gifts, 68
   Fairy Tales for Grown Ups, 68
Mass Observation, 157, 167
Maxwell, Gavin, 160–1
medievalism
   as cultural phenomenon, 124–5
   LR's interest in, 121–4, 127–8, 133–4, 140, 143–5
Mellor, Leo, 14–15
   Reading the Ruins, 81
Methodism, 126
Miller, Lee, 170
Miller, Tyrus, 213
Mitchison, Naomi, 122, 128
modernism
   Caradoc Evans pioneers, 101–2
   and cyclic effects, 159
   Edith Sitwell and Constant Lambert suggest needs simplicity, 211–12, 214
   and 'formation', 102
   in *Gods with Stainless Ears*, 85, 89, 105–7, 156, 178
   and imperial decline, 124
   as literary-historical category, 44n10, 213
   in LR and David Jones, 105–14
   LR's, 8–10, 15, 62, 121, 192, 211
   in LR's *The Endeavour*, 14, 198–9
   and medieval past, 122–3
   and national identity, 50
   and poetic structure, 106–7
   in Welsh literature, 102
modernity: effect on local Welsh culture, 85–7, 98
monasticism, 143–5
Moore, Marianne, 212
'Moorhen' (LR; poem), 188
Moran, James, 10
Moretti, Franco, 85–6
Morgan, Clare, 133
Morgan, Eluned, 45n14
Morris, William, 140–3, 145
Morys, Twm: 'My First Love was a Plover' (poem), 192
Movement poets, 8, 208, 214
Mundye, Charles, 14–15, 127

N

Nancy, Jean-Luc, 14, 178, 194n13
'narrative of community' (literary sub-genre), 72–3
Nash, Paul: *Monster Field* (painting), 160
National Library of Wales: granted royal charter, 68
National Museum of Wales: granted royal charter, 68
nationalism, 123–4, 126
Nazism, 127, 147n27
neo-Romanticism, 133–4
New Apocalypse school, 70, 73
New Directions (US publication), 7
'New World, The' (LR; poem), 64n13
New Zealand: in Katherine's Mansfield's writing, 57–8
Nicholls, Peter, 160
Noë, Alva, 186
'Notes for an Autobiography' (LR), 2, 46n17, 47

O

'Orange Charger, The' (LR; poem), 200
'Out of the Paw of Night' (LR; uncollected poem), 203
Owen, Peter (publisher), 200, 210, 214

P

Parkinson, Sydney, 202–3, 205, 207, 209, 214, 216n22
Parry, R. Williams, 41, 166, 191
Parry-Williams, T. H., 45n15
Pasmore, Victor, 3
Patagonia: Welsh colony, 32–5
Pattern, Father Hope, 135
Peat, Alexandra, 137
Peate, Iorwerth C., 71, 140
   The Welsh House, 42, 71, 76
Pendine Sands, 80
Phillips, Katherine, 7
piepowder: as term, 131
Pikoulis, John, 8
pilgrimages, 134–6
Piper, John, 125, 133
Plaid Genedlaethol Cymru (Welsh National Party): founded, 20n53, 126
Plain, Gill, 143
'Plasnewydd' (LR), 64n30
Plate, Liedeke, 123
'Poem' ('For my house is clothed in Scarlet'; LR), 23, 166
'Poem from Llanybri' (LR), 26–7, 55, 60–1, 122, 134–7
'Poem on moorhen and its scarlet garters' (LR), 27
Poems (LR: 1944), 4, 26, 60, 85, 134
Poetry London (magazine), 7
Pound, Ezra
   Bel Esprit scheme to free Eliot from bank employment, 198
   as exile, 50
   on Midi, 129
   modernism, 124, 192
   and past, 122
Powell, Michael and Emeric Pressburger, 125
Power, Eileen: *Medieval People*, 144
Powys, John Cowper: *A Glastonbury Romance*, 125
Pratt, Mary Louise, 73
Pre-Raphaelites, 141, 143
Proverbs, Book of: LR borrows from, 25
'Pub' (LR; story), 79–80
Pwyll Pendefig Dyfed, 38

R

Radford, Jean, 212
'Radio Talk on South American Poems' (LR), 2, 31, 35, 203
Raine, Allen: *All in a Month*, 67
'Rainshiver' (LR; poem), 192–3
Ramazani, Jahan, 10
'Raw Salt on Eye' (LR; poem), 157, 185
Rebecca Riots, 53
Red Book of Hergest, The, 96, 126, 133
Reed-Danahay, Deborah, 73
Rees, W. J.: *The Lives of the Cambro-British Saints*, 102
'Rhode Island Red' (LR; poem), 38
Rhodri Fawr (Rhodri the Great), 38
Rhys, Angharad (LR/Keidrych's daughter), 43, 215
Rhys, Ernest, 28, 50
Rhys, Jean, 6, 12
Rhŷs, Sir John, 181
   Studies in the Arthurian Legend, 125, 126

INDEX

Rhys, Keidrych
  edits *Life and Letters Today*, 7
  edits *Wales*, 7, 23, 47, 69, 103, 127, 179
  enquires about LR's Welshness, 47
  on invoking tradition, 145
  on LR's stories, 69
  marriage to LR, 3, 23, 48, 62, 90, 157
  military service, 36, 162
  modernism in, 102
  overshadows LR, 9
  publishes LR's *Introduction to Village Dialect*, 56
  separation and divorce, 199, 203–4
  wartime identity number, 92
  and Welsh identity, 179
  'The Curlew' (poem), 166
  Modern Welsh Poetry (ed.), 102
  'The Van Pool, Tichrig' (poem), 25–6
Rhys, Prydein (LR/Keidrych's son), 103
Riding, Laura, 212
Roberts, Cecil Arthur (LR's father), 2, 24, 48, 203
Roberts, Glyn, 68
Roberts, Gwyneth Tyson: *The Language of the Blue Books*, 77
Roberts, John (coracleman), 139
Roberts, Kate, 68
Roberts, Lynette
  accommodates to Welsh language, 179–80
  applies for grants and scholarships, 197
  attitude to war, 27, 29, 53–4, 79–80, 85–8, 93–4, 98, 109–12, 128, 156–7, 162
  attracted to ballad form, 33–4
  becomes Jehovah's Witness, 62
  birth and early life in Argentina, 2–3, 24, 27, 29–33, 47–8, 203
  children, 43, 62, 103, 215
  as conservationist, 42
  death, 62
  diary, 102, 186, 200
  divorce, 199, 203–4
  on false misinterpretations of Welsh-speaking peoples, 70
  family background, 48
  given names, 2
  gravestone inscription, 66n61
  images of estuary and tides in, 155–60, 164, 168, 171–4
  impressionist style, 61
  interest in birds and bird-life, 157, 165–71, 177, 179–80, 185–8, 200
  interest in Welsh coracle, 37
  interwar travels, 157
  and Keidrych Rhys's 'Van Pool', 26
  life in rural Wales (Llanybri), 3, 6–7, 14, 24, 26–30, 32, 36, 38–43, 48–9, 53–6, 63, 80, 90, 119n12, 128, 132, 135–7, 157, 180, 188–9
  listening and representation of sound, 177–81, 185–6, 194
  literary earnings, 201
  marriage to Keidrych Rhys, 3–4, 23, 48, 62, 90, 157
  meets Edith Sitwell, 211
  on memory, 73
  mental decline, 7, 62, 63n3, 103
  modernism in, 9–11, 101, 121, 178, 192, 212–13
  moves to caravan, 4, 17n13, 199
  on nationhood and history, 126–7
  obscurity, 4–5, 7–9, 11
  as outsider, 3–4, 90, 145
  paintings exhibited, 206
  peripatetic life, 24

Roberts, Lynette (continued)
  place in, 58–9, 129, 136, 157–8, 173, 185, 194
  plans move to Mallorca, 199, 215
  poetic style, 8–10, 13, 28, 38
  political-social views, 6, 127
  preference for clarity and precision, 28, 140, 206–7
  preoccupation with medieval past, 121–4, 140–1, 143–5
  qualities, 1–2
  quotes from Bible, 189
  red cloak, 3, 24–5, 59
  refers to Welsh 'peasants', 49–50
  relation to Wales, 6–7, 11–13, 34, 47–52, 54–5, 60, 62–3, 104, 117–18
  relations and correspondence with David Jones, 4, 102–4, 117
  reputation, 8, 15
  runs aground on board cruise ship, 202
  sets up florist's company, 204
  short fiction, 67–83
  and simplifiction in modernism, 211–14
  speaks no Welsh, 56
  suffers miscarriage, 49, 94, 119n22
  training as artist and decorator, 5, 24, 74, 140
  use of Welsh myth, 96–7
  uses Welsh quotations, 189–91
  ventriloquizes local Welsh speech, 53–4
  view of environment, 179
  visual richness, 206
Robichaud, Paul, 129
romance: William Morris on, 154n129
Romanticism, 125
  see also neo-Romanticism
Rousseau, Henri ('Douanier'), 153n99
Royal Air Force: wartime effect on Carmarthenshire, 89–90
'Royal Mail' (LR; poem), 64n13

S
St Fagan's National Museum of History, 71–2
Savage, Mike and others: *Globalization and Belonging*, 50, 52, 55–6
Schliemann, Heinrich, 138
'Seagulls' (LR; poem), 36
'semi-periphery'
  and cultural changes through capitalist modernity, 85–6
  in LR's writing, 88
'Seven Stories' (LR), *see Introduction to Village Dialect With Seven Stories*
'Shadow Remains, The' (LR; poem), 122, 142–3
Shakespeare, William: *Richard II*, 158
Shell Travel Guides, 134
short stories: English-language by Welsh women, 67–9
Simms, Colin: *Hen Harrier Poems*, 165
'Simplicity of the Welsh Village' (LR; essay), 45, 52, 63n8, 71
Sitwell, Edith
  correspondence and relations with LR, 4, 14, 199, 211, 215
  LR dedicates *Gods with Stainless Ears* to, 4, 211
  and modernism, 211–14
  Gardeners and Astronomers, 211
  I Live under a Black Sun, 201, 210, 212
Skokholm (island), 158
Skoulding, Zoë, 11–12, 14
Spry, Constance, 204
Stanislavski, Konstantin, 130

'Steer' (LR; story), 60, 70, 77–8
Sutherland, Graham, 160
Swansea: wartime air raid on, 40–1, 61, 81, 164
'Swansea Raid' (LR; story), 61, 70, 79–81, 88, 163–4
Swift, Jonathan, 212
Synge, J. M., 184

T

Taf, Afon (estuary): in LR's poems, 155–6, 174
Taliesin, 23, 37, 125, 139–40
Taylor, C. S. M., 113
Taylor, Elizabeth (author), 213
'Tea with the Sitwells' (LR; essay-memoir), 211–12, 215
'Temple Road, The' (LR; poem), 162
Thomas, Bertha: *Picture Tales from Welsh Hills*, 67
Thomas, Dylan
  attends LR–Keidrych Rhys wedding, 119n12
  death and grave, 103, 168, 211
  in London and New York, 103
  and LR as bird-woman, 168
  on LR's background, 2
  meets Caradoc Evans, 101
  modernism in, 102–3
  Deaths and Entrances, 11
  'Prologue to an Adventure', 103
  'Return Journey' (broadcast), 66n53
Thomas, M. Wynn, 12–13
Thomas, R. S.
  and bird-life, 165
  poetic style, 8
  and rural past, 178
  'Pietà' (poem), 189

'Tiles' (LR; story), 61, 70, 75–7
Times Literary Supplement, 209
'To Keidrych Rhys' (LR; poem), 23
Tobias, Lily: *The Nationalists and Other Goluth Studies*, 68
Towy (Tywi), Afon (river), 156
traddodiad, 126
Treece, Henry, 70, 73
  'Two at the table', 70–1
Tribune (journal), 7
Tschiffely, A. F.: *This Way Southward*, 44n10
Turner, Victor and Edith, 135–7

U

Ustinov, Peter, 211

V

Vyvyan, C. C.
  Down the Rhone on Foot, 201
  Temples and Flowers, 201

W

Wainwright, Laura, 4
Wales
  bardic tradition, 126
  cultural identity, 179
  effect of war and modernity on culture, 85–9, 92
  land appropriated in war, 91
  LR's and David Jones's culture and identity, 104
  in LR's poems, 56, 107, 130
  LR's relation to, 6–7, 11–13, 34, 48–50, 52, 55, 60, 63
  medieval, 122–3
  mythic origins, 138
  nationalism, 126
  pilgrimage sites, 136
  rural life depicted in LR's 'Seven Stories', 71–9

Wales (continued)
    settlers in Patagonia, 32–5
    violated by English/British in war, 107–9
    women short story writers, 67–8
    see also Welsh language
Wales (journal), 7, 23, 25, 47, 69, 102–3, 126, 139, 179, 193
Walkovitz, Rebecca L., 10
Wallace, Diana, 207–9
Wallerstein, Immanuel, 85
Walsingham pilgrimage, 135
war: in LR's writings, 27, 29, 53–4, 79–80, 85–8, 93–4, 98, 109–12, 128, 156–7, 162
Warwick Research Collective (WReC), 86
Webb, Andrew, 13, 181, 193
Welsh language
    forms, 191–2
    LR champions, 41
    LR does not speak, 56
    LR quotes in writings, 42, 189–91
Wheale, Nigel, 8, 143, 169
Whistler, Peggy ('Margiad Evans'), 9, 102, 144
Whitman, Walt, 38
Wigginton, Chris, 10
Wilkinson, John, 137
Williams, Daniel: *Black Skin, Blue Books*, 140
Williams, Revd David, 51
Williams, Glyn, 32
Williams, Kyffin, 216n24
Williams, Raymond, 20n53, 118
    Culture, 102–3
    Marxism and Literature, 104
    'Welsh Culture', 104
women
    experience of war, 128
    in LR's 'Seven Stories', 69
    and modernism, 15, 144, 213
    and monasticism, 145
    status in Wales, 5
    wartime work, 90–1
    Welsh short story writers, 67–8
    write historical fiction, 212
    write on medieval past, 123
    writers in Wales, 9
Woodcock, George, 87, 93
Woolf, Virginia
    on past, 128
    'Anon' (essay), 125
    Between the Acts, 132
    'Modern Fiction' (essay), 62
    'Monday or Tuesday' (story), 62
    Three Guineas, 132
    The Waves, 62
World War II
    effect on Welsh cultural life, 85–9, 91–2
    in LR's writing, 27, 29, 53–4, 79–80, 85–9, 93–4, 98, 109–12, 128, 162
    working women, 90–1
Wykes-Joyce, Max: *Triad of Genius*, 210

X

'Xaquixaguana' (LR; poem), 64n13

Y

Yeats, W. B.
    on curlew as harbinger of death, 165
    LR denies influence, 25
    modernism, 124, 159

Z

Zagarell, Sandra A., 72–3, 76